MISSION
AND
APOLOGETICS

edition afem
mission specials 4

PETER BEYERHAUS

VTR
Publications

This book ist part of the series edition afem – mission specials,
ed. by Klaus W. Müller, Bernd Brandl and Thomas Mayer.

Bibliographic information published by Die Deutsche Bibliothek
Die Deutsche Bibliothek lists this publication in the Deutsche National-
bibliografie; detailed bibliographic data are available in the Internet at
http://dnb.ddb.de.

ISBN 3-937965-44-0
Stock Number: 860.544

Cover illustration: VTR
Printed in the UK by Lightning Source

Table of Contents

Preface

This book is based on a series of lectures which the author delivered during the fall of 2003 as a guest professor at the prestigious Yonsei University in Seoul, Korea. Aware that the Korean Church has now taken over the lion's share of the recruitment and world-wide deployment of trans-cultural missionaries, the author seeks to equip students spiritually for the encounter with adherents of non-Christian belief systems and of anti-Christian movements. Avoiding mere alarmism, the intention is to give positive guidelines for persuasively presenting the biblical truth. Today the Gospel's claim that Jesus Christ is the way, the truth and the life, apart from whom salvation cannot be attained, is contested not only externally by rival religions and quasi-religious ideologies; it is challenged within Christendom itself by those who deny the objectivity of biblical revelation and advocate an inter-faith dialogue aiming at a mere friendly sharing of spiritual experiences.

Giving in to such a mentality severs the very roots of the Christian missionary vocation, as we see, alas, within a large segment of Western Christians today. Since the days of the Apostles and Church Fathers, evangelistic witness to and apologetic defence of the truth have always constituted two inseparable prongs of missionary outreach. The publication of these lectures is guided by the hope that the book may open many minds to the urgent relevance of this insight.

Chapter 1

The Church's Apologetic Task Today

Introduction

Two experiences in my childhood have made a lasting impression on my mind. They have helped me to determine the spiritual task and direction of my later professional career.

The *first* experience was the annual mission feast which my parents arranged in the large garden of our rural parsonage in Eastern Germany. I was fascinated by the missionaries' exciting reports about their evangelistic work in Africa, China and India. I was especially impressed by the unshakable fidelity with which they preached the Gospel in season and out of season regardless of pagan opposition from incredulous audiences, witch doctors, governors or even robbers. For these courageous missionaries trusted in the protection of their heavenly Lord whose presence they felt, especially in dangerous situations.

The *second* experience was the bold stance which the *Confessing Church* in Germany took against the anti-Christian propaganda of Hitler's Nazi-Regime (1933-45). One night in 1938 a political agitator delivered a speech in a political gathering in our community hall. He magnified Hitler's achievements under the new national emblem, the *swastika*. To this he contrasted the weakness of Christianity which – in his opinion – had shrunk to the state of an outdated religion. At the climax of his talk he roared: "The cross of Calvary has faded away; now we are illuminated by the *swastika*!"[1] Everybody in the assembly – all parishioners of my father – kept silent, either out of fear or of mental submission. This was unbearable to my father. He rose and shouted in protest: "The cross of Calvary has not faded! It is still the power unto salvation for everyone who believes!" The "brown" orator angrily responded: "Who dares to disturb this important assembly? Throw him out!" Immediately two uniformed members of Hitler's paramilitary guard rushed to my father and pushed him roughly to the exit. A few months later he was cited to the court for a trial. Only through the out-

---

[1] The swastica (a cross with hooks) – which originated from Buddhism – was the emblem of the Nazi ideology and formed the center of the German flagg during the reign of Adolf Hitler.

break of World War II was this case dismissed as a minor matter, and it finally fell into oblivion.

These two experiences taught me an important spiritual lesson: I learned first of all that the Gospel of Jesus Christ has to be proclaimed in all parts of the world irrespective of the costs. Moreover I learned that the Christian faith is always contested by rival religious or ideological claims for universal validity. Followers of Jesus, therefore, have to stand up for their convictions even when the Gospel meets with resistance.

This early insight was substantiated later on by our confrontation with *Marxism* during my study in the eastern part of Germany (1947-50). It was confirmed again in my missionary encounter with remnants of animistic superstition amongst our South African church members (1957-65). The third and more prolonged confirmation of my insight I received after my return to Germany (1966) in our "second church struggle" in the post-Christian situation of the once "Christian West." On the basis of these personal experiences I realized that it was my specific calling in my missiological teaching to combine the *evangelistic* and the *apologetic* concern.

This was also my intention when giving the *Yong Jae lectures* at Yonsei University during the two terms of 2003. Whilst in the Spring term I put the main emphasis on the evangelistic side, during the Fall term it rested on the apologetic side. But the two aspects are clearly interrelated. They must never be separated in all our encounters with people who adhere to a non-Christian belief system. We have a double task: as Christ's witnesses we are obliged firstly to *affirm* the Gospel in order to win people for the Saviour Jesus Christ; secondly we have to *defend* its truth in order to prevent the Church from betraying her message of salvation

I. Apologetics and Its Biblical Foundation

A. Definition

What do we mean by "apologetics?"[2] It is a theological theological term which is derived from the Greek word "*apologia*" (ἀπολογία)

---

[2] C.H. PINNOCK: Art "Apologetics" in: New Dictionary of Theology (abreviated NDT), IVP Leicester 1988, pp. 36 f. – C. van TIL: The Defense of Faith, Philadelphia 1955. – Avery Dulles: A History of Apologetics, Philadelphia 1971.

which means "defense." It can be used both in secular and in spiritual connections. When an accused person is put on trial, he or his advocate delivers an "apology." That means he tries to persuade the judges of his innocence and of the justice of his or her client's cause against the accusation of the opponent. In the metaphorical use an *apologia* is made positively in order to give convincing arguments for a truth claim. Negatively we seek to refute the erroneous arguments and unfounded accusations of the opponent.

Apologetics is a branch of academic theology in which the rules of an erudite defense of one's own faith are taught both in general and with regard to particular divergent positions. It is practiced in all major religions, but it has its oldest traditions in the Christian Church with roots already in the Old Testament and in Judaism. An American missiologist, *Harold A. Netland,* defines[3] "Christian apologetics is the response of the Christian community to criticism about the truth-claim of God, human beings, sin, salvation and Jesus Christ, which are said to apply to all people in all cultures at all times."

Theologians distinguish between *theoretical* and *applied* apologetics, the former one being cultivated in dogmatics under the name "Fundamental Theology," the latter one being explored in "Practical Theology" and in "Missiology." We may also distinguish between *negative* (or *destructive*) apologetics and *positive* apologetics. The former refutes the errors, prejudices and contesting view in other positions (2 Cor 10:4-5). The latter attempts to persuade skeptics of the credibility of Christianity and to remove intellectual obstacles to it. It presents convincing arguments for the intellectual plausibility of the Gospel.

B. Biblical Foundation

1. Already in **Old Testament** times God Yahweh charged his elected people of Israel to guard the faith. This meant positively to remember that God, the LORD, is One, and to love Him with all their heart and with all their soul and all their strength, and to keep His commandments (Dt. 6:4-9).

Negatively it meant to shun all idols and to oppose false prophets who seduced Israel to idolatry (Dt. 18:20-22).

Particularly the biblical prophets and apostles were apologists commissioned and empowered by the Holy Spirit unashamedly to affirm the faith and to defend it against seduction and apostasy.

---

[3] Evangelical Dictionary of World Mission, Baker Books 2000, p. 70

In the Old Testament *Israel* testified to God as personal creator and ruler of history, against all pagan mythologies (Ps 19:1ff; Jer 10:11f). Yahweh's prophets defended His sovereign claim and position against the "nothingness" of the pagan gods (Is 44; Ps. 115:1-4). The prototype of all apologists was the prophet Elijah. On mount Carmel he challenged Israel to make a clear choice between Yahweh and Baal and consequently confounded the vein confidence of Baal's prophets in His alleged dominion of nature (1 Kings 18). The entire history of Israel is the dramatic account of God defending the validity of the First Commandment and His determination to punish all syncretism (blending of religions) and apostasy (2 Chron 36:15-21).

2. In the **New Testament** it is first of all *Jesus* himself who proves his divine authority and life-giving power against unbelieving Jews (Mk 2:1-12; John 8:12-20; 10:22-25). He sharply denounces the hypocritic legalism of the Pharisees who replaced the supreme commandment of love by human made ceremonial rules (Mt 23). Instead he invited graciously all those who were weary and burdened to find rest under his gentle yoke (Mt 11:28f).

Later on the *Apostles* both positively and negatively witnessed about Jesus Christ to their own disobedient people (Acts 22) and affirmed unashamedly the reality of Christ's resurrection and the claims of the Gospel (Acts 4; 26) before Jewish and pagan courts. Paul and John uncompromisingly denounced intruding Judaistic and Hellenistic heresies as *"a different gospel"* (Gal 1:9; Phil 1:7.16).

In accordance with Jesus the Apostles warned the early church of a future increase of false teachers. They saw in their doctrines the working of *demonic spirits*, preparing the emergence of the *Antichrist* (2Tim 4:1-5; 1 John 4:1-4). Thus the apostolic defense of the faith initiates a spiritual battle. The prospects of winning it are hopeful on account of the spiritual armour with which Christ's believers are equipped (Eph 6:10-18), as Paul states "The weapons we fight with ... have divine power to demolish strongholds. We demolish arguments and any pretension tht sets itself up against the knowledge of God, and we take captive every thought to make it obedient to Christ" (2 Cor 10:4).

3. *The NT emphasices apology as a **general Christian duty**.* The classical place where the nature of apologetics is expressively described is found in 1 Peter 3:15: "Always be prepared *to give an answer* (Greek: ἀπολογίαν) to everyone who asks you to give reason for

the hope that you have. But do this with gentleness and respect, keeping a clear conscience ...".

The context confirms that the early Christians often had to confess their faith in a hostile situation. But the apostle encourages his congregation not to be frightened. Rather they should be ready to explain for what reason they were filled with hope even in trials. For this would make an impression on the mind of their adversaries. In some cases it would even leadthem into a similar experience with Jesus Christ. The primary function of Christian apologetics is to witness joyfully and gently to our Lord and Savior and at the same time to give convincing reasons for this. We should, therefore, not have a narrow concept of apologetics which sees its place mainly in heated debates, perhaps even in a fanatical and arrogant mood. For here the saying would apply: "You have won an argument, but you have lost a friend."

Still apologetics in the NT understanding clearly also aimed at defending the faith against misunderstandings, prejudices and deceptive infiltration of heretics. Therefore, all Christians are charged to be watchful, discern the spirits whether they are from God and to fight for the faith entrusted to the Church once for all (Jude 3b). The Church is the temple of the living God, the pillar and foundation of the truth (1Tim 3:15). In her alone eternal salvation can be found. Thus every believer in general and a Christian minister in particular has to safeguard it from confusion and destruction. This we cannot achieve by our natural capacity, not even by intellectual sharpness alone. This work of persuasion is ultimately the ministry of the Holy Spirit. He is working through the testimony of Christ's faithful servants and he convicts (ἐλέγχειν) the world "of sin and of righteousness and of judgment" (John 16:8). God's Spirit is driven by a "holy jealousy" which he imparts to Christians as well (2Cor 11:2; James 4:5). For Christ loves the Church as his mystical bride and wants to present her to himself as a radiant Church, without stain or wrinkle ... but holy and blameless (Eph 5:25-27).

We realize: apologetics is a spiritual task entrusted to the Church by Christ himself. It will be necessary to be mindful of that task both in pastoral and in missionary situations. Its practice is a battle for life and death, because behind non-Christian religions and ideologies we are facing demonic powers which are opposed to God and His biblical revelation. Apologists, consequently, might even end up as martyrs, which is the ultimate way of contending for the faith. The history of Korean martyrs[4] gives radiant illustrations for this serious truth.

II. Apologetics in Church History

1. **Apologists** put their mark especially on the 2nd and 3rd Christian centuries. During this time the post-apostolic Church struggled boldly to conquer the Roman empire and to prove the spiritual superiority of the Gospel over the syncretistic Pantheon of occidental and oriental cults and religious philosophies. To take up the challenge of the latter was the specific calling of those Christian scholars who expressively were called "*apologetes.*"[5] But their concern was taken up even later on by the Greek and Latin Church Fathers in the 4th and 5th centuries. Outstanding names are Justin the Martyr († 165), Tertullian († 220), the Alexandrine scholars Origin and Clement († after 215) and later on Ireneus and Augustine. They both defended the Christian faith and explicated it to educated people. They addressed themselves to Rabbinic scholars, Greek philosophers, and also to the Roman persecutors of the Church.

The apologetes were challenged by the critical argument that Christianity was but a recent, intellectually crude and even hypocritical religion. It was denounced as being dangerous to the venerable traditions of Greece and Rome and even a menace to the cultural foundation of the Empire. Against this the apologetes tried to prove the ancient origin of Christianity, the purity of its moral code and the virtues of its confessors. Moreover, they even tried to persuade the Greeks that Christianity was perfectly compatible with the noblest elements of their heritage. In fact they prepared a creative syntheses between the Christian creed and the thought forms of Greek philosophy. Thereby Christianity finally could be transformed into an indigenous religious institution without sacrificing the central elements of the Biblical message. This was achieved, however, only through a costly theological struggle in order

---

[4] R.G. PAIK: The History of the Protestant Missions to Korea. Pyongyang 1929, pp. 41-45.

[5] T. G. DONNER: Art "Apologists," in: New Dictionary of Theology, eds. Sinclair B. FERGUSON et. al., Intervarsity Press, Leicester/Downers Grove, Illinois, 1988, pp. 37-39. – The Grek texts of the apologists' writings are collected in E. J. GOODSPEED: Die ältesten Apologeten, Göttingen 1914. – English texts in: C. C. RICHARDSON, (ed.): The Early Christian Fathers, Philadelphia 1953.

to safe-guard creedal expressions like "Trinity" or "Christ's equal essence to that of his Father "ὁμοούσιος."[6]

The apologetes also had to fight against the sublime intrusion of religious heresies into the Church herself. The most dangerous spiritual enemy was the *"Gnosis."* It presented an alternative way of salvation, rather similar to the Hindu *yoga* patterns, a kind of spiritual self-redemption. The Gnostic heretics could even refer to Christ as God's revelation. But at the same time they denied both: his incarnation and his atoning death on the cross. The apostle John both in his letters and in his gospel unmasked the tactics of such pseudo-Christian ideas. They identified those teachers as spiritual fore-runners of the coming Antichrist (1John 2:18). Thereby St. John established a special apologetic tradition which is relevant anew in our time, where the Church is confronted world-wide by several neo-gnostic occurrences as e.g. the esoteric New Age Movement.

2. In the **Medieval Age** the post-Constantine Church now had become the established religion and saw little need for apologetics in her own realm. But soon a new religious rival to Christianity arose – in form of aggressive *Islam*. Therefore some outstanding theologians such as *Thomas Aquinas* (1214-1274) conceived their dogmatic textbooks as a systematic unfolding of the revealed truth. Christianity, he taught, is not contrary to human reason, but transcending it. Thus Thomas wrote his main work *"Summa Contra Gentiles"*[7] against the rationalist attacks of Muslim scholars. In it he distinguished such concepts which are common to Christians and Muslims and those doctrines which Christians have received by special revelation.

The most famous apologist of the Christian faith over against the Muslim criticism was *Ramon Lull* (Raimundus Lullus, 122-1316).[8] He devoted his life to prove the superiority of Christianity over Islam and to educate missionaries for the Muslim world. Being faithful to the biblical concept of apologetics, Lull did not advocate a military crusade against the Muslims. Instead he tried to convince them by philosophical and even mathematical arguments and by a humble missionary ap-

---

[6] Christian GNILKA: Chreesis. Die Methode der Kirchenväter im Umgang mit der antiken Kultur I. Schwaben-Verlag Basel/Stuttgart, 1984.

[7] Thomas Aquinas: Summa contra Gentiles, tr. A. C. Pegis et al., On the Truth of the Catholic Faith, 5 vols. (Garden City, NY, 1955-57), reprinted Notre Dame, IN, 1975.

[8] Larry POSTON: Article "Ramon Lull" in Evangelical Dictionary of World Mission, p. 585. – E.A. Peers: Ramon Lull. A Biography.

proach. Ramon Lull was quite successful even amongst educated Muslims. But finally, in 1215, he ended up as a true martyr. He was stoned to death by an angry crowd in Bugia, North Africa.

3. The **Reformers** concentrated their defense of the Gospel on the inter-confessional controversy with their Roman-Catholic opponents. *Martin Luther* (1484-1546)[9] defended his biblical protest by showing that the Roman emphasis on good works and acts of penitence contradicted the Pauline doctrine of justification by faith alone. The evangelical concerns were codified in the famous fourfold "*alone*" (solus/sola): Christ alone, the Bible alone, by grace alone, through faith alone.[10]

In his polemical writings Luther could attack his opponents rather forcefully. But he, too, realized that the evangelical faith had to be safeguarded positively. This he accomplished by creating systematic catechisms and by writing popular church hymns like "A mighty fortress is our God," which were translated into numerous languages. Thus they served to establish the identity of the Evangelical faith for all continents.

4. **Rationalism and Pietism.** Nearly contemporaneous with the Reformation, the Christian faith in the West began to erode under the influence of the *Renaissance* (ca. 1350-1550) and *Humanism* (14th and 15th centuries). Both drew their ideas from the antique philosophies and mythologies of the Greeks. They introduced an *anthropocentric* world viewwhich came in conflict with the *theocentric* world view of the Judaeo-Christian tradition. This trend unfolded tremendous force in the age of *Rationalism and Enlightenment* (1680-1850). From now on the highest position was attributed to the capability of human reason vs. divine relation. This modern trend culminated in the triumph of anti-religious skepticism and in the bloody event of the French Revolution (1789-93): The beheading of the Catholic monarchy and the enthronement of the "Goddess of Reason," symbolized by a notorious prostitute sitting on the altar of Notre Dame-Cathedral in Paris. This rang in the age of *Modernism*:[11] the rapid secularization of the formerly Christian world view and value system.

---

[9] Luther's Works, 55 vols., (St Louis and Philadelphia, 1955 -).

[10] John ATKINSON: Martin Luther and the Birth of Protestantism, Basingstoke 1982. – Paul WETTER: Der Missionsgedanke bei Martin Luther, Culture and Science Publication, Bonn 1999.

[11] A. M. G. STEPHENSON: The Rise and Decline of English Modernism, London 1984. – H. P. V. NUNN: What is Modernism? London 1932.

Unfortunately, *orthodox Protestant* theologians generally withdrew from the philosophical battlefield and developed a rather sterile conservatism. It were the European *Pietists*[12] and the Anglo-American Evangelicals who hastened to affirm the validity of the biblical faith. They did so not so much by intellectual arguments. Rather they re-assured themselves of the reality of their spiritual experience with Christ in their hearts and with His living word in the Bible. This was done, to start with, in the fellowship of likeminded brethren and sisters. Moreover they also tried to put it into practice by deeds of charity and Christian pedagogic and by spreading devotional literature. Later-on, with the breakthrough of the *Evangelical Revival*[13] in the middle of the 18th Centur, they assumed a strong sense of responsibility both for evangelism at home and for missionary preaching overseas. In doing so they also rediscovered the need of an apologetic encounter with the proponents of non-Christian belief systems: rationalism in the West, Islam and Hinduism in the East. *Jonathan Edwards* (1703-58),[14] a main agent of the Great Awakening in North America, wrote also one of the finest works of apologetics in modern times: "The Great Christian Doctrine of Original Sin," 1758.

During the 19th century conservative theologians struggled hard to come to terms with the vexing problem of the relation between religious belief and science, especially in its popularized demagogic forms. Many textbooks on apologetics were written during this time. Some of them became a welcome help to young students who tried to safe-guard their conversion experience by undergirding their evangelistic witness to their fellow students by plausible arguments. Some of the famous evangelists, especially those in the academic world, were outstanding apologists as well: *D. L. Moody* (1837-1899),[15] *E. Stanley Jones* (1884-1973)[16] *Henry Drummond* (1851-97)[17] and *Karl Heim* (1874-1958).[18]

---

[12] F. E. STOEFFLER: The Rise of Evangelical Pietism, Leiden 191965. – Martin BRECHT: Geschichte des Pietismus. 4 volumes, 1993-2003.

[13] E. E. CAIRNS: An Endless Line of Spendour. Revivals and their Leaders from the Great Awakening to the Present. – C. G. FINNEY: Lectures on Revival of Religion, ed. By W. G. McLaughlin, Cambridge MA 1960.

[14] I. H. MURRAY: Jonathan Edwards. A New Biography, Edinburgh 1987.

[15] S.N. Gundry: The Life and Work of D.L. Mood, 1910. – W. SMITH: An Annotated Bibliography of D. L. Moodey, 1948.

[16] E. Stanley Jones: The Christ of the Indian Road, 1925.

[17] G. A. SMITH: Henry DRUMMOND, 2 vols., London 1899.

[18] I. HOLMSTRAND: Karl Heim: Philosophy, Science and the Transcendence of God, Stockholm 1980.

5. *The Confessing Church in Hitler's "Third Reich".*[19] In my autobiographical introduction I did already mention the struggle of the
faithful wing of Germany's Protestant Church against the efforts of
Hitler's brown champions to establish the racists ideology of National
Socialism as the dominant world view in Germany. But there was also
another wing within the Church – the "German Christians" – that advocated a synthesis between the National Socialist vision and seemingly
compatible elements of the Christian faith. Hitler was admired to be
Germany's saving leader, sent by God himself. The Church should
become fully patriotic and contribute to the fulfillment of his racist
vision of an "Arian" empire. Against this betrayal biblically oriented
theologians under the leadership of *Karl Barth* (1886-1968)[20] rose in
protest. At a historic gathering in *Barmen*, the *Confessing Church* was
inaugurated in 1934. Its climax was the proclamation of an actual confessional statement, called the *Barmen Declaration*[21]. This became the
"Magna Charta" of all confessing Christians. It is quoted respectfully
even today as an authoritative doctrinal document. The Declaration
revived the apologetical tradition of the classical creeds and confessional statements of the Reformation. This was done by affirming the
authentic biblical teaching in six affirmations (thesis) and by defending
it against the current heresies by six corresponding refutations (antithesis): "We affirm – we reject." A similar pattern, inspired by the Barmen
Declaration, was later adopted for the evangelical declarations on
Christian mission in Wheaton (1966), Frankfurt (1970) and Seoul
(1975).

III. Contemporary Christianity Challenged by Modernism and Post-Modernism

When we try to describe our apologetical task today, we have to realize that our cultural situation has become more complex then it was
30 years ago. Up to that time the dominant force in controlling and
shaping the Western Society was *Modernism.*[22] It built on the assump-

---

[19] German Empire 1933-45.

[20] G. W. BROMILEY: Introduction to the Theology of Karl Barth, Edinburgh 1980. –
Biography by Eberhard BUSCH: Karl Barth, London 1976.

[21] A. BURGSMUELLER/R. WETH (Eds.): Die Barmer Theologische Erklärung. Einführung und Dokumentation, Neukirchen 1984.

[22] Os GUINNESS: "The Impact of Modernization," in: J. D. DOUGLAS (ed.): Proclaim Christ Until He Comes. Lausanne II on Manila, IcoWE, 1989, Minneapolis 1989,
pp. 283-288.

tion that the world was a closed, three-dimensional system, ruled immanently by the laws of nature. By utilizing these laws, it was assumed, mankind would be able to establish its control over the universe and assure the constant progress towards the utopic goal of a better world. No reference was made to a transcendental God interfering with the course of history. In fact the metaphysical concept of an invisible, transcendent reality was wholly abandoned from the Modernist world view. God and other extra-sensual beings and events were transferred to the realm of religion. Some people might cultivate such ideas in their private life. But religion was seen to be irrelevant to the task which people had to cope with in technology, science, medicines, politics and business. To talk about religious beliefs in these contexts was regarded to be out of place. Consequently most Christians became ashamed to do so. This situation still prevails in large sections of European Society. By the international spread of Western technology it is also imported to the educated class in African and Asian countries. This is detrimental to the evangelization of the Two-thirds world, and it constitutes an intellectual barrier to Church growth.

The Scottish Missiologist and Missionary bishop *Leslie Newbigin* (1909-98)[23] was one of the outstanding apologists in our day. In the final period of his life he meditated and wrote much about the devastating effect of Modernism to the spiritual foundation of European culture. He also worried about its dangerous effects on the evangelization of the East. He often quoted the penetrating question of an Indonesian church leader, General *Simatupang*, put to him in an earnest conversation: "Dr. Newbigin: How can the West be converted?" Simatupang had come to the conclusion that the evangelization of Eastern nations, especially the intellectual elite, may be frustrated in the long run. That would happen, if Christianity in the West could not overcome the fatale cleavage between science and belief that had been introduced by the philosophers of the Enlightenment and their forerunners: *Francis Bacon* (1561-1626), *Thomas Hobbes* (1588-1669) and *John Locke* (1632-1704).

The answer which Leslie Newbigin had found for himself and tried to convey to the Western church in his apologetic writings was clear and impressive: He argued that the clue to a new spiritual revolution and genuine revival was to reinforce the message of *Christ's resurrection*.

---

[23] L. NEWBIGIN: Unfinished Agenda. An Autobiography, Eerdmans, Grand Rapids 1985. – Idem: Foolishness to the Greeks. The Gospel and Western Culture, Eerdmans, Grand Rapids 1986.

This he held to be the most decisive event in world history. For it has shattered – once and for all – the grip which the dark forces of evil, the cosmic powers, held on all creation, humanity in particular. The resurrection is the beginning of the new eschatological creation. Newbigin regards it as a real event in history which has been testified to by credible witnesses. It cannot be refuted scientifically, as already young Lesslie once had argued successfully in the Student's Debating Society. The risen Christ is also the head and origin of a new mankind. Being incorporated in His Body Christians are called and able gradually to transform miserable social conditions of this fallen world into a new state where the coming Kingdom of God is already foreshadowed. According to Newbigin the Gospel has not only a bearing on individual souls. It is relevant also for all sectors of human life. Therefore it is to be preached as *"public truth,"*[24] addressing itself to the representatives of political, academical, technical and economical institutions.

How shall we evaluate Newbigin's theory? I believe we should welcome it as a help for the development of a wider concept of mission, as long as we remain mindful about the end-time prophecies in the NT. Such mission in a modern world should contain both: the primary appeal to sinners that they be reconciled to God and also the apologetic demonstration that their personal reconciliation also has a *cultural significance*. For in the power of Christ's resurrection the battle against social evils like corruption, social suppression, alcoholism and sexabuse can be fought effectively. Satan's capturing power is broken wherever Christ is accepted as Savior and Lord.

But many people to whom we preach are still obsessed by an immanent epistemology and by ideologies of Modernism. How can they be persuaded to open up for the credibility of an event like the resurrection? Does this not presuppose the existence of an invisible, supernatural reality that surpasses and pervades the three-dimensional reality of our physical world?

Here two recent developments in the history of ideas can come to our assistance. Both have not ended the age of materialistic Modernism, to be sure. But they effectively challenge its intellectual monopoly. One is the *revolution in science*, brought about by the new theoretical paradigms of physicians like *Albert Einstein* (1879-1955), *Max Planck* (1858-1947), *Niels H. D. Bohr* (1885-1962) and *Werner*

---

[24] L. NEWBIGIN: Truth to Tell: The Gospel as Public Truth, Grand Rapids/Geneva, 1991.

Heisenberg (1901-76). They have shown that the laws of nature known by us have abiding validity only under certain limited conditions. It all depends on the subjective position and perspective chosen by the scientific observer. We cannot exclude entirely that our empirical world in which the so-called laws of nature normally apply is surrounded and penetrated by a fourth dimenson or even more such. Those quite freely can interfere with the movements within our three-dimensional space. The well known Korean evangelist *Paul Yonggi Cho* (*1936) has written a book called: "The Fourth Dimension."[25] Here he makes use of these scientific innovations for his plea to accept the plausibility of science and miracles wrought by the Holy Spirit.

In the cultural context of a Shamanist world view his arguments were quite acceptable. For Koreans and people in Asia and Africa generally always believed in the reality of an invisible world. From here both good and evil spirits can interfere with our earthly life, according to their assumption.

But nowadays even in the West a growing number of people are opening up for extra-sensual perceptions (ESP), coming from a mysterious realm not accessible to empirical science.

The Esoteric Movement is one aspect of a new cultural mega-paradigm called *"Post-Modernism."*[26] It was named so because it has done away with central elements of Modernism, which it tries to replace. Although this cannot succeed, in the public mentality, by now, it runs side by side with Modernism. The term "Post-Modernism" is oscillating. It may contain various contradictory elements. Therefore no definition, but only a description can be attempted.

In Post-Modernism we *negatively* observe a fundamental skepsis against the superiority ascribed by Modernists over human reason. It also denounces the optimistic evaluation of technological and commercial progress. For such alleged progress has not fulfilled the great hopes which Western people once placed upon it. On the contrary, it has caused the cultural, political and ecological dissolution and the crisis of meaning in the Western world.

---

[25] Paul Yonggi CHO: The Fourth Dimension, vol. 1; (South Plainfield, NJ, Bridge Pubishing 1979.

[26] Peter Beyerhaus: „Das Zeugnis vom Heil in unserer multikulturellen Gesellschaft," in: DIAKRISIS 17 (4/1996), pp. 200-213.

Positively, Post-Modernism means a shift of balance towards the aesthetic talents of the human brain over against its intellectual and volitional functions. It strongly emphasizes the right of the *individual* to make one's own choices independent from doctrines and values commonly held. Established authorities are disregarded in favor of personal self-realization. In defiance of universal conventions everyone is entitled to develop his/her own lifestyle. Even the possibility of transcendental experience is advocated over against an empirist epistemology. The *"new search for spirituality"*[27] is a characteristic product of Post-Modernism.

In a way the Post-Modernist climate has made it easier to present a message which does not confine itself to the boundaries of empirical experiences and scientifically proved facts.

Therefore, anti-religious criticism is not the prevailing obstacle to an evangelistic presentation of the Gospel. Post-Modernists would not dismiss the miraculous accounts of the Bible and the testimony of one's personal experience of the presence of Christ in our life as absurd claim. Thus the spiritual frontiers in the contemporary world are moving again.

But this does not allow us to become too optimistic either. Openness to transcendental experiences does not automatically mean sympathy with the Biblical message of God's self-revelation in the unique event of the incarnation of His Son in the man Jesus Christ! For Post-Modernism places all religious claims on the same level. They **may** prove their significance to those who venture an experience with them; but people have complete freedom to attempt a synthesis between Christianity and other religious ideas or to abandon it altogether. Postmodern humans are principally anti-authoritarian also in the fields of religions and ethical behavior. They do not respect absolute truth-claims or universally binding norms.

The result is an ever expanding *religious pluralism* and a general attitude of *relativism.* This is, of course, completely incompatible with the faith in God's definite self-revelation by His inspiring the Biblical authors. And such relativism may eventually turn into scorn, indignation or even hostility when confessing Christians proclaim Jesus Christ

---

[27] James A, Henrick: The Making of the New Spirituality, InterVarsity Press 2003. – Harvey COX: Turning East – the Promise and Peris of the New Orientalism, Simon and Schuster New Yorl 1977. – Dave HUNT/T. A. MacMAHON: The Seduction of Christianity, Harvest House Publishers Eugene, Origon, USA 1985.

as THE way, THE truth and THE life, apart from whom nobody can come to the Father (John 14:6).

Therefore our central concern in missionary apologetics today must be, undauntedly to uphold the objective truth in the Biblical relation of God's eternally plan of salvation. This can, of course, not be done by a mere appeal to respect a sacred tradition or the doctrine of scriptural inerrancy; for other religions and ideologies have their own venerated books, too. The contemporary apologist has to present and to defend God's deeds of redemption as real events, testified to by credible witnesses in their time. He must give plausible arguments for their reality and show their significance in conformity with the Apostolic interpretation. He or she should proceed to point out the continuity of similar liberating experiences which people individually or corporately have made with the crucified Saviour at all times and places. He, Jesus Christ, remains the same yesterday, today and in eternity (Hebrews 13:8). The most effective apologetic argument will always be a combination of the authentic truth, faithfully presented, and the existential experience of it in the life of the evangelist himself. I admit: this is no scientific proof in the Modernist sense. But the truth of the Gospel will unfold its convicting force by the confirmation through the Holy Spirit and the readiness of the Christian witnesseseven to suffer and to die for it.

IV. The Apologetical Concern in the Evangelical Movement Today

When theological Liberalism that originated from Germany and Britain started to unfold its full vigor also in the United States and to capture most of the established theological seminaries, a group of respectable Evangelical scholars got alarmed. They decided to stem the Modernist tide by publishing a number of theological volumes and tracts that defended the main tenets of Biblical Orthodoxy as being absolutely essential and non-negotiable. Accordingly these were called *The Fundamentals*.[28] They included such doctrines as the creation in six days, Christ's virgin birth, physical resurrection and bodily return and the atoning significance of His death on the cross. The Fundamentalists also affirmed the trustworthiness and inerrancy of Scripture against both higher biblical criticism and scientific objection. During

---

[28] G. M. MARSDEN: Art. "Fundamentalism," in: NDT, pp. 266-268. – Idem: Fundamentalism and American Culture. The Shaping of Twentieth-Century Evangelicalsism 1870-1925, New York 1980.

this stage the Fundamentalists contributed much to solidify the Evangelical position. But later on account of the fanaticism of some of the proponents and their attempt to resort to court trials rather than to academic arguments, Fundamentalism fell into discredit in public opinion. That harmed the Evangelical Movement also as a whole. The Evangelical faith was, from then on, often taken to be old-fashioned, anti-intellectual and an expression of a primitive worldview.

A. The "New Evangelicals"

Since the 1940ies, however, successful attempts were made by the Movement of the "*New Evangelicals*" to rehabilitate their position. They raised educational standards in their new institutions and attempted to reconcile belief in the creation with authentic science. Theological research was taken more seriously. Evangelical thinkers of high academical caliber emerged, men like *Carl Henry*, *James Montgomery* and *Harold Ockenga*. They confidently joined public intellectual debates and expressed their views in substantial monographs and respectable new magazines like "Christianity Today."

An American scholar with worldwide influence who devoted his ministry to the upholding of the faith was **Francis Schaeffer** (1912-1984).[29] He can be called the "Pioneer of Modern Evangelical Apologetics." In accord with the NT usage of the word "*apologia*" he combined both "destructing" and "constructive" aspects. The task of the former is to refute error and distortion. The latter consists in the attempt to build up an all-embracing Christian worldview. For Schaeffer this was the more important side. He tried to integrate theology, philosophy, science, arts and – not to overlook! – an ethical lifestyle. For this purpose he founded a model community in *L'Abri*, Switzerland. he invited people to this colony who searched for reliable answers to the ultimate questions of life. Coming himself from a fundamentalist church, he tried to maintain the basic concerns of original fundamentalism without sharing the later tendency of separatist fanaticism. Even skeptics were attracted to him by his sympathetic, winning approach, in which he was congenially supported by his charming wife *Edith*.[30] Amongst his many publications his standard work "How Then Shall We Live?" (1977) is a historic analysis of the disintegration of Western

---

[29] Francis SCHAEFFER: Complete Works, 5 vols., Westchester IL, [2]1985. – L. T. DENNIS: Francis Schaeffer. Portraits of the Man and His Work, Westchester IL, 1986.

[30] Edith SCHAEFFER: L'Abri, London 1969.

culture under the influence of anti-metaphysics, anthropocentricity and atheistic Humanism.

Towards the end Francis Schaeffer became concerned about a kind of superficial Evangelicalism that reduces the Christian faith to individualistic piety. He found that it builds its evangelism on emotional appeal, often leaving aside the aspects of repentance and ethical renewal. In his book "The Great Betrayal" (1988) he critically accuses the mainstream of the Evangelicals of their succumbing to the spirit of the age. He illustrated this by the compromises made by many Evangelicals with regard to abortion, ecumenism, biblical criticism and feminism.

From this we can learn that true apologetics is not directed to unbelieving outsiders alone. Rather it starts with an honest self-analysis of established Christendom. Peter warns us (1Pt 4:17a): *"It is time for judgment to begin with the family of God."*

B. Re-allignment for Biblical Mission

In close connection with the solidification of the worldwide evangelical community, there emerged a new sense of calling to world evangelization. It was negatively provoked by the diminishing dynamics in conciliar (ecumenical) Christianity, due to its theological crisis. The famous *Wheaton Congress* in 1966[31] marked the beginning of the new alignment of the Evangelical mission movement. Its final manifesto, the *Wheaton Declaration,* strongly reaffirms the biblical foundation of mission. On the other side, it deplores the intrusion of soteriological *universalism* (= all mankind will be saved eventually or is already saved) and of *syncretism* into the mainline churches and missions. The Wheaton Declaration, thereby, sets a new pattern of combining evangelistic motivation with anti-modernist refutation.

I have mentioned already that Wheaton was echoed from the European continent by the *Frankfurt Declaration* in 1970.[32] Partly this was a reaction to the changed direction of the WCC's Uppsala assembly in 1968. The fact that the sponsors of the Frankfurt Declaration had reestablished the ancient confessional pattern *"we believe – we reject"* (formerly *"damnamus"* = we condemn) aroused a tremendous shock –

---

[31] Harold LINDSELL (ed.): The Church's World-Wide Mission, 1966. – Christianity Today XI, 13 May 1966, pp. 48 ff.

[32] The text of the Frankfurt Declaration is documented in Peter BEYERHAUS: Missions – Which Way? Zodervan, Grand Rapids 1971, pp. 107-120.

but also a glad excitement all over the world. We had dared to violate against the conciliatory inclusive spirit in modern ecumenical thinking!

C. The "Second Confessional Struggle" in Germany

The Frankfurt Declaration is a typical expression of the spiritual concern of the new **Confession Movement** in Germany, established in 1966 as a reaction to the neo-rationalistic dissolution of the biblical Gospel by *Rudolf Bultmann*'s program of *"demythologizing the New Testament."* Its brain trust became the *"Theological Convention,"* founded in 1969 by a Lutheran professor in Systematic Theology *Walter Künneth* (1901-1996), who formerly (1937) had distinguished himself as one of the champions of the *Confessional Church* in fighting the Nazi ideology. The Theological Convention takes up the apologetical battle with biblical criticism, to start with. The subsequent target were a variety of anti-biblical cross-currents emerging in the wake of it.

Since most of those had worldwide influence, we sought cooperation with like-minded conservative Christian scholars and mission leaders in other countries and continents. At an international meeting 1978 in Westminster Chapel, London, the *"International Christian Network"* was established. Several European and international congresses were held subsequently. Usually we publish our findings in theological tracts and books, dedicated to to give the readers specific, Bible-based orientation and help them to face the challenge of theological, ideological and religious cross-currents. The name of our magazine conveys our spiritual program: *"DIAKRISIS – an aid to the confessing church for spiritual discernment, renewal and fellowship."* Here again you find the combination of both aspects of Christian apologetics: affirmation and defense of the faith.

One of the earliest insights we have gained in our confession movement was: Apologetics is not just an intellectual exercise. It is a spiritual battle (Eph 6:10-18). It anticipates here and now the final encounter between Christ and Antichrist.

V. The Need of Korean Christians to Uphold Their Faith against Distortion

The Protestant Churches in Korea are acclaimed all over the world for three spiritual qualities:

Firstly their ardent prayer life, secondly their evangelistic dynamics, and thirdly their biblical orthodoxy.

The sequence could also be reverted; for the acquaintance with the Word of God can be seen as the source both: for prayer and witnessing. Very early in the history of the Protestant mission to Korea, the Bible was translated into the Korean language and made readable by the translaters' use of the revived *Han'gul* alphabet. Already the first generation of converts received a solid biblical education with help of the Bible Class system. In this way they learned clearly to distinguish between the new faith and the indigenous religions, and to avoid the danger of relapsing into them.

But spiritual temptations have always been accompanying the way of the Korean Church, and today they come with increased force. Therefore, safe-guarding and defending the faith remains an important task, and if theologians, ministers, church workers and members do not learn to practice apologetics, the church might be infiltrated and gradually lose its biblical identity. Let me briefly mention some of the main dangers as I have observed them during my visits to your country:

1. Korean Christians are constantly tempted by *Shamanism* as a basic folk religion still influencing the subconscious mind. It can shape a spiritistic and magic mentality disguising itself as the work of the Holy Spirit.

2. *Syncretistic movements* have occurred very early. The first one was the semi-religious revolutionary *Chong Do Kyu* (Tonghak) Movement during the 19th Century. Korea has even exported – and with great success – an ill-famed syncretistic movement: the "Unification Church" of *Sun Myung Moon*[33] who raised messianic claims to his own person as "Lord of the Return."

3. Some churches became infected by shamanistic ideas when mass movements into Christianity were motivated partly by *magic hope* to find a material good life in the church. In the airplane from Frankfurt to Seoul I was seated next to a Korean student who smilingly admitted to me that she sometimes sought advise from Shamanist soothsayers, believing that God was speaking through them.

4. During their occupation of Korea the Japanese installed the *Shinto-cult* on all Korean institutions, including the churches. Heated debates took place in the synods whether Shinto was just a patriotic ceremony or must be resisted as idolatrous worship. Outstanding mar-

---

[33] Dong-Joo LEE: Koreanischer Synkretismus und die Vereinigungskirche. Edition VLM, St. Johannis-Druckerei Lahr 1991.

tyrs like pastors *Yang-Won Sohn*[34] and *Ki-Cheul-Choo*[35] struggled hard but largely in vain to warn their fellow Christians against timid compromising and crowned their witness by becoming martyrs.

5. Ever since the liberation of Korea in 194, there was the *Communist threat from the North*. Today North-Korea has a strategy to conquer South Korea from within by sending agents that infiltrate all public institutions. They try to condition the minds towards accepting Marxist ideas.[36]

6. *Buddhism* has become a resurgent major religion in Korea. Under the influence of the Pluralistic Theology of Religions, even Christian students are wondering whether Buddhism – and other Asian religions as well – should not be regarded as alternative ways of salvation.

7. Under the veil of a *"wider ecumenism"* universalistic ideas are spreading worldwide and make an impression on the minds of Christians even in Korea.

8. *Modernist Western theologies* – both historio-critical and political – are imported by Korean theologians who took their doctoral degrees in the West. Now they develop the new impulses in the Korean context as professors at theological seminaries. *Minjung Theology*[37] is a typical example for this.

This may occur, however, even in sublime forms. Some modernist theologians carefully express themselves in a biblical vocabulary and adapt themselves to Korean charismatic piety. Sometimes not even their more orthodox colleagues and large evangelical assemblies discern that "a different gospel" (Gal 1:6.9; 2 Cor 11:4) is communicated to them.

---

[34] Dong-Hee SOHN: My Cup Overflows, Christian Literature Crusade, Seoul 2001.

[35] Kwang-Cho CHOO: My Father, Rev. Ki-Cheul Choo, the Martyr (Korean and English), UBF Press, Seoul 1997.

[36] Thomas BELKE: *Juche* – A Christian Study of North Korea's State Religion, Living Sacrifice Book, Company, Bartlesville, OK 1999.

[37] Yong-Bock KIM, ed.: Minjung Theology. People as the subject of history. Christian Conference of Asia, Singapoor 1980. – Committee of Theologicl Study/KNCC (ed.): Minjung and Korean Theology, Seoul 1982.

Conclusion

These observations show already my intention when publishing this series of *Yong Jae lectures*: I hope that they will contribute toward sensitizing my auditorium to the enormous spiritual dangers which are threatening contemporary Christianity in general and Korean churches in particular.

But my ultimate purpose is not to frighten my listeners and readers. Rather I want to let them discover that such encounter also constitutes a welcome opportunity, in the first place, to rediscover the authentic biblical truth which is attacked and distorted by a particular non-Christian movement. We need to be deeply grounded in the revealed Word of God in order to encounter the heretical challenges.

But moreover, if we seek a take serious and friendly encounter with our partners, we may also discover some elements of biblical truth in their views. At least we may sense a spiritual quest that can only be satisfied if our partners get to know what God has in store for them by offering to them his gift of salvation in Jesus Christ.

If taken in this sense, apologetics will not appear as a tiresome and unpleasant duty to you, as a mere emergency action. Rather it will let you make a thrilling experience of what it means to be Christ's faithful ambassadors. You are witnesses to a world which opposes Him but nevertheless can find true life in no one else but Him.

Chapter 2

Overcoming the Rationalistic Foundations of Historical-Critical Theology

A few decades ago, Christians in Germany were stirred up by the appearance of a book with the provocative title: *Alarm about the Bible.*[38] It soon became a bestseller. The reason for publishing it was not so much that academic theologians had begun to question the authenticity of biblical texts. Many had already done that for 300 years. What worried the author was rather the fact that the proponents of higher criticism had started to propagate the results of their research among ordinary Christians. This they did through popular literature, radio and television. In view of these determined efforts of modernist theology to penetrate the Christian community, Dr. Bergmann wrote, "Alarm must be sounded to the followers of Jesus."

The adherents of modernist theology, however, eagerly continued their publicity campaign. They regarded it almost as a missionary endeavor. They pressed forward rapidly and thoroughly with a barrage of information launched on the largest possible scale. They claimed that the churches during past decades had heaped upon themselves a great burden of guilt by neglecting to inform their members of important results of literary, historical and textural criticism of the Bible. Consequently, they insisted, ordinary Christians were kept in a state of immaturity and even superstition. The modernists held that the Church had closed off the Gospel to people who are unable to combine infantile belief with sound reason.

Thus, in the same churches two groups confronted each other as to their attitude towards biblical criticism. One group deplored the process as detrimental to the congregation; the other welcomed it as educative and evangelistic.

In this chapter, I do not try to dodge the serious issues or to retreat to the golden middle way. Rather, I confess that from the outset that I shared the deep concern of *Dr. Bergmann.* So did those like-minded conservative colleagues who in 1969 founded the *"Theological Con-*

---

[38] G. BERGMANN, 1963: (5th, revised edition 1974).

vention" of the new *Confession Movement "No other Gospel."*[39] But I do not want to limit myself to sounding an alarm. I want to attempt to go deeper; to expound some other basic issues and to suggest a remedy.

I. The *Sola Scriptura* Principle of the Reformation

Very soon, the "battle about the Bible" started to cross the borders of Germany. German theology was and still is highly respected all over the world, for better or worse. So, very soon, it also reached those churches who owed their existence to the modern evangelical movement of world missions and had a deep trust in the reliability of the Bible as the Word of God. Now theological skepticism was introduced to them by the representatives of their mother churches overseas.[40] This makes it obvious that the "hermeneutical question" is not simply a case of scholastic hair-splitting, as I once was told by ecumenical leaders at the 8th World Missionary Conference at Bangkok in 1973.[41]

This becomes all the more evident if we remind ourselves of the central place given to Holy Scripture in the Protestant-Evangelical Churches even since the days of the Reformation.

The decisive question in *Martin Luther*'s controversy with the papists was this: what must Christians in general, and more specifically, what must teachers of the Church, regard as the source and yardstick for their doctrinal statements? His opponents endeavored to refute him by arguments taken from the tradition of the fathers and councils. Luther held fast to the principle that Scripture alone was the normative foundation of all preaching and teaching within the Church. Thus the slogan *"sola scriptura"* (Scripture alone) became the bedrock of evangelical faith and action. The tremendous emphasis on the authority of the Bible is brought out in the Introduction to the Formula of Concord of 1577:[42]

We believe, teach and confess that the sole rule and criterion by which all doctrines and teachers are to be judged are the prophetical apostolic writings of the Old Testament and the New Testament only. ... Other writings of ancient and modern teachers, however famous they might be, should not be held equal to Holy Scripture but should alto-

---

[39] R. BÄUMER, P. BEYERHAUS, F. GRÜNZWEIG (eds.) 1980, pp. 24-35.

[40] Peter BEYERHAUS 1972a: Ch. 6.

[41] Idem, 1973: pp. 119f.; 180-182.

[42] Die Bekenntnisschriften der evangelisch-lutherischen Kirche, [2]1955: vol II, p. 767.

gether be subjected to it, and should not be accepted otherwise than as witnesses ... "

Similar affirmations were made in all other confessional statements at the age of the Reformation. I just mention the Calvinist "(Second) Helvetic Confession" (1566),[43] the "39 Articles of the Church of England" (1571),[44] and the Westminster Confession (1647).[45] In our generation this tradition is renewed in the Mission Declarations of the Evangelical Movement, e.g. Wheaton 1966, Frankfurt (1970), Lausanne 1974, Seoul 1975.

The Reformation believed Scripture to be the only fountain of doctrine. The Bible held the supreme teaching office in the Church. Orthodox Lutherans consequently considered it most important to prove that the Bible, because of its inherent quality, was fully able to exercise its ministry. Lutheran theologians strove to refute the Roman Catholic argument that the Bible was, for laymen, an obscure book full of confusing ambiguity. For this purpose they developed a very minute doctrine of the inspiration of the Holy Scriptures saying: as they had come into being, not out of a human decision, but as the Holy Spirit breathed on their human authors, the Holy Scriptures had necessarily the quality of complete inerrancy, for the Holy Spirit is infallible. This doctrine was applied not only to statements about faith and ethics, but also to statements concerning history, chronology, and geography. Some theologians even affirmed that the Bible had been dictated by the Holy Spirit during a complete suspension of the human personality of the writer.

Since Scripture was given to men as the sole and authoritative record of God's saving acts, the Bible was declared to be not only completely reliable but also clear and sufficient for all knowledge necessary for salvation. Thus the affirmation of the *"claritas et perspicuitas scripturae sacrae"* (clarity and lucidity of the Holy Scriptures) could be called the central Protestant dogma in theological epistemology.

In order to understand the Scriptures, it was believed, no supplementary means of interpretation taken from outside are required. Even if the internal evidence of the Scriptures is not everywhere the same, they are their own and sole interpreter. The dark and more difficult passages are to be understood in the light of the plain and clear pas-

---

[43] Hans STEUBING et. al., 1977, p. 155.

[44] Ibid. p. 240.

[45] Ibid. pp. 209 f.

sages. This procedure would invariably resolve any seeming contradiction which might appear in the different statements of the Bible.

II. The Changed Hermeneutical Situation Today

If, after this glance into the past, we direct our eyes to the present, the contrast could not be more striking. In Germany today – and in other lands also – there is hardly a faster way to ruin one's reputation as a respectable theologian than to speak of the inspiration of the Bible, its inerrancy,[46] and the absence of self-contradictions in it. The doctrine of the authority of the Scriptures is openly questioned by our present theological generation and its intellectual leaders. This started remarkably during the late 1960's and early 1970's. At that time, radical movements within the churches, and even the Geneva leadership of the WCC, turned their attention one-sidedly to social and political involvement. Because of this, secular analysis of the world situation seemed much more important than biblical orientation. This fact could and still can be seen in many different connections. In one of the preparatory texts for the Fourth General Assembly of the World Council of Churches at Uppsala (1968), we could read:

"... some Christians look upon the processes of secular history as furnishing new divine revelations which the church must accept: They discern the activity of the Spirit in the emergence of free nations and international solidarities and undertakings where Christians and non-Christians cooperate in seeking justice or peace in the new social structure created by the technological revolution. Such attitudes contest the claim that the Church alone is entrusted with the power to announce the Kingdom of God and that its life and witness is the only true anticipation of the Lord's coming."[47]

More radical in tone, but in thorough agreement with the WCC document, a few years later a conference of German junior ministers produced the following statement: "We cannot naively gauge the way we seek orientation from contemporary social and personal concerns. In contemporary discussion, the Bible meets us as one partner amongst others."

---

[46] James I. PACKER: Art. "Infallibility and Inerrancy of the Bible," in: NDT pp. 337f. – J.D. Hannah (ed.), 1984. – N.L. Geisler (ed.), 1979.

[47] World Council of Churches 1967, p. 10.

Some church leaders wondered how those young theological candidates could arrive at such shocking conclusions! They appeared to reveal acute Marxist influence on their thinking. This was obviously true. But those responsible officials did not consider that this could have happened only because the theological pattern built up during their university studies had suffered severe structural damage. The watering down of their belief in the authority, reliability, and internal unity of the Bible had been caused by the critical approach and arbitrary reinterpretations of several successive schools of academic "exegesis." But to this the leaders of our established churches had been blinded. We need to look at this problem more closely.

III. The Bible Viewed at as a Piece of Literary History

During the *Enlightenment*[48] of the eighteenth century, a great change took place in the theological approach to the Bible. Biblical research came under the powerful influence of *Rationalism*,[49] the modern way of thinking. Man become conscious of himself within his world and gained great confidence in the ability of his own reason. He developed a new interest in history, understood himself in historical perspective, and evaluated history in the light of his own problems. The new contact with other cultures brought to Western Christendom an insight into other religions. This greatly stimulated the study of comparative religions and the quest for their common content. Scholars no longer looked for biblical texts to prove their dogmatic systems. Rather, they sought out the *human side* of the Bible. Its historic origin received the most attention. The Bible was seen as only one book among others. The analytical and comparative methods of modern literary art were applied to it.

The first Protestant theologian who developed a purely rationalist approach to biblical exegesis was *Johann Salomo Semler* (1725-91),[50] a scholar widely respected at his time. In a negative reaction against his pietistic education, he opened himself to the influence of the deistic philosophy of the Enlightenment. From 1752 Semler taught as a professor at the University of Halle, which otherwise had been a center of Pietism where the first evangelical mission board was established by

---

[48] E. CASSIERER 1951. – P. GAY 1970.
[49] H. TITTMANN 1816.
[50] G. HORNIG 1961.

August Hermann Francke (1663-1727)[51] in 1706. His successor Semler taught biblical disciplines, Church History, Dogmatics and Ethics. To him, human reason was the highest authority in all realms. In this way, he came to the following convictions:

1. The divine inspiration of the Bible is refuted in principal. Criticism of the biblical Canon, i.e. the collection of authentic documents, is exercised by means of historical science.

2. Each individual erudite Christian decides for himself which biblical writings are important for his personal faith.

3. The Old Testament is significant only for the Jewish nation; the universal religion of Christianity however is contained in the New Testament.

4. The task of scientific exegesis is to discern and discard such elements in the biblical writings which are conditioned by the circumstances of their time. The exegete has to decide what may be of enduring significance.

5. Only the "religious-ethical truths" in the Bible are of divine origin.

6. Academic theology must be granted complete freedom for its scientific research and teaching.

7. All theological statements – including the Churches' confessions – are historically conditioned by their times and accordingly merely relative expressions of truth. There is no binding force in them that may infringe individual liberty. Consequently, Semler refuses to present a clear definition of Christianity.

8. Christianity and non-Christian religions as well are elements of the "divine world plan." – Thus, the distance between them is reduced considerably.

This summary of Semler's ideas can lead us to a surprising insight: Most of the assertions of later theological schools that practiced "historical-critical Bible research" were already anticipated at the heyday of Enlightenment! At the end of the *eighteenth century* rationalistic ideas practically dominated both, at the theological faculties and even in church life.

The **nineteenth century** may be called the classical "age of historicism." In it the "historical method" achieved a dominating role in Bible

---

[51] Erich BEYREUTHER, 1958. – Arno Lehmann (ed.) 1957: pp. 33-45.

exegesis. Only this method was regarded as intellectually honest and acceptable. This value judgment prevails even today in university theology. The "historical-critical method" of exegesis was – and is – regarded as scientifically indispensable to any legitimate theological insight. Thus this twisted view of the Scriptures has actually now assumed the position which in older Protestant orthodoxy was occupied by the doctrine of inspiration! Its aim is to secure the intellectual validity of any theological statement basing itself on a biblical text. Accordingly, the famous theologian *Gerhard Ebeling* (1912-2001) called the development of this method "the most important achievement of Protestant theology since the Reformation."[52] He held that the genuine mission of the Reformers could be fulfilled only by the use of the historical-critical method.

On the other hand, many Bible-orientated Christians fear that this method may deeply endanger their faith. They regard it as the root of all evil. In order to decide who is right, we have to ask: what is this method exactly?

IV. The Historical-Critical Method[53]

1. The Meaning of the Terminology.

When we use the term "*the* historical-critical method" in the singular, we must realize that it refers to a whole complex of instruments used in the scientific research in the Bible. The collective term "historical-critical-method" is somewhat misleading. It has contributed to a false understanding. Some state naively that the consistent application of the historical-critical method is the only adequate way for modern man to reach a genuine understanding of the biblical texts!

It is important to realize that the hyphenated combination of the two adjectives "historical" and "critical" is not common practice in other arts and sciences. The term has been specifically coined by a certain school in liberal theology. The two adjectives express two distinct concerns. A *historical* interest traces the complicated origins of the biblical books. It asks what situations and traditions have influenced the biblical authors.

---

[52] Gerhard EBELING 1950, pp. 1-46.
[53] E. KRENTZ 1976.

A *critical* interest searches for the authenticity and validity of a particular text as to its form and content. The historical-critical method is usually divided into *three main branches*: *textual* criticism, *literary* criticism, and *higher* criticism:

Textual criticism compares the ancient biblical manuscripts and attempts to establish the probable original wording of the text.

Literary criticism tries to establish the literal integrity of a biblical book: has it an inner unity? Has it been written by one author only? Is it really written by the person to whom it is ascribed? Can we trace a history of oral tradition and revision? What interest can be discovered in such different historical layers? – An important part of literary criticism is *form criticism*. It asks, of what nature are the different literary units that make up a particular biblical book? They may be historical accounts, hymns, legal documents, creeds, or theological discourses.

Finally, *higher criticism* arises from the fact that certain internal tensions seem to exist between different biblical texts. Two biblical authors or even one may have two sets of diverging historical data. For example, there are three different accounts of the conversion of Paul (Acts 9, 22, and 26). – Furthermore, theologians feel entitled to establish a certain normative criterion, i.e. a central theological principle within the Scripture. On its basis they evaluate all other theological statements in the Bible. For example, it could be asked: is man justified by faith without works, as Paul teaches in Romans (Rom 3:28), or by works and not faith alone, as James (2:24) affirms? Can these two views be brought to a synthesis (as I believe), or do we have to opt for one of them, as even Luther thought (mistakenly, I think)? For it all depends from how you define "faith" and how you understand "works:" Are they our human achievement or a fruit of the Holy Spirit?!

2. The Rightful Use of Historical Perspectives

The Bible is not an easy book, if we realistically and objectively seek to interpret it with all the problems we find in it. Nobody can honestly deny its theological riddles and its inter-relatedness with its contemporary world. Therefore, we should recognize the desirability of approaching biblical texts in a scholarly way. The faith of the Christian community has always been enriched by serious research.

The biblical accounts of creation and Christ's crucifixion as well as resurrection are not placed in a closely knit dogmatic system nor re-

corded in an unbroken chain of historical events. Their primary intention is not to satisfy the desire of philosophical speculation nor the interests of historical science. Rather, they testify to the mysterious way
in which God led His people, the ancient and the new Israel, according
to His sovereign plan of salvation. They also show how Israel's understanding of God was gradually shaped by His unpredictable intervention in acts of salvation and by his revealing his purposes for them to
the prophets and apostles.

The discovery of the historicity of the Bible is a truly liberating experience for us. It shows us that the Bible does not want to be treated as
a textbook with stereotype formulations of rules and doctrines. It rather
sets forth the manifold offer of God's grace and His calling of each
new generation to obedience. But in all changing situations, He remained faithful to His promises and consistent in His commandments.
He did so in reference to the specific cultural and political context of
those particular times. Therefore, the biblical texts reflect these historic
and personal circumstances. An inflexible "dictation theory" of inspiration, however, could prevent people from understanding the unfolding
of God's revelation in history, and prevent them from understanding
the living human personalities of the writers and their responsible share
in formulating their messages.

3. The Illegitimate Application of Critical and Historical Viewpoints

Granting all this, we must not overlook the fact that a historical-
critical examination of the Bible entails *tremendous dangers*. These
arise from a fact which many theologians are not aware of: no science
or art can work absolutely objectively and without any presuppositions.
On the contrary, both the selection and the evaluation of the methods of
study – and thus also its results – are predetermined by the position
which the observer himself has chosen. This principle applies in different degrees to the various branches of arts and sciences. But the *complementary theory* of the Danish physicist and Nobel prize winner *Niels
H. D. Bohr* (1885-1962) has shown that even exact science in its explo-
ration and description of the same natural phenomenon may arrive at
different and contradictory statements. For statements made depend on
the perspective of the scientist. Thus, the beam of light can be understood both, as an immaterial wave and also as a close succession of the
smallest units of a light "substance." The two different findings are
complementary, but they are *not contradictory*.

Theologians who stumble over the seeming contradictions in the Bible should heed this insight. They should confess with shame that their colleagues in science have surpassed them in their critical self-examination of the presuppositions of their epistemological principles. Many a time, the working methods of historical-critical research have been secretly predetermined by the critical theologian himself. For he held an unreflecting and unwarranted belief in the absoluteness of its concepts of reality and its way of obtaining knowledge. All this has constituted nothing more than a pseudo-scientific justification of a certain philosophical position, whether it is rationalism, idealism or - nowadays - even dialectical materialism! Theologians have thereby often fatally blocked the true way of gaining divine insight.

4. Three Fatal Presuppositions

We can discern three fatal presuppositions by which representatives of the historical-critical method have abandoned and are abandoning the basis for fruitful and legitimate research into Scripture. None of these presuppositions is demanded either by Scripture itself or by a true scientific epistemology.

The *first presupposition* links up the theological method of attaining insight to the epistemological theory developed by the philosophers *René Descartes* (1536-1650) and *Immanuel Kant* (1724-1804). They have been explicitly applied to theology by *Ernst Troeltsch* (1865-1923).[54] This theory of attaining knowledge places at its center "man as subject" who faces that which he wants to know as his object. But – Kant and Troeltsch claim – it is not possible for man to gain absolute insight into the thing he wants to know. He is limited by the categories of attaining knowledge inherent to his human nature. Thus he can only attain insight into things as they *appear to him.*

In the existentialist school of *Rudolf Bultmann*[55] this idea of the empirical limitation of our knowledge is central. Here it is maintained that by revelation we cannot receive objective knowledge of metaphysical objects like heaven or life after death. Only those experiences which touch me deeply in the center of my personality are relevant.

Another aspect of this adherence to a general empirical theory of knowledge is that the student of the Bible must accept the closed sys-

---

[54] Ernst TROELTSCH 191,: pp. 729-753.
[55] R.A. JOHNSON 1974.

tem of the scientific world-view. Each event is seen as caused by an impulse in accordance to scientific law. Theologians often overlook the fact that modern science no longer attempts to subject the totality of reality to such a closed system. They admit that we are not really sure that all processes in nature are determined by unchangeable laws. But curiously, by an act of voluntary subjection to an outdated pseudo-scientific world view, modernist theologians demand that all biblical miracles are to be judged according to the closed system understanding of nature. They apply this norm to everything in the Bible from the creation account to the prediction of Christ's bodily return. It is obvious that, under such circumstances, the historical-critical approach can end up in a wholesale elimination of biblical affirmations. In his famous demythologization program of 1941, Bultmann has catalogued them under the label *"discarded."* He wrote: "Discarded are the stories about Christ's descend to hell and ascend to heaven. ... Discarded is the expectation of the "Son of Man" coming with the clouds of heaven and the rapture of the faithful to meet him in the air. ... Discarded is the belief in spirits and demons because of our knowledge about the forces and laws of nature. You cannot use electric light and razors, seek for medical help and at the same time believe in the NT's world of spirits and miracles. ... Discarded is mythical eschatology simply because Christ did not return immediately, as expected. On the contrary world history went on and is going to go on, as every person with a sound mind will agree."[56] We see how the consistent application of the rationalistic view point leads to an elimination of central affirmations of the Christian Creed!

What is the *second dangerous presupposition* of the historical-critical method in the conviction of many of its representatives? It is the assumption that understanding a certain biblical author or text basically consists in discovering the individual peculiarity over against all other authors and traditions. Thus the essence is sought in a nominalistic way in the isolated individual. By this process the inner coherence of all biblical texts is frequently overlooked. Many historical-critical scholars, applying their radical methods of form criticism and higher criticism, have gone so far that they have split the Old Testament and the New Testament into smaller and smaller units, deriving from different sources. Sometime these units may consist of only half a verse!

---

[56] Rudolph BULTMANN ³1954: pp. 17 f.

In the process of studying these particularities the scholar finally discovers so many seeming contradictions in the texts, that he ends up with losing his sense of the organic wholeness of the Bible. Thus in many quarters it has become impossible to speak of a common theology of the Old Testament or of the New Testament, and even more impossible to speak of a theology of the whole Bible.

Instead, "biblical theology"[57] has been dissolved in a vast number of theologies or personal concepts, opinions, or conscious reinterpretations by individual authors. By the mutual exclusiveness of their several concepts, all these authors seem to question and criticize each other. Bible readers who follow such "theologians" lose any sense of the authority and normative standard of the Scriptures. Carrying this line of thinking to its logical conclusion my late Tübingen colleague *Ernst Käsemann* (1908-98) stated to the Faith and Order Commission of the WCC in 1964: "The New Testament is in a shocking degree non-authentic, full of fictions and contradictions."[58]

Such chaotic results of the historical-critical method cannot satisfy these modernist theologians in the long run. They seek for an integrating principle which can serve as a center or as a norm of theological evaluation for all the seemingly heterogeneous texts. They introduce a *distinction between* the actual *wording* of the biblical texts and their real *intention*. While the wording is conditioned by the historical circumstances and thus transitory, the intention, it is claimed, is of abiding value.

But here we meet the *third most dangerous presupposition* introduced by representatives of the historical-critical theology: the presumed intention of the texts is "discovered" by way of abstraction from their real wording and by means of a guiding question or principle not gained from the texts themselves.

Such a hermeneutical clue is usually taken from the interpreter's own philosophical predilection and forced upon the biblical text from outside. Although this is true, the modern theologian would not admit it. Rather he would point to many biblical texts which (by means of his hermeneutical approach) start radiating truth before our eyes in an amazing fashion. The hermeneutical principle which one uses seems at first glance to produce exactly those relevant answers to our contempo-

---

[57] B.S. CHILDS 1970. – W.J. HARRINGTO, 1973.
[58] E. KÄSEMANN 1964: pp. 58-63.

rary problems which we had been searching for. But what do you find when you look a bit more thoroughly at the quoted texts and start exegeting them in their original setting? You will soon discover that no genuine exegesis is offered to us but rather an ingenious, but alien, reinterpretation.

Such an integrating hermeneutical principle was introduced by Bultmann and his school in form of the "existential interpretation." Bultmann's disciples ask in what way the intention of a certain text was to change the perception man had about himself. In describing such human "self-understanding," Bultmann to a large degree made use of the existential analysis which had been developed by the modern philosophy of existence of *Martin Heidegger* (1889-1976).[59] It had become widely popularized in Europe by existentialist novels and dramas of modern writes like *Albert Camus* (1913-60) and *Jean-Paul Sartre* (1905-80).[60] According to this view, man is thrown into a world which is full of riddles and dangers; we are faced by inescapable death, filled with anxiety or illusion. Now it all depends on how man realizes his own position. According to Bultmann himself, human beings might either be enslaved in their self-centered inclination or become liberated from it by opening up for a new dimension. He believed that his idea of a basic change in man's self-perception through his encounter with the Kerygma, the message of redemption, was in fact the very center of the Gospel according to both Paul and Martin Luther. Thus he claimed to have restored the authority of the theology of the reformers over against its idealistic perversion by theological liberals at the end of the last century, who believed human beings can develop their true selves by striving for the highest moral ideals in their strength.

This actually was the reason for the amazing influence of Bultmann's theology: it appeared to be modern and still genuinely Lutheran at the same time!

But his existentialist concept of justification by faith differs substantially from Paul's doctrine of justification. According to Bultmann, man (after the change in his self-understanding) actually remains alone in his world. The newly gained "openness to the future" appears as a rather vague and impersonal feeling. In the New Testament, however, justification by faith constitutes a new personal fellowship with a living God in Jesus Christ. Bultmann expressly declares such fellowship to be

---

[59] M. WARNOCK 1970. – J. MACQUARRIE 1955.
[60] Jean-Paul SARTRE 1948.

mythological. Consequently, a prayer of petition and intercession becomes meaningless; at its best it could be replaced by meditation.

5. The Theologies of Socio-political Involvement

Bultmann's hermeneutical principle was time-bound, however. This is clearly seen by the historical fate which has befallen it. During the late sixties and early seventies, avant-garde German scholars like *Jürgen Moltmann* (1926)[61] firmly committed themselves to leave behind the age of a pessimistic existentialist individualism. They confidently entered into a seemingly new epoch where mankind as a whole embarked upon strenuous efforts to reshape the structures of the socio-economic and political world order. Little attention now was paid to the individual and the understanding of his own existence. Contemporary ecumenical interest focused on terms like "history," "social structures," or "utopian vision." These determine men's political actions. Thus, in the new generation, the existentialist school had to give way to the new theologies of revolution, liberation, or feminism which articulated the neo-Marxist "principle of hope"[62] dressed in the terminology of biblical eschatology.

Christians who used to be opposed to "modern" theology were well advised to be careful not uncritically to rejoice at this change. There was no reason for spiritual optimism. For the basic method of interpretation still remained the same in both schools of thought. They are both recklessly using the results of radical literary and higher criticism. Both of them recklessly used the alleged historical conditioning and pluralism of the biblical texts. They did and still do so in order to introduce their various philosophical keys, with the help of which they construct their own hermeneutical system. And they do so on the basis of some arbitrarily selected and reinterpreted texts. Both, existentialist and political theologies, are inclined to silence the real message of the documents of biblical revelation. Both do a superb job of proof-texting. The exegesis of both is, however, highly colored by predetermined results.

In the Bultmann era, an existentialist chamber orchestra played variations on one single theme: the call to make a decision for a new understanding of oneself. In the neo-marxist climate, a band of trumpets led by the Old Testament prophets sounds an "ultimate challenge"

---

[61] J. MOLTMANN 1969. – Idem, 1975. – R. BAUCKHAM 1987.
[62] Ernst BLOCH 1947ff.

to the whole church, calling her to participate in world revolution, thus ushering in the Kingdom of God into this world.

The average congregation, however, finds itself unable to recognize the voice of its Good Shepherd in it. Believers hear it neither in the charming tunes of the existentialist chamber concert, nor in the piercing sounds of the revolutionary trumpets. They sadly face the torn document of its traditional faith looking like a battlefield in which bombs and shells have gouged deep trenches.

V. Pneumatic Exegesis – a Renewed Spiritual Approach to Scripture[63]

1. Reaffirming Biblical Authority

It is not my intention merely to unveil the shocking picture of the desolate theological scenery we find in Western theology today. One must go on to explore the ultimate consequences of such exegetical methods.

I would also plead for a new understanding of the Bible which relies completely on the interpretive power of the Holy Spirit.[64] It is necessary to do away with an approach to the Bible which sees in it nothing else but a literary collection of contradictory bits of documents, reflecting merely the existential self-understanding, or the political utopias, of past generations in remote cultural surroundings.

Today's challenge is, to rediscover the Bible as (1) the normative embodiment of the revelatory words and acts of God with His elected people in the *history of salvation* and (2) as the witness of the people's exemplary response in faith or of their regrettable response in disobedience. We are called upon to take up our Bible not to do socio-religious studies, but to ask the Lord to speak His living word directly to us through it. With the same authority with which He once spoke to the prophets, evangelists, and apostles, God speaks to us today. He is still able and willing to shepherd, console, exhort, and warn our present generation.

We must liberate ourselves from the dictatorship of theological scholars, especially those who declare that their allegedly scientific

---

[63] Hellmuth FREY [2]1972.
[64] P. BEYERHAUS, 1996b, pp. 338-351.

approach is the only possible one for attaining a true understanding of the Bible. Protestant churches recognize no papal office. Nevertheless, by regarding the propositions of modern exegetical scholars as infallible results, we are in danger of coming under the control of a multitude of "popes" who are contradicting and superceding each other. I refer to theologians who are imperiously absolutizing their academic methods. Although their views are always hypothetical and opposed by their colleagues or successors, they offer them as "indisputable results of scientific research." They declare them to be normative for all honest Christian faith which wants to cleave to the truth.

Not all modern theologians speak this way, but they do exist. Their ambition to be the teachers of the Church is unbendable. They produce around themselves an atmosphere either of fascination or of intellectual terror. Nobody dares to break this spell. Nobody wants to risk his reputation as an enlightened contemporary or as a respectable modern theologian.

In my own personal experience and by contact with students, I have discovered what a hypnotic effect can originate from such a pressured belief in "the latest insight of theological science." Therefore, my Bible-orientated colleagues and I never tire of explaining to our students that there is nothing less scientific than to declare theological hypotheses to be "scientifically established." I found that such explanation achieved almost a kind of exorcism under modern circumstances. It had a wonderful liberating effect. Those young theologians, depressed by the latest persuasive hermeneutical system, had almost lost their sense of humor. Now they became overwhelmed with the joy of the spiritual life which a re-opened Bible had given them. They were enabled to pray again. They heard in the Scriptures anew the voice of the living Lord. They experienced personal fellowship with Him who has risen from the dead, both spiritually and bodily. They realized that just as His death could not keep Him in the grave, neither can an outdated scientific theory evaporate Him into a vague philosophical idea. Nor can it transform Him into a fashionable model for admiration: Jesus, the "man for others," the "revolutionary," the "superstar."

2. The Holy Spirit and Hermeneutics

I have already anticipated the positive step which must follow the refutation of a philosophically pre-conditioned hermeneutical approach in modern academic exegesis. We could call that negative first step the "demythologization of demythologization."

Those modernist theologians who introduce their own philosophical principles of understanding into their methods of exegesis have made one correct observation: there is no understanding of the Holy Scriptures without presuppositions. We all need a hermeneutical key which gives us access to a consistent understanding. True, historical approaches to biblical texts might, to a certain degree, clarify the external circumstances under which a biblical book has been written. Therefore already *August Hermann Francke* practiced what he called the grammatical method, and recently evangelical scholars speak of their "grammatical-historic" method. They accurately analyze both the wording of a given biblical text and its original historic situation. But they know that this indispensable exercise cannot give us access to the inner understanding of the sacred texts. It is just cracking the shell of the nut, as Francke remarked. But from there you must proceed to taste the sweetness of the kernel. Nobody is touched or overwhelmed by having identified the literary species or historical setting of a biblical text. No preacher receives a striking message for his sermon in this way. The decisive act of understanding takes place rather at the moment in which that authority which is speaking in and through the text meets something within me which is already predisposed to be spoken to by this authority.

In the same way, an unmusical scholar may be able to compile some bibliographical or statistical data from the history of music. But he will never be able to enjoy an oratorio or even to understand it. This also explains why true believers often feel untouched when they listen to a modernist sermon. Possibly the preacher himself did not experience that essential inner understanding! In that case, he does not transmit on the wave length the congregation is tuned to. In John 10:3-5 Jesus identifies himself as the Good Shepherd whose sheep follow him because they know his voice. *"But they will never follow a stranger; in fact they will run away from him, because they do not recognize a stranger's voice."*

We have to add, however, that the communication gap can also originate with those who listen to the sermon if they are not genuine sheep of Christ!

Communication between the Bible and the congregation is made possible by the fact that both are created by the same divine force, the infusion of the Holy Spirit. He takes his abode in them as a living divine personality. Just as the congregation is the temple of the Holy Spirit, the Scripture (according to II Timothy 3:16) is – called *"theo-*

pneustos" or "inbreathed by the Spirit of God." The Greek word *"theopneustia"* is translated into Latin by the term *"inspiratio."* It means exactly the same: that the Scripture is blown through – inbreathed – by the Holy Spirit. From this we can conclude that the future advance or the downfall of our churches is dependent on our readiness to say a clear "yes" to the inspiration of the Scriptures. Only in this way will our minds regain that unity and authority lost to us by our misdirected hermeneutical approaches.

3. The Decisive Task

By this I do not mean that we can return to the doctrine of inspiration in the form in which it was developed by classical Protestant Orthodoxy in the 16th and 17th centuries, which was not yet fully aware of the historical conditioning of the biblical books. But I maintain that the demand for a new acceptance of the inspiration of the Bible is placing a decisive task before the entire field of theology in the immediate future. That task is to relate the genuine result of literary research to the authoritative claim of the Holy Scriptures to be the essential literary embodiment of God's self-revelation in history. If theology should prove unable to solve the task, it would have lost the right to be called theology. It is no longer scholarly occupation with the *Logos tou Theou,* the Word of God. It would then by its own efforts have eliminated itself as superfluous and irrelevant.

The resolution of those young German ministers, quoted in the beginning, was no mere slip of the tongue. It was the inevitable consequence of a line of approach to which they were introduced by their theological teachers. Thus it is a *"mene tekel upharsim"* ("numbered, weighed and given away," Dan 5:26-28) for much modern theology.

Scientific literary research into the historic origins of the Bible can be good and useful, but only as long as we remain aware that the originator of the biblical texts is the Holy Spirit. It was He who gave us this text in its final normative shape in the canon of the Old Testament and New Testament, conceived and accepted by the early Church. The Holy Spirit has given the impulse to all who have been engaged in conceiving, keeping, copying, compiling, and revising the biblical texts. He also preserved them from distortions and false additions. Thus, in the word which has been received and written down by mortal men, we encounter the living voice of God – sometimes directly, sometimes in a manner more obscure to our present understanding. God's word does not need to be rewritten or reshaped at every cultural change. It does not need to be reinterpreted by any philosophical principles. God's word is able to speak to us in our space age as directly as it did to the Greeks in the first century and to the Papuans in their Stone Age culture at the beginning of this century.

Sometimes we meet people who try to discredit the method of making direct use of a biblical text by asking such vexing questions as: "Sure that is what is written, but what does this mean today?" or, "How can we speak about God today?" These questions are based on wrong presuppositions. But they do point us, against their own intention, toward a correct observation. True understanding presupposes an inner likeness of that which is to be understood and the subject who wants to understand. The hermeneutics of modernist theology tries to accomplish this task by reformulating the text in philosophical or sociological terms taken from our situation, but leading to falsification and even to an offence against God's majesty!

That which needs to be changed is not the text but rather the inner attitude of men which causes their difficulty in understanding. God himself offers to make this change in us. It can take place when the Holy Spirit himself takes possession of us from within, makes us receptive to God's voice, regenerates and illuminates our distorted reason, and transforms us into the image of His Son. All those who have received the offer of salvation in Jesus Christ, have by faith and baptism also received the Spirit of sonship (Rom 8:23). It is this Spirit of Christ within us who, in hearing the word of the Bible, hears and recognizes His own word.

The person who has not received the Spirit of sonship is, according to the words of Paul, still a "natural man." To him the judgment applies: "The unspiritual man does not receive the things of the Spirit of God, for they are folly to him, and he is not able to understand them because they are spiritually discerned." The Christian, however, is entitled to confess: "We have received, not the spirit of the world, but the Spirit that comes from God, in order that we may know the things which God has freely given us" (1 Cor 2:14f.).

Now the relationship between the spiritual and the natural man is not one of sociologically separated groups. Christians who rely solely on their own natural reason are leaving the spiritual realm and become natural men again. Thus, a Christian theologian can gain genuine insight into the Bible only to the degree in which he approaches the Scriptures in the Spirit and in the obedience of faith.

The *misery of modernist theology* is that it has participated in the original sin of the Enlightenment, the idolization of man's reason. In a hidden way, the tendency to ascribe an absolute authority to our un-enlightened reason is still influencing all our theological work, even the work of many conservative scholars.

The *healing of our theology* and our churches in Europe, America and partly in Asia as well can only take place if in faith we penitently subject our intellect to the guidance of the Holy Spirit. This guidance can be gained only by a personal life in the Spirit and by listening to the continuous self-explication of the divine Word within the fellow-ship of the Church of Jesus Christ. Theologians can never claim to be teachers of the Church as long as they act as autonomous interpreters of the Bible who respect only the thorough application of their "scientific" methods. They can become valid teachers of the Church only to the degree they enter the field where the Holy Spirit is displaying His ener-gies. This means at the same time that they carefully study the living history of biblical interpretation which is the special field of the Holy Spirit's work. They must humbly join the chain of witnesses, not so much as historical critics, but rather as the faithful stewards of God's mysteries.

Chapter 3
The Truth Encounter with
Semi-Religious Ideologies

Introduction

Have you ever looked at a modern world map showing the regions that are occupied by the major religions? Then you may also discover areas which are seemingly void of any religion. Instead they are dominated by ideologies, such as secularism, Marxism or Maoism, and formerly by National-Socialism. This indicates an important fact: During the 20th century ideologies have sprung up and spread so forcefully that over wide areas they replaced those religions that once had prevailed there.

I. What is an Ideology?

The semantic analysis shows its two components: The first one *"ide-"* is derived from the Greek verb ἰδεῖν (*idein*) = to see and from the noun εἶδος (*eidos*) = visible appearance, or more specifically **image**.[65] We find it also in our words "idea" and "ideal." – The second component is derived from λόγος = word and from λόγια = doctrine. An ideology thus is the doctrine about significant images or visions that appear in human minds. Thinking people are induced to understand them and to work for their practical realization. We may think of *Plato's* (427-347 b.C.) famous teaching about the *eternal ideas* of which the empirical things are only imperfect counterfeits.[66] The ideas embrace the metaphysical nature of the empirical objects: e.g. a visible dog is just an imperfect model of the eternal idea of the dog. The idealist tries to transform our imperfect physical world, especially society, to become more concordant with the eternal ideas beyond it.

But already in the 18th century the term "ideology" was used from a secular point of view. The French philosopher *Antoine Destutt de Tracy* (1754 – 1836) taught that we have to gain our ideas and values exclu-

---

[65] Gerhard KITTEL: Art. *"eidos"* in: Theologisches Wörterbuch zum Neuen Testament, vol. II., p. 372.

[66] Wilhelm WINDELBAND, [14]1950, pp. 98ff.

sively from the perception of our external world. The ideologist presents himself as a realist. He critically examines the objective truth of the theories which underlie our social and political actions: Do they conform with the scientifically established reality? Or are they just expressions of unaccountable speculation?

Today, the word "ideology" often is used in a very vague sense. It may refer to any attempt to analyse a problematic political situation and to suggest a solution for it. The different political parties in Korea each have their own "ideology," which in this context means "programmes."

But in our context we speak of "ideologies" with a more characteristic meaning. We are referring to modern world views that attempt to explain the total reality from one, single, this-worldly principle. Moreover they try to change the present situation according to wishful imaginations of their founders and adherents. Since the time of the *Enlightenment* and the *French Revolution* (1789-92) there has been a constant series of changing ideologies. They recommended themselves as the solution to all fundamental problems. Since Christianity has lost its former influence as the one authoritative world view, ideologies have more or less successfully took its place in public opinion. During one recent epoch, at least,[67] there arose ideologies of a different nature. Some were philosophically or scientifically oriented types of deistic or atheistic *humanism*. They might build on psychological experiments or propose an autonomous moral value system. Others again as e.g. *Liberalism* followed a certain market strategy to provide for the common welfare. The most influential ideologies in the 19th century were Conservatism, Nationalism, Liberalism, Socialism, Hegelianism, Positivism, Evolutionism (=Darwinism) and Marxism.

Particular brands were the ***totalitarian ideologies.*** Their champions were deeply or even fanatically convinced of their doctrines as the only remedy for the public misery. Consequently they resorted to violence. They did so when less docile people did not follow voluntarily or if the enemy did not surrender unconditionally. The most widely spread ideologies which managed to establish complete control of the political systems were the socialist or communist movements of *Marxism, Leninism, Maoism* to the left, *Fascism* and *National-Socialism* to the right.[68] Nowadays even *Islamism* is taking the shape of a totalitarian ideology.

---

[67] Daniel BELL, 1960. – Fernandez de la MORA, 1955.

[68] Heinz KARST, 1979, pp. 86-93.

Thus we realize that ideologies appear in manifold shapes; but all justify their doctrines by a claim on "truth." How do we evaluate and approach ideologies from a biblical position?

II. The Unalterable Truth Claim of the Gospel

1. A Unique Proof

The word **truth** (ἀλήθεια = uncoveredness) is a biblical key term. In John's Gospel in particular it contains the totality of the Gospel.[69] Jesus says about himself: "I am the way, **the truth** and the life ..." (John 14:6).

Yet this truth claim of Christ and of biblical revelation in general has been contested throughout the history of his Church. For other people also claim truth for their deepest convictions. I remember reading a red poster in the formerly Communist East Germany, carrying a famous dictum of Lenin: "Marxism is almighty, because it is true!"

As Christians, therefore, we are asked, whether we are prepared to stand up for our truth and to face contradiction, scorn and even persecution for it. Why is this so important? How can Christians in spite of such totalitarian claims dare to protest? How can we confess like Peter before the Jewish Sanhedrin: "Salvation is found in no one else, for there is no other name under heaven given to men by which we must be saved" (Acts 4:12)?

The reason is that the truth of the Gospel does not originate from the philosophical reflections of our limited and erroneous human reason. It does not build upon the experiences or illuminations which the founders of non-Christian religions claim to have received. No, the truth of the Gospel is a divine gift. The eternal, almighty and all-knowing God Himself has bestowed it to us. It came from His heavenly abode, from that light which is inaccessible to any human grip; God did not send to us an idea or a system of doctrines. No: He sent His own co-existing Son. He came into our world in order to bear witness to the truth (John 18:37). Out of his own deepest knowledge Jesus has proclaimed God's counsel of salvation to us. His entire existence was transparent to God's holiness and love. Thus he could say about himself: *"He who sees me, sees the Father"* (John 14:9).

---

[69] Rudolf BULTMANN: Art. „Aleethei," vol. I, pp. 233-251, 245-249.

This majestic claim of Jesus immediately provoked opposition and even the murderous hatred that brought him to the Cross. But God miraculously confirmed that claim; He raised His Son from the dead! He let him, the Risen One, appear bodily to his disciples. Thus He assured them that He was really alive. Consequently they followed his Great Commission. They went as his witnesses into the whole then known world and boldly confessed: *"That which was from the beginning; which we have heard, which we have seen with our eyes, ... and our hands have touched – this we proclaim concerning the word of life"* (1 John 1:1-3). No other religion, no philosophy, no ideology has ever been able to base itself on such a proof as the Gospel message has.

2. Truth as an Evangelistic and Apologetic Obligation

To become a Christian means to acknowledge and grasp the illuminating, liberating and life-giving truth which God has sent us through the Gospel of Jesus Christ.

The Church has been called into existence by that truth. Therefore she is destined to be a stronghold, a pillar and a foundation of truth (1 Tim 3:15). She is the place where mankind perishing in its errors can find that infallible truth which alone can give life to it. Therefore the Church is commissioned to take the truth of the Gospel out into the world. For it wants to perform the same liberating work amongst all peoples, irrespective their race, culture, social standing or religion.

But on the way Christians will experience that they are not the only ones who come with an offer of truth and salvation.[70] Rather they meet rival offers from other ways of salvation, both religious and ideological ones.[71] Others, too, maintain (as stated earlier), that they bring the truth to mankind, and together with it redemption and historical change.

III. Various Religions and Ideologies and Their Common Origin

1. The Ultimate Root Causes

How do religions and ideologies come about? And how shall we evaluate them in the light of the Gospel of Truth? Since the Fall of

---

[70] Leonore BAZINEK, 1990.
[71] Klaus BOCKMÜHL 1986.

Adam, all mankind shares in the groaning of unredeemed creation. Man has been created in the image of God (Gen 1:27). As such he is destined to enjoy communion with Him and to receive eternal life. But in consequence of the disastrous separation from God he finds himself fettered by the forces of alienation, of suffering and killing. These fetters bind him together with all other creatures, which also groan because of their subjection to the forces of destruction (Rom 8:20-22).

But human beings always remain somehow conscious of their lost paradise, no matter how deeply they have fallen and how remote they are from God. They have a shadow-like sense of it, although they do not know exactly what that home looked like; neither do they recognize the real reason of their rejection. At the same time they cannot give up hoping that there will be an exit road out of their misery. Therefore man cannot cease to look around for a message that gives an answer to their riddles. He constantly seeks for ways which can lead him out of this damage.

St. Augustine in his "Confessions"[72] writes about our human heart that it is restless in us until it finds rest in God. In this unquenchable longing even in our alienation we still are connected with our heavenly Creator. This is caused by the light of truth which mysteriously enlightens everyone who comes into this world (John 1:4-7). And this longing is fulfilled by the appearance of the illuminating truth in the God-Man Jesus Christ.

But as well as that valid divine answer by God's revelation through the Gospel, other answers spring up. They seek to push into the same gap. They were suggested by a spiritual force hostile to God and man. That opponent sneaked into paradise and pretended to present a "better" truth than that of God. These alternative answers are at the roots of non-Christian religions and ideologies.

Both share, inasmuch as they are imitations of the divine truth, some formal elements with the Gospel: Firstly they try to inform man about the *root cause* of his present miserable state. Secondly they seek to point out to him a *new goal*, in which this misery will be overcome. Thirdly they offer *ways of salvation*, which people should go in order to reach that goal.[73]

---

[72] Aurelius AUGUSTINUS.

[73] Walter KÜNNETH, 1979, pp. 22-36.

2. The Difference between Religions and Ideologies

As to the peculiarities in their ways of salvation, the particular religions differ amongst each other; likewise ideologies too appear in different shapes.

The distinct point in which all **religions** differ from ideologies is their *supernatural orientation.* They try to direct themselves at an invisible reality that transcends our empirical world. This may be concepts of personal Gods like *Allah* in Islam or *Shiva* and *Vishnu* in Hinduism. It may also be a less tangible idea of an impersonal divine reality like *Brahman* in Brahmanism or an eternal world law like *Karma* in Buddhism. A knowledge that is conveyed by religion will always refer to an experience of divination or illumination.

In contrast to this, an **ideology** does not recognize any other kind of reality than that which can be found in our visible earthly nature, in human history and in the forces and laws that can be discovered here. Ideologists *claim a scientific character* for their doctrine, and they proudly abstain from faith experiences. They derive their insights from their own research or from the ingenious insights of their founders. They maintain, however, that the same insight can be arrived at by any human being that uses its reason.

However it is debatable whether the ideologists really are capable of maintaining their fundamental distinction between ideology and religion. We shall come back to this question.

IV. The Basic Elements of an Ideology

1. Ideologies are Secular Ways of Salvation

Ideologies are movements that seek to win people as loyal followers. They entice them by offering to show to them a way to liberation from their present miserable conditions into a satisfactory future. In analogy with religions, they present themselves as ways of salvation. But in a modern age where *reason* is strongly emphasized, ideologies recommend themselves to the human capability to gain *scientific knowledge.* Their point of departure is the actual or alleged state of misery in which individuals and communities have to exist. That state of emergency is generalized as being the basic cause for human suffering in its entirety. Depending on the chosen diagnostic perspective, an ideology might bear socio-economic features as with *Karl Marx* (1818-

83).[74] It can also bear psychological features as with *Siegmund Freud* (1856-1939), racial and biological features as with *Adolf Hitler* (1889-1945) or sexist features as with feminism.

Ideologists spend a lot of time trying to raise people's consciousness of their misery. They should be filled with indignation and impatient to cast off the shackles of their imprisonment.

Once this has been achieved, ideologists show to their adherents the way to "freedom." They encourage them to form coalitions to fight for their liberation. They point out the steps to be taken to change their present intolerable conditions: underpayment, oppressive structures of society and even prevailing moral standards. At this point ideologies are less concerned about intellectual explaining the truth. Rather they give *instructions for revolutionary action*.

Karl Marx expressed this in his the famous dictum:[75] "The philosophers have only interpreted the world. But the real task is to change it." Thus we can summarize: Ideologies are methodological directions to make people discontented and allow them to achieve their redemption by using their own potential.

2. Ideologies Show Goals of Hope

In order to mobilize the necessary inner forces and the readiness to endure, ideologists also have to inspire their followers with concrete hopes. They point out targets for them which they should strive for by all means. And they should be firmly persuaded that these goals lie within their reach. Therefore such goals are painted with radiant colours. Political ideologies try to excite the masses by inflammatory speeches, by pictures, spectacles, music, festivals and military parades. By these means, *stereotype slogans* are repeated over and over again. They should impress themselves deeply into the minds of the masses and fill them with ardour.

Once the stage of enthusiasm has been reached, the people become willing to discipline their life. They are prepared even to sacrifice it for the attainment of the ideological goal of hope. We call this *fanaticism*. Modern history is full of examples how ideologists by their mass manipulation have been able to inflame nations with a spirit of fanaticism so that they became ready to go to war. I had that experience in my

---

[74] See chapter IV.
[75] Karl MARX, 1971, p. 341.

youth when Hitler was able to turn our German nation into fanatics. He even drove it to commit collective suicide for the cause of the German "Third Reich" (=Empire). When the Second World War was nearly lost, the Nazis made a final desperate attempt to mobilize the last reserves of the German nation for resistance. In a mass meeting in Berlin's Sport Palace *Joseph Goebbels* (1897-1945), Hitler's State Minister for Propaganda, challenged his audience: "Do you want the total war?" Unanimously the crowd responded roaringly: "Yes!," thus provoking a total disaster for our country.

3. Ideologies are Pseudo-Religions

At this point it becomes obvious that the supposed difference between religion and ideology is only an apparent one. For the ideological goals of hope for which the ideologists try to capture their followers are not attained by scientific insights. They are fantastic ideals, objects of wishful thinking. Therefore they can only be accepted by faith in them. This becomes apparent by the terms which are used to describe those goals of hope: Ideologists speak of their *"vision"* (i.e. prophetic sight), their *"utopia"*[76] (which literally means "no-where") or their *"dream"* which one day, as they are fully convinced, will be fulfilled. People are called upon to share in these dreams in order to become inspired for action.

Karl Marx dreamt about the forthcoming "classless society;" Freud and the Freudian Marxists dreamed and are dreaming still about a psychological state of complete harmony, attained by the release of sexual instincts. Hitler conquered and destroyed Europe because he was inspired by his vision of a Germanic empire, stretching from the Atlantic Ocean to the Ural Mountains. This should just be the beginning of a future world empire. The Neo-Marxist philosopher *Ernst Bloch* (1885-1945) was able at an age of 90 years to get our Tübingen students to become thrilled about his "concrete utopia" of an imminent "Reign of Freedom."

At this point **Christians ought to be perceptive!** Such ideological visions are not just curiosities which people might be enthusiastic about for a short while and then drop them. No, they can develop an immense force. They are able to instigate people to quit their entire lifestyle and motivate them to perform incredible actions, including murderous threats to their opponents.

---

[76] Karl MANNHEIM, [2]1962.

How does the Bible interpret this phenomenon? When God created man to His own image, he indeed wanted him to devote his life to a vision that transcends the conditions of his everyday life. That vision should encourage us to strive for a higher purpose with all our capacity. The question is, however, whether we dedicate our life to striving for a genuine goal of hope which we only can receive from the truth of biblical revelation. Or do we allow ourselves to be blindfolded by trickery and delusion? That might entertain us for some time; but eventually it will pull us into disaster and then dissolve itself into nothingness.

4. Totalitarian Ideologies have Demonic Sources

By now, we are able to unmask the innermost secret of pseudo-religious ideologies: their guiding *ideas* originate in ghostly apparitions.

They have not simply been invented by certain individual thinkers; for in that case they could not unfold such force. We rather should speak of demonic delusions. This is especially the case when ideologists employ terms and imagery which clearly remind us of their appearance in biblical revelation. The ideological description of a forthcoming "reign of freedom" is a counterfeit of the messianic kingdom as announced in OT and NT prophecy. But it is separated from the person and the saving work of God in Jesus Christ. It is transmuted into a creation of self-determined, rebellious man. The great ideologists – like some founders of religions or sects – are people who spiritually went astray. By their arrogance and obsession for power they mixed up the truth of God with lies, and they replaced it by a fraudulent substitute. In this state of disobedience and rebellion they became mediums for a satanic inspiration. This can clearly be demonstrated from the life of young *Karl Marx*, to whom we shall turn in our next chapter. Likewise in the inner vocation of *Adolf Hitler* and at the emergence of National-Socialism, occult influences have been traced historically.[77]

Satan is able to use both non-Christian religions and ideologies to bring people under his spell by blindfolding their founders and fill them with demonic inspiration. His purpose is to make people worship him through the mediation of pagan idols and modern ideologies. This will be a decisive step towards the implementation of his ancient aspiration for world dominion.

---

[77] J.A.E. VERMAAT, 1975.

Under such auspices, ideologies can only react in hostility when the genuine truth of the Gospel is presented. They must do their utmost to block the road of the Gospel to the world of nations. Wherever a totalitarian ideology like Marxism-Leninism or Maoism has conquered a country, the messengers of the Gospel are shut out, and its steadfast followers will be persecuted.

V. Convergence of Religions and Ideologies in the "One World"-Utopia

In contemporary developments within the world of ideas we make an exiting observation: we can discover the beginnings of a magnificent process towards the convergence and amalgamation of all formerly contradicting religions and ideologies. They flow into a spiritual super-power that tries to suck in all mankind. The hermetically sealed borders between particular religions and between particular ideologies have become porous. They embark on mutual sharing and transformation. Consequently, the previous distinction between transcendental religion on the one hand and this-worldly ideologies on the other hand gets weakened. Religions are opening for political concerns, ideologies adopt transcendental elements. The emerging spiritual super-power seems to be a world religion penetrated by an universal ideology. It is the "religion of the secular gods," as my teacher Walter Freytag (1899 – 1959) has called it.[78]

1. The Religion of Secularism and of Occult Experiences

The characteristic of such an ideologized religion is that it places the human being at its centre. It is the collective man who unites in himself the resources of the whole mankind in order to redeem himself. He tries to change the world into a paradise on earth according to his own imagination. Everything which various religions have attained as partial insights to improve psychological, social, economic and political conditions is merging here. But even the secret forces which people have discovered by means of extra-sensory perception, and which enable them to have ecstatic peak experiences are utilized. Under the slogan "new spirituality" they are incorporated as common elements in that universal religion.

---

[78] Walter FREYTAG, 1961, p.122.

2. Moving towards the One World-Religion

We meet such efforts to amalgamate religions and ideologies at several places at the same time. Important organizations, both religious and secular, can be mentioned here. I mention just a few typical examples: The United Nations, the Club of Rome,[79] the WCC and the World Conference of Religions for Peace. Frequently we hear the slogan *"Survival of Mankind."*

We are told from various sides that the very existence of our planet earth and of mankind is severely endangered. The main reasons were our irresponsible use of technology, the exploitation of the resources of our ecological system and population growth.[80]

Some of these warnings are well founded. If they are taken as a call to repentance in accordance with Rev. 8:13 (and 9:20-21) they are surely warranted. Such calls should be heeded by joint actions of the responsible authorities. But some suggested solutions are precarious. It is concluded that the imminent universal disaster can only be avoided under one condition: The speakers of mankind in all realms of life: in politics, sciences, economics, philosophy, religion must unite. Together they should draft a global strategy for the survival of mankind. Such strategy is to be built on three pillars:

1. All existing orders of national law, economy, education, including the standards of sexual morals, are to give way for a new global order. Many influential politicians both in the East and in the West like to speak about the coming *"New World Order"* (*NWO*) they are working for.

2. This global order is to be enforced by the creation of a *World Government*. It should be invested with sufficient authority and military power to secure peace and to establish justice.

---

[79]The Club of Rome is a German-based global think tank that deals with a variety of international political issues. It raised a lot of public attention with its report The Limits to Growth, (ed. D.Meadows et al., published in 1972), which predicted that economic growth could not continue indefinitely because of the limited availability of natural resources, particularly oil. The oil crisis of 1973 increased public concern about this problem. The second, equally alarming report of the Club or Rome was edited by M. Mesarowich and E. Festel: Mankind at its Turning Point, Stuttgart 1974. – Today the Club of Rome has 100 members from ore than 50 nations, amongst them several present or former heads of states: Richard von Weizsäcker, Vaclav Havel, King Juan Carlos, Queen Beatrix of the Netherlands, Michail Gorbatchew. Their avowed "goal is the common concern and responsibility for the future of mankind."

[80] P. BEYERHAUS, 1976, pp. 128-132; 314-328.

3. The New World Order should be enhanced by a spiritual foundation and a unifying bond of allegiance. A kind of *world religion*, sometimes called "United Religions" is proposed.[81] All existing religions and world views should be encouraged to make their particular contribution to it without making absolute truth claims for themselves. For that purpose they should start or in fact have already started to engage in dialogue and cooperation.[82]

3. Theological Evaluation

How, then, shall Christians evaluate these ideas – we may call it the *One World-Ideology* ? At a first glance they appear rather plausible and intriguing. It is surely true that the constant arms race, the widening gap between the rich and the poor, population explosion, waste of energies and air pollution may finally lead to the self-destruction of mankind. Likewise it is true that we become guilty if we simply keep silent in face of collective selfishness which destroys God's good creation and exploits the underprivileged. Here we are called to act responsibly as God's stewards.

But we act only responsibly if we never forget that the real dominion over our world belongs to God and that He still rules its history. In His revealed Word and in the laws of nature, God has given us commandments and ordinances which we must respect. We must not suspend them in favour of a new self-determined morality.[83] The decisions concerning our survival and the end of this age abide solely with God. Therefore, man is never entitled to proclaim himself as the highest authority, who can determine the course of history. He is never allowed to change the ordinances of creation, the ethical laws and even the biblical faith according to his own judgement.

For as a fallen being, man is prone to deception, – to being deceived by others and even by himself. Here lies the fundamental hollowness of all ideologies. In their trust in the capability of man to save himself ideologists disregard the corruption of human nature by sin. Equally treacherous is their modernist belief in progress as inherent in secular history. For they overlook that God himself has doomed this present eon to final destruction (2 Peter 2:7).

---

[81] E. LASZLO, 1974.

[82] We shall return to this theme in chapters VII and XI.

[83] See our chapter XI.

Seen from the empirical point of view we arrive at the same conclusion. Historical experience shows that human beings never are able to discern clearly between responsible policies and their own instinct for power. Accordingly it is to be feared that the suspension of authority on the national level finally may end up with a conglomeration of power on a global level. But then mutual accountability will not be possible anymore.[84] Thus, the serious danger comes into view that under the pretext of securing human survival a new totalitarian ideology is emerging. It is the One World-Ideology which will subjugate mankind under a total world dictatorship.

4. The Strategy of Antichrist

It is our task as Christians to discern the signs of the time and try to interpret crucial developments in the light of God's prophetical Word. Here, we have serious reasons to observe contemporary ideological tendencies with great apprehension. For in John's Revelation (Ch. 13: 17; 18) we find predictions that amazingly agree with these movements. They depict a universal dictatorship to which the ten kingdoms of mankind transfer their powers (Rev. 17:12f.). That will be the final stage of that anti-God process that started with the Fall of our first parents, and even before that with the original rebellion of Lucifer himself. In religions and ideologies self-exalting man wrests some isolated elements from God's truth and promises. He incorporates them into his anthropocentric world view and subordinates them to his autonomous plan of self-redemption. Human beings arrogate to themselves the role of their Creator. Man refuses to recognize any binding commandments of God. Instead he becomes his own lawmaker - which is, in God's sight, "lawlessness" (see II Thess 2:7 and already Matth 24:12). He puts himself into the position of God as Saviour and Lord of the world.

But man does not do this out of his own impulse; rather he is used by Satan as an instrument in his demonic strategy. In the contemporary plans to establish a New World Order on the basis of a universal semi-religious ideology we can recognise an age old intention of Satan. He wants to remove Christ from His throne as the supreme Lord of the

---

[84] The Korean Herald (Sept. 20, 2003) carried an article about the problem of replacing national sovereignty by a global authority with the right to intervene whenever it appears necessary. The author William Pfaff wrote: "What is this international community that will take such decisions? The U.N.? Of the five permanent Security Council members, China is a party dictatorship, Russia is a dubious democracy. The General Assembly majority consists of dictatorships and failed states."

universe and replace Him by the Antichrist. It is that apocalyptic person whom Paul calls the *"man of lawlessness"* (2 Thess 2: 3, see also V. 8a). That means it is the one who does not recognise any other law except those which he autonomously gives himself in defiance of God's Lordship.

The **strategy** by which Satan will try to secure the subjugation of all mankind to such demonic system of government will be a **twofold** one. It will build both on **fascination** and on **fear**. Mankind will be fascinated by the miraculous achievements which Antichrist will accomplish, assisted by the False Prophet (Rev 13:11-17; cf. II Thess. 2:9f.). At the same time mankind will tremble for fear in view of the apocalyptic catastrophes and obediently submit to him who promises to avert them by his powerful government.[85]

Anticipating this final scenario, the Dutch author *John E. Vermaat* wrote in connection with the WCC's Fifth Assembly at Nairobi in 1975: "Antichrist will push through his utopia of universal unity against the frightening background of total destruction. In view of that imminent destruction both religions and ideologies will be driven to unite. The ideology of the last times predominantly will be an ideology of survival. Anyone who dares to resist that ideology will be regarded as obstructing the welfare of humanity. Coming together and cooperation will be the supreme law. A person who opposes this law will be expelled from mankind."[86]

VI. Ideological Infiltration into the Christian Church

1. Instrumentalized Churches

One more step is needed to implement this plan. In the general melting process of religions and ideologies and in the globalisation of political, economic and cultural systems even the Christian Church and her message must be integrated. Such plans have been conceived and devloped since the end of the 19th century.[87] Only then the unification of mankind will be perfect; because one third of mankind are counted as Christian. The ideological foes of the Christian faith have recognised long ago that the Church cannot be abolished by external violence

---

[85] This was also predicted as a vision in 1898 by Wladmir SOLOWJEW, 1968.

[86] J. A. E. VERMAAT, 1976: pp. 212-220, esp. p. 217.

[87] George F. DILLON, ⁵1965: (see especially pp. 89 ff.).

alone. Therefore they try to undermine the fortress by cunning infiltration in order to finally to take it over.

The greatest menace to the churches today is not open persecution. True enough, there are martyr churches in many parts of the world. Yet more dangerous is their ideological conquest from inside. This fulfils the warning of Jesus: *"Beware of the false prophets!"* (Matth 7:15). Illustrations can be found from the German church struggle under Adolf Hitler and from the Soviet era in Russia. In Germany the party of "German Christians" tried to mix up the biblical Gospel with elements of the Nazi ideology. In the Soviet Union and other east European states the Communist government managed to make numerous priests and bishops act as its agents and to use the Orthodox and even Baptist Churches as instruments to spread its ideology. I have witnessed this myself at the ecumenical Assemblies at Nairobi '75[88] and Vancouver '83. The official delegates from the Communist bloc appraised the social achievements of their governments and denied emphatically that there existed anti-Christian persecution in their countries.

But in Western countries today, too, churches and their individual members are tempted to adapt to the ideologies of global transformation. This process moves on various ways.

2. Ideological Climate

There is such a thing as *ideological infection.* Ideologies are spiritual powers. They catch people often in unconscious ways. They can be compared with the viruses of a Chinese flew epidemic that pollute the air at crowded places. Ideological viruses pollute the entire contemporary life. They communicate themselves through the mass media: Radio, TV and pictorial magazines, through music, education and also by a provocative lifestyle, including clothes and hairstyles.[89] Even Christian families are not immune against such subtle ideological infection. Many churches, too, adapt their worship service to the spirit of the age in order to reach the present generation and not to miss the latest trend!

3. Ideology Instead of Theology

Since the time of Enlightenment modernist theology always has adapted itself, and become an ecclesial mouth piece for the ever-

---

[88] Helena Posdeeff, 1976, pp. 240-248.

[89] Blue-jeans e.g. have contributed much to level national cultures and gender distinction!

changing spirit of the present age. Rationalistic doubt undermined trust in the reliability of God's biblical revelation. What were left were mere biblical words, being robbed of their genuine meaning. Those empty shells were refilled with the favourite ideas of current thought. The result was an ideologized gospel, which was presented by the churches as an actual translation of the Christian message.

Sometimes when you listen to a sermon, you might soon get the impression that this is not the biblical Gospel. It sounds rather a gospel which has been reinterpreted in accordance with current thought. Perhaps you might rediscover the main content of a political article you read last week in the newspaper. The same phenomenon we encounter in modern creeds, hymns and prayers. Central biblical terms like "salvation," "kingdom of God," "resurrection," "new man," and "fellowship" are detached from their original context in the biblical plan of salvation. Instead, they are associated with inner-worldly goals and slogans of the main stream ideology. In this way, these biblical terms seem to gain a new relevance for our present situation. But in reality they are deprived of their genuine content and exchanged for a fraudulent surrogate.

The final stage of this project is reached when the very person of *Jesus Christ* himself is subjected to an ideological re-interpretation.[90] In some political theologies Jesus is deprived of his divine dignity. Instead he becomes a symbol for a modern political liberator like some of the heroes of Latin American. Jesus is styled as the champion of a modern ideology of political change; but he ceases to be the Redeemer of the sinful world sent by God the Father.

Many modernist, especially socio-political, theologies are in fact ideologies, poorly dressed up in a Christian vocabulary, often with a Marxist leaning.[91] In their variety they have three features in common:

1. They do not start from Scripture and the Church's confessions, but from a Marxist social analysis, emphasizing the human misery of "suppression."

2. They systematically contradict the entire genuine Chrisitan tradition, which is denigrated as "white" or "Western" theology.

---

[90] Rolf SCHEFFBUCH, 1976, pp. 133-141.
[91] Dale VREE, 1976.

3. They hide their heterogeneous origin by means of "semantic deception," i.e. by wrapping their ideas in a language that partly sounds biblical.

Unfortunately even the WCC during the last 4 decades has been acting on the assumptions of such ideological theologies like Liberation Theology, Black Theology, and Feminist Theology.[92] Employing their services, the WCC tried to win the support of its member churches especially in the Two-thirds World.[93] to pursue its new ecumenical goal: The utopic kingdom of this world, called the *New Humanity* or the coming *World Community*.

4. The Two Beasts

What is happening here strongly reminds us of the predictions of Jesus and the Apostles about the anti-Christian dominion of the end time. John speaks of the two beasts which he saw coming out of the abyss: the first beast is the symbol of a political world ruler to whom all power on earth is bestowed (Rev 13:1-10; 17:17), the *Antichrist*; the second beast (Rev 13:11-17) is the symbol of the *false prophet* (Rev. 20:10) who by his deceptions and miracles seduces mankind to follow and worship the Antichrist.

That false prophet obviously will be the one who succeeds in fusing all religions and ideologies, including occultism, with a type of Christianity that is completely distorted by modernist theologies.

But both figures are already foreshadowed long before their final appearance. As Jesus' warns us in his eschatological sermon in Matthew 24 (v. 5 and 11), and as John does in his first letter (2:18; 4:1), antichrists and false prophets are the permanent, insidious companions of the Church throughout her history. Some of them emerge from inside, others intrude from outside. Christians, therefore, are charged at all times to examine the spirits (1 John 3:1-3) and to resist any confusion of the Gospel with other religions and ideologies. This is also our task today. How can we succeed?

---

[92] See chapter VI.
[93] P. BEYERHAUS, 1988a.

VII. The Christian Response to Anti-Christian Ideologies

1. Divine Enabling and Support

As Christ's followers we are fortunate that we need not fight the battle in our own strength. For Jesus has promised to support us by sending his Counsellor, the Spirit of Truth (John 15:26; 16:13). It is He who will convict the world of sin, righteousness and judgment (John 16:8). He will enable the Christians to testify to the truth by cleansing them and giving them authority them. How will that take place? Let us listen to a saying of Jesus in John 8:31-32: "If you hold to my teaching, you are truly my disciples. Then you will know the truth, and the truth will set you free." Jesus points out three steps: to hold to his teaching, to know the truth, to be liberated by the truth.

2. Remaining in the Words of Christ

The *first step* is to continue in Christ's teaching and thereby prove to really be his disciples.

Jesus calls us out of our self-centredness and of our fascination with the authorities and systems of this world. He lets us look at Himself, the Redeemer and Lord of the world. For on His Cross he has already acquired a perfect salvation for all mankind, and by his Resurrection he has been installed as the Lord above all created authorities in Heaven and on earth (Matth 28:18!) Now we are to enter into a living relationship with Him. A true disciple is simply someone who remains in continuous conversation with Christ. By his living word, he will daily guide us. When we pray and meditate about His word, His features will deeply impress themselves on our mind as our authentic model. We shall follow Him obediently step by step without being led astray by ideological confusion to the left and to the right.

Following Jesus as his true disciple includes *daily repentance*, because every assault against God's holy will, even in thought and imagination, blurs our spiritual discernment and makes us receptive to ideological fascination. Eventually this can even be God's punishment! He himself may send upon disobedient people *"strong delusions* [e.g. ideologies!] *to make them believe what is false"* (1 Thess 2: 10-12).

3. To Know the Divine Truth

Daily attention to the Word of Christ leads us to the *second step*: *"You will know the truth."*

Let us be fully submitted to Jesus, in hearing, serving and testifying! Then He will give us insight in the meaning of those biblical statements which at the first glance appear strange to us. We penetrate into the depths of God's mysterious plan of salvation. In such perspective we might – at least partly – understand some of the present riddles and oddities that encounter us (Rom 8:28).

By the anointing of the Holy Spirit (1 John 2:20 and 27) we can even perceive the significance of the ideologies; for they, too, involuntarily play a role in the great drama of salvation, which will end with the triumph of the returning Lord Jesus Christ.

4. Liberation from Ideologies

Thus He leads us to the *third step*: *"The truth will set you free."* The truth of the Gospel liberates us from such ideological constructs that by enticing or frightening seek to push us into a wrong direction. For the Gospel unmasks their impotence in view of the One to whom all power is given in heaven and on earth.

The truth of the Gospel will even encourage us to approach our seduced fellow human beings in order to disentangle them from the snare of seduction[94] We can point out to them the vanity of all self-chosen ways of salvation and testify to that salvation which Jesus Christ has already wrought at his Cross once and for all: it is redemption from estrangement from God, and – as a consequence – also from meaninglessness, isolation and anxiety. It is that redemption which opens up a new life for us in the power of which we can become agents of genuine renewal.

Yet being aware of the realism of the Bible, we are also sober enough to tell our fellowmen bluntly that, in this fallen world, not all of its problems will be solved during the present age. The structures of death cannot be removed from this creation until the end, when even our ultimate enemy, death itself, will be destroyed (1 Cor 15:26). The problem of how to secure the survival of mankind cannot attain the first priority on our agenda. God has not promised us our survival in the old

---

[94] See even the command given in Jude 22 and also Rev. 3:2 to do this!

eon. But He has promised something greater: eternal life and a new creation! The political, social and ecological problems today that vex us so much will all be solved in due time, but not by autonomous humanity. They will be solved – to start with – when the returning Christ will set up his messianic kingdom on earth. Finally, they will be removed entirely when God the Father will create a new heaven and a new world (Rev 21:1). Then all of His outstanding promises will be fulfilled. All tears will be wiped off, death and mourning will disappear (Rev 21:4), and the new creation will reflect the glory of the Triune God.

Chapter 4
Rise and Downfall of Marxism

Introduction

In 1920, when looking back at his Bolshevik October Revolution in Russia, its leader *Vladimir Iljitsh Lenin* (1870 – 1924) coined the boastful slogan: "Marxism is almighty because it is true." It was an expression of the gigantic aspirations of the Communist Party that its ideology soon would be the dominant world view, having been universally adopted. 70 years later, in 1990, the unexpected historical turnover took place: the Communist Party lost its control over the Soviet Union and the other Eastern Bloc states, and thousands of statues of Lenin were overturned. That ended the Communist era at least in Eastern Europe.

Why then do we still include a discussion of Marxism into our book on apologetics?

The reason for this is that, first of all, that Marxism still survives openly in Red China and Vietnam, in some parts of Russia and Latin American countries, and last but not least in North Korea. Theoretically it is cherished in leftist circles and movements also in Western countries which were never under Communist rule, even in churches and in theology! Theologians are divided on this issue. Some acclaim Marx as a great humanist and champion for social justice. They blame the established churches for cooperating with the capitalist system and for their social indolence. Genuine Marxism, they claim, can be evaluated apart from its atheistic trends and be used for scientific analyses. For basically, they say, it contains a humanist world view. Such opinions stem, however, from a deficient insight into the real character both of Karl Marx himself and his ideology. This shows - in the second place - that Marxism has still to be fought and overcome intellectually and spiritually.[95]

---

[95] Konrad LÖW, 2001.

I. The Life, Work and Spiritual pProfile of Karl Marx (1818-1883)

The nature, history and fate of Marxism are all embodied in its main founder *Karl Marx*.[96]

His forefathers on both sides had been respected rabbis in Trier for 150 years. But his parents converted to Christianity. Karl, born in Trier 5th May 1818, owed his sharp logical mind to his Jewish heritage; and perhaps also his instinct of what future may keep in store.

The family belonged to the wealthy middle class. Karl had never suffered from poverty; on the contrary: he drew freely financial support from his parents.

He studied philosophy, strongly influenced by *Hegel*'s idealistic philosophy of history,[97] later on by *Ludwig Feuerbach* (1804-72), a notorious critic of human religion, interpreting it as a mere psychological projection, and by *Charles Darwin* (1809-82), the pioneer of evolutionism.

Marx' first employment was to become an editor of the liberal newspaper *Rheinische Zeitung*. In Trier he lived near the French border. Thus he keenly observed and commented on the political and ideological development in revolutionary France.

Later he moved to London, the heart of the British colonial empire and centre of international commerce. Here he lived as a freelance writer and wrote many voluminous books.

The most famous of them were the "Manifest of the Communist Party" – better known as the *"Communist Manifesto"* – in 1848. Nineteen years later he published successively 3 volumes of what became his main work *"Das Kapital."* He interacted much with leading revolutionary ideologists of his time, especially his only abiding friend *Friedrich Engels* (1820-95) who is the co-founder of Marxist Communism.

Marx died in London on 14th March 1883 and was buried there.

What can we know about Marx' religious disposition? In his childhood and early youth Karl started out as a pious Christian. His first written work was a school essay: "The Union of the Faithful with Christ." Here we read the beautiful words:

---

[96] Klaus HORNUNG, [3]1978. – Jean-Yves CALVEZ, 1964.
[97] Konrad LÖW, [2]1985: pp. 233f.

"Through love of Christ we turn our hearts at the same time towards our brethren who are inwardly bound to us and for whom He gave Himself in sacrifice ...

Union with Christ could give an inner elevation, comfort in sorrow, calm, trust and a heart susceptible to human love, to everything noble and great, not for the sake of ambition and glory, but only for the sake of Christ."[98]

Yet his natural character was, indeed, very ambitious and self-asserting. This is one reason why his life soon took a very different turn. He grew to be prouder and prouder, and in connection with this he behaved ruthlessly in the choice of his words and means. Now his father became concerned; he wrote a warning letter to his son when he was 19 years old.[99] The father deplored that he had been too lenient in education.

By then it was already too late. Karl Marx had already chosen another, dangerous avenue. A sudden, mysterious change took place. He became passionately anti-religious and he followed an inner lust **to destroy**. In an essay written for his matriculation he used the verb "to destroy" 6 times, whilst none of his fellow class mates used it even once! Thus they give him the nickname "destroy."[100]

It seems that he had experienced a personal disappointment which he could not cope with. For Marx had started out with artistic ambitions, but his poems and drama received no recognition.[101] At that time he writes in a poem under the title: "Invocation of one in despair:" *"I wish to avenge myself against the One who rules above."* So Marx still believed in the existence of a God above him, but he quarrelled with him about his fate. And now he proceeds by assuming an attitude of frightening hybris:

> *"So a god has snatched from me my all,*
> *in the curse and rack of destiny ...*
> *Nothing but revenge is left to me. ...*
> *I shall build my throne high overhead,*
> *cold, tremendous shall its summit be ..."*

---

[98] K. MARX: The Union of the Faithful with Christ. MEW, Suppl vol. 1, p. 600.

[99] Werner BLUMENBERG, [5]1967: pp. 25 ff.

[100] Richard WURMBRAND, 1985: p. 12.

[101] The following information and quotations are mainly taken from the study of Richard WURMBRAND, op. cit., pp. 11-18.

Marx dreamt of ruining the world created by God. So he wrote in another poem:

"Then I will be able to walk triumphantly,
Like a god, through the ruins of their kingdom.
Every word of mine is fire and action.
My breast is equal to that of the Creator."

These words remind us of Lucifer's proud boasting, as recorded in Isaiah 14:13:

"I will ascend to heaven, I will exalt my throne above the stars of God."

How could such blasphemous thought come into young K. Marx's mind? *Richard Wurmbrand*, a Rumanian pastor who was imprisoned many years and "tortured for Christ," has written a fascinating book: "Marx and Satan."[102] In this he expounds his thesis that Marx at a decisive juncture got in contact with a Satanist sect and became a practicing Satan worshipper himself. He concludes this from a drama written by Marx at that time under the name *"Oulanem,"* which is an inversion of Christ's title *"Immanuel"* = "God with us." In this we find descriptions of some elements typical for the Satanist ritual. This is confirmed by another poem called "The Player" in which he wrote:

"See this sword? The prince of darkness gave it to me." Here Marx doubtlessly refers to the rite of initiation into the Satanist sect.

From now on Marx really acts like a loyal servant of the devil, whose whole intention is to hate God and to draw as many creatures as possible with himself into the pit of everlasting damnation. He knew that this was his fate. In his poem "The Pale Maiden" he wrote:

"My soul, once true to God,
is chosen for hell."

Accordingly every note of warm human emotion disappeared from his character.[103] He became a very hard personality, cynical, abusive towards all beauty, without love and compassion even against parents and friends. Both he and Engels wrote about their own parents only in contemptuous language as "my old ones," and they were interested in their death only to get at their heritage! Marx did not even attend the funeral of his father, whose financial aid he had squandered on frivo-

---

[102] See note 6.
[103] Arnold KÜNZLI, 1966: p. 169.

lous pleasures. Likewise Marx had a poor relationship with his wife. Twice she wanted to leave him. When she died, he did not attend her funeral either.

Thus he develops a demonic pride combined with hatred against God and mankind.

It is therefore very important to notice: Marx's primary motive was not to help the poor or to improve social conditions when working as newspaper editor in Trier. On the contrary, he regarded Communism as a severe danger.[104]

His deepest motive was to avenge himself on God by hating Him and everything He had created. In particular he hated the human beings as miserable creatures. He despised whole nations and races – including the Jews! With Wurmbrand and others we can state: Rebellion against God and His creation preceded the socialist ideology. Marx received his Communist ideas not before 1845, when he had a decisive meeting with *Moses Hess* (1812-75),[105] founder of the Social-Democratic Party of Germany (SPD). Hess was both a forerunner of Jewish Zionism and a pioneer of revolutionary socialist ideas. He tried to combine the two elements by ascribing to the Jews the historical role of erecting a messianic kingdom on earth – without God however. For Hess, too, was an atheist. He took pleasure both in Marx and Engels, persuaded them of his revolutionary ideas and joint them in writing the "Communist Manifesto" (1848).

We can observe a similar historical development in Russia: forerunners of the Bolshevik party of Lenin were the *"Anarchists,"* fierce opponents not only to the Tsarist regime but to any government in general. They, too, were obviously demon inspired. This is described prophetically by *Dostoyevsky's* novel: "The Demons."[106]

The anarchists fought for a world revolution. Their leaders *Michail Bakunin* (1814-76) and *Sergej Netschajew* (1845-82) founded the "World Revolutionary League." Their Magazine bore the title: "Hell!" In their writings you find a brutal language: "Slaughtering, burning

---

[104] Karl MARX: "Der Kommunismus und die Augsburger Allgemeine Zeitung," in: Die Rheinische Zeitung, quoted in MEW I.1 (1), p. 263: "Attempts to by masses to carry out Communist ideas can be aswered by a canon as soon as they become dangerous."

[105] Moses HESS, 1841 – Ernst KUX, 1967: p. 23. – K. VORLÄNDER, 1929, pp. 47 f.; 55.

[106] Fjodor M. DOSTOJEWSKY, 1922.

down" were favourite expressions. They assassinated Tsar Alexander II on 13 March 188. Destruction was the chief primary motive of those Russian anarchists.

We can clearly identify the trade marks of the Marxist movement in its revolutionary phase from its inception throughout its history They are: extreme pride, demonic aspiration, even a tendency towards occultism, hatred against God and his creation, the brutal desire to destroy everything. This could and still can be observed in all parts of the world.

Marx died in despair, like all Satanists do. Just a few days before his death he wrote to Engels: "How pointless and empty is my life, but how desirable."[107] When he died 1883 in an isolated existence in London, not more than six people followed his coffin to the grave.

Yet: historically seen, he became successful, at least for one epoch. Seventy years after his death, one third of the world was dominated by economic and political systems shaped by Marx's thought.

II. The Main Ddoctrines of Marxism

A. The Key Concept of "Surplus Value"

Marx's reflection starts by his observation of the widening gap between the rich and the poor. Indeed at the height of the Industrial Revolution social conditions of labourers were rather deplorable. They were underpaid and suffered badly, even children having to work for 10 hours daily under unhealthy conditions. Marx sensed the popular discontent in the lower classes. He explained this unjust situation by the concept of *"surplus value."* According to it the trade value of a certain product is determined by the amount of labour time invested in it from the original state of raw material. The employer, who sells the product, gives only a small part of the gain as wages to his workers The main portion of the surplus value he keeps for himself. Thus he exploits the time and manpower of his employees for his own private benefit. He accumulates the capital in order to enlarge and improve his factory by introducing modern techniques. Only thus he can compete with other factory owners. In the long run only the most effective enterprises can survive, others have to close down. This results in an enlarged offer of cheap labour; consequently the social conditions of the working class

---

[107] Karl MARX, 1882: p. 65.

get even worse. In this connection Marx develops his theory of the *"reduction to misery"* (Verelendung = pauperisation) of the proletariat. That increases the tension between the upper class of the owners and the under class of the workers.

At the same time, by the economic *"law of concentration,"* monopolistic capitalism will steadily reduce the number of independent firms. At the end only one huge capitalist concern will remain, unable to find buyers for its products. Thus the whole system of capitalism will collapse. Then the capitalists will be compelled to hand over the means of production to the workers. Marx calls this the "expropriation of the expropriators." This introduces the *"stage of socialism,"* which finally will be replaced by the *stage of Communism.*

B. The Theory of "Historical Materialism"

Another key concept of Marx and Marxism is the term *"class struggle."* It was not invented by Marx, but he radicalised it. To him it became the main single moving factor in human history. According to Marx and Engels and all later Communists history is motivated and proceeds not by spiritual factors but rather material interests, leading to succeeding class struggles. Depending on the state of production, classes are formed in relation to possessions: small farms in early times, large estates in the age of "feudalism," factories in the age of the possessing middle class, monopolistic industrial concerns in the near future. There has been and always will be a conflict of interest. The upper class tries to secure its status quo, the lower class tries to get its share in the possessions. In critical times these tensions are sharpening to such an degree that a revolution is staged.

Marx had a keen interest in social revolutions; for he taught that by them the historical progress is speeding up. Therefore he was opposed to the social reforms introduced by responsible European governments, for they diminished social tensions. He maintained that by now the general situation had become revolutionary. He regarded himself as a prophet of the coming world revolution. By his inflammatory writings, starting with the Communist Manifesto, he placed himself at the head of the revolutionary process. Marx called his own system a "system of mockery and contempt." He said: "For us hatred rather than love is necessary." Marx and his collaborator Friedrich Engels wrote in the revolutionary year 1848, with reference to France:

"The unsuccessful slaughtering since June and October ... the Cannibalism of the counterrevolution will convince the people that there is but one means to shorten the bloody labour pains of the old society: It is revolutionary terrorism."[108]

To his great disappointment the big revolution did not come off during his life time, because social conditions were improving. Furthermore, the masses proved to be both unwilling and unable to stage a real revolution. For that he cynically despised them. So he retreated to his academic studies in order to further develop his materialistic philosophy. On account of that most of his former followers regarded him as a traitor.

C. The Philosophy of Dialectical Materialism

Karl Marx became a disciple of the great German philosopher *F. W. Hegel* by studying his works. He shared with him a basic concern for world history and an interest in the forces by which it moves. He also was intrigued by Hegel's concept that this happens by a dialectical process according to the triadic pattern: *thesis – antithesis – synthesis*. This says: Each present state of affairs is challenged by a new factor that negates it. But as soon as the negation has taken place, a new, stronger factor emerges which opposes the new position. Thus the negation itself is denied. It is, however, not completely revoked, but rather – together with the original thesis – absorbed in a higher synthesis. This happens on all levels: the social, the cultural and the political. Everything on earth is moving step by step towards integration into a larger unit: A comprehensive philosophy, a world culture and a world state.

The decisive difference between Hegel and Marx is that according to Hegel's idealism the fundamental reality is *spiritual;* to Marx – in contrast – it is *material.* The world process is not for Marx shaped by lofty ideas coming from a transcendent realm. Rather it takes place by the evolution of the material substance of which it consist. Human beings are not a divine creation; rather they created themselves out of intelligent apes that made tools for themselves to get at their food. Thus man has created himself by his labour and is still developing by it.

The history of mankind is moving by conflicting material interests, articulating themselves in new formations of socio-economic organisa-

---

[108] Works of Marx and Engels (WME). Volume 5, p. 457.

tion. This proceeds by an innate law of history. Finally the "classless society" will be established, a state of abiding peace, happiness and cultural creativity. Then everyone will work according to his abilities, and everyone will receive according to his needs.

To Marx ideas, philosophies, ethical codes and religions are not inspired from above. They do not influence the historical process. They rather are a secondary "superstructure" of human consciousness. They simply reflect and try to justify the present empiric reality, the prevailing socio-economic system. Therefore there are no abiding ethical codes which the workers have to respect.

Religion, according to Marx, is invented to stabilize the existing order by making the oppressed class submissive. It lets the poor hope for a heavenly compensation for what they missed on earth. He therefore calls religion *"the opium of the people."* Since it – supposedly – prevents them from fighting for their rights, it should be attacked by all means.

In the former Soviet Union the philosophy of Dialectical Materialism was the official ideology. Thereby it occupied the place of the Orthodox faith, the former state religion.

D. Strategy

The Communist Manifesto states as final goal **World Revolution**. Tactically, this is to be approached openly by partial revolutions, and secretly by infiltration. One means is to associate with other interest groups and together with them create "frontier movements" with acceptable common aims, e.g. improved labour conditions. At the same time Marxist indoctrination takes place. One ingenious means is "Semantic deception." It is to use traditional terms with a changed intention. Thus a Marxist led "Peace Movement" prepares the people for neutrality and disarmament, facilitating the final takeover. Marx wrote: "The first task of the press is to undermine all foundations of the present political state."[109] Basic elements of the present order that are to be eliminated are private property and consequently the institutions that guarantee it: the state, the church and even the family. "The abolition of private property is the abolition of all human alienation. It is the return

---

[109] WME vol. 6, p. 234.

of human beings out of religion, family and state into their human, i.e. social existence."[110]

F. Dictatorship by the Proletarian Class, as Represented by the Communist Party

According to Marx the process towards socialism is irresistible and irreversible. But it will not come into being by spontaneous action of the poor masses. It can only be brought about by that portion, *the proletariat*, which has developed a revolutionary consciousness.

The proletariat, again, needs to be spurned and directed by an inner circle, a *"party of a new type"* which assumes the leadership. It speaks and acts as the self-appointed (!) representative of the people. This must, of course, consequently lead to the establishment of a new dictatorship. That was evident to Marx himself. He justified it as a necessary transitory period in the revolutionary process, called *"the dictatorship of the proletariat."* But as a matter of fact this concept has led to the establishment of totalitarian states, autocratically and even tyrannically controlled by the Central Committee of the Communist party. The party built on the fraudulent assumption that its leaders represented the people in the s.c. "Peoples' Democratic Republics" like East Germany and North Korea. In Germany the marching columns used to sing "The Party, the Party is always right!" But to the shock of the Communist leaders, in 1989 the great turnover took place. Suddenly, during a huge political rally in Leipzig, indignation broke out publicly. Somebody shouted unashamedly: **"We** are the people!" This became the battle cry not only during that rally but of the entire peaceful revolution. That ended the "dictatorship of the proletariat" in East Germany!

III. The Anti-Christian Nature of Marxist Systems

1. Similarities between Marxism and Christianity

Analogies in appearance

If one compares the ideology and self-presentation of Marxism, one easily can discover a number of formal similarities with Christianity. To mention a few apparent ones:

Both have their *authoritative book*, here the Bible, there *Das Kapital*.

---

[110] WME Suppl. vol 1, p. 537.

Catholic Christianity has the *supreme teaching office*, the bishop of Rome, whilst Karl Marx is treated as the "Pope of Communism," who believed himself to be infallible. Christianity venerates its *saints*, the "spirits of the righteous men made perfect (Hebr 12: 23); Marxism adores its human idols: pictures of Marx, Engels, Lenin or Mao are born in demonstrations, similar to the icons carried in Orthodox processions. Both have also their annual *celebrations*.

Analogies in doctrines

Both teach an *original state of harmony*, here man in paradise, there human beings in original freedom. *Man's fall* into sin corresponds to the introduction of private property. Both speak of a *state of misery*, here human captivity to sin, there to exploitation. Both focus on redemption, here from sin, there from expropriation. Both adore a *redeemer*, here Jesus the Messiah and Son of God, there a deified leader: Lenin, Stalin, Mao, Kim Il-sung, or Ho Chi Min. The faithful followers both of Christ and of Marx are assembled in an *elect community*, here the Church, there the Communist party. Both have a *mission* concept: Christian evangelism corresponds to Marxist agitation and propaganda (*"agitprop"*). Both have *eschatological expectations*: the Judgment Day prior to the establishment of the Kingdom of God is replaced by the World Revolution leading into the "classless society."

A very similar observation could also be made with *National Socialism*: Hitler borrowed ideas from Marx and from the Bible. This confirms our thesis that ideologies are semi-religions, ultimately and basically influenced by Christianity.

2. Sharp Criticism of Christianity

The seeming similarities between Christianity and Marxism are, as stated, only formal ones. As far as content is concerned, they sharply contradict each other. I mention just the most crucial contradictions:

Firstly there is a great difference in the *concept of man*. According to Genesis 1:27 man is God's image, whilst according to materialistic Marxism the human being is essentially a stomach: "Man is what he eats." The Bible teaches that he has been created by God, Marx dared to insist that man created himself by working. He admired Darwin for his doctrine of evolution which makes no essential distinction between animals and human beings.

Secondly there is a different *concept of redemption*. Man as a sinner, separated from God, has been redeemed by the blood of Christ, shed for us on the Cross. He freely accepted suffering and death on our behalf. – Marx on the other side does not regard man as sinner, but as a victim of social oppression. Therefore man has to redeem himself as a basically social being by using revolutionary violence.

Thirdly the basic objection of Marxism to Christianity is the negative assumption: "There is *no God*, science has proved it." This the Bible finds ridiculous, because God essentially is a transcendental reality to which physical science has no access. Even if human beings were the outcome of an evolutionary process, the question arises: by what intelligent unseen force does that process move forward to reach such a wonderful result?

Since Marx denies the existence of God, to him the Supreme Being is *autonomous man*. This conviction is shared by the chief Marxist ideologists at all times. *Lenin* said:

"Atheism is an integral part of Marxism. Marxism is materialism. We must combat religion." This is the ABC of materialism and consequently of Marxism."

In his book, "Atheism in Christianity," the Marxist philosopher *Ernst Bloch* wrote:

"The original sin consists in the fact that man does not wish to be like God ... The belief in a personal God is the fall of man into sin. This fall must be repaired."

The entire ideology culminates in the self-deification of man, in obvious concordance with the insinuation of the snake: *"Ye shall be like God ...!"*

If there is no God, there can be *no eternal moral code* either. In Dostoyewky's novel "The Karamasov Brothers" the nihilist Ivan remarks: "If there is no God, everything is permitted." Much earlier Marx agreed: all ruling morality is hypocritical. Therefore to him ethics becomes an object of mockery and contempt. Likewise his Marxist followers do not have any permanent binding moral rule. The only undisputable law is to believe in the Communist Party and obey it.

Marx has *no concept of Truth;* he substitutes his dialectics, by which any thesis is suspended by its antithesis. Thus any action can be justified as correct, if it suits the class struggle!

All basic *social institutions* which Christians respect as God's ordinances of creation and preservation are denied as to their legitimacy, particularly the state and the family. They may be tolerated provisionally; but eventually they must be replaced by new forms of organization and education. Therefore the primary right of parents to bring up their children is disclaimed. The responsibility rests with society at large. Consequently in Communist states children who received a Christian education could be separated from their parents and were sent into camps. This happened to the children of the famous Don Cossacks, who had been killed or deported because of their staunch Orthodox faith.

There is a profound contradiction in *ethics*: Marxism does not approve of "love" as supreme principle. It is substituted by hatred for the class enemy. The Stalinist author *Lunarsharskij* wrote in the spirit of Marx:

"We hate Christianity and the Christians. Even the best ones we must regard as our worst enemies. Because they teach love for our neighbours and compassion, which contradicts our principles. Christian love is a hindrance to our spreading the revolution. Thus down with love! We need hatred. We must learn to hate, for only then we can conquer the world."[111]

Already Marx and Engels had called Religion the *"opium of the people,"* because, they complained, it appeases them. It lets them accept their unbearable conditions in hope for a heavenly compensation after death. Religious otherworldliness blindfolds them for the material realities.

3. Open Persecution of Churches and Christians

The Communist fight against Christianity did not only consist in verbal attacks. In several countries like Russia, China, North Korea, Romania the anti-Christian programme was, after the Communist victory, carried out with physical violence. This was often done under cruelties too horrible to be described in detail. But I recommend to Korean readers the book of *Dong-Hee Sohn* "My Cup Overflows."[112] Here the author gives a most moving account of the martyrdoms first of her two brothers and then her father *Young-Won Sohn* (who had already

---

[111] Quoted by K. ANDERS, 1963, p. 101.
[112] Christian Literature Crusade, Seoul 2001.

before suffered in Japanese prisons). They happened during a Communist uprising in Soonchun, South Korea in October 1948, and again early in the Korean War, in September 1950. The pretext here was that Christians were accused scornfully of being "Yankee boys," cooperating secretly with the American capitalists.

Likewise in Russia religious persecution was justified politically. The Russian Orthodox Church was accused of having been an instrument of the repressive Tsar-regime, helping to exploit the masses. Massive antireligious propaganda was staged. Christianity was ridiculed as mere superstition, believing in a Jesus who never had existed!

Here again hostile words soon were accompanied by hostile actions. Already in March 1922 Lenin killed 8000 priests; numerous monks and nuns were executed likewise. Many churches and monasteries were vandalized or profaned and turned into stables or swimming pools. In Moscow one church was changed into a "Museum of Atheism."

Congregations were dissolved and readmitted as "registered churches" only under untenable conditions. All baptisms had to be reported. Infant baptism was forbidden entirely. Pastors of the dissident "unregistered churches" who met secretly in forests were arrested, severely sued and sent into Siberian labour camps.

In some cases the worst aspect of the persecution was not physical torture and execution. Attempts were made through the psychological techniques of brainwashing to make confessing Christians betray their brethren. Moreover they were brutally forced to deny Christ, even to blaspheme against God and thereby go to hell! This goal was cynically stated by the torturers. Here anti-Christian Marxism unveiled its satanic nature!

4. Other Methods

The Sovjet Union and other Communist states guaranteed "religious liberty" in their constitutions, but an extremely restricted one. After World War II the Soviet government discovered the strategy of achieving their aim by granting a limited tolerance. They started using churches for Communist purposes. Granting limited liberty to Christians could make them pliable and cooperative. Official delegates should act as mouth pieces at international, e.g. ecumenical conferences. I have experienced this with my own eyes and ears at the WCC's Assemblies at Nairobi 1975 and Vancouver 1983.

The Soviets also developed a system and strategy to infiltrate and undermine churches and other Christian organizations even outside Russia. It was called *"Orginform."* It should establish secret cells in every country and every large religious organization. Communist agents specialized in clever propaganda, infiltrated churches and missions to prepare the ideological disarmament of the faithful. One highly successful strategy was the cooperation between Communists and Christians in the s.c. "Peace Movement," the final aim of which was not and still is not to establish genuine peace with freedom. Rather it was designed to blind the Christians to their revolutionary aim and planned take over of control. This is what has been going on in South Korea for quite some time!

In North Korea some representative churches are kept open for the purpose of demonstrating to foreigners that no persecution exists. Naïve visitors believe it. They do not know that N. Korea is still the country with the worst persecution going on; around 100,000 Christians are imprisoned. Baptism can only be practiced secretly, if at all. But one never reads about it in the South Korean press. Nor is it mentioned in sermons.

IV. History, Expansion and Diversification of Marxism

Until the First World War the ideology of Marxism was spread theoretically through the channel of the "First International Network." Most of the Social-Democratic and Communist parties and groups kept contact through it. The world historical change came by the October Revolution 1917 in Russia. It was achieved after heavy fighting between the Red and the White Armies. When the Bolsheviks won, the imposition of the Soviet system cost terrible human sacrifices. During the collectivisation of agriculture 10 million of "kulaks" (small farmers) were killed! It is estimated conservatively that during the entire Soviet era about 60 million people were killed. Another 60 million people were executed by the Maoists in China.

This showed that Marx's writings which had an unveiled terrorist dimension, led logically to a system with cruel consequences. It became embodied in the characters of most Bolshevik leaders, particularly in *Joseph Stalin* (1879-1953). He, the "iron man," was described by his own relatives as a person with no human emotion. He believed only in organised power and a system of control and deterrence. This was enhanced by a comprehensive spy system which was also applied in all other Communist countries.[113]

Communist parties were established in most countries on four Continents (Europe, Asia, Latin America), unless they were outlawed by authoritarian states. After the defeat of Germany in World War I, the Soviet Union forced Eastern Europe into the Communist Bloc of "People's' Republics." The same happened to North Korea. After the decolonisation of the Third-World, Communist states were also erected in several South East Asian, Central American and African countries. In other regions Marxist revolutionary movements expected their chance. 50 years after the October Revolution one third of mankind was under harsh Communist control. Marx' vision of a world revolution appeared to have come close to its universal implication. Had it not been for the counter-threat of the United States of America as the rival super-power and also by NATO, the total takeover might possibly have succeeded. What happened in this part of the world during the Korean war (1950-53) was a regional foreshadowing of a threatening Communist-democratic confrontation on a world scale.

Marxist Diversification

The Communist system was, however, *not monolithic*. Due to different historical circumstances and personalities a diversification of applied Marxist ideology occurred. In many cases Communist and nationalistic ideas were merged into particular Marxist ideologies and state systems. We can only mention the major ones: *Maoism* in China; *Castroism* in Cuba, Potpolism in Kampuchea, *Ho Shi Minism* in Vietnam, and Kim Il-Sung's *Juche,*[114] the semi-religious ideological blueprint for tyranny in North Korea, which appears as an amalgamation between Stalinism and Fascism.

But in all cases there were common features: totalitarianism and terror. Wherever the Communists came, they indulged in unprecedented mass slaughters, and especially in anti-Christian persecution.

During the later 1960's in Czechoslovakia an attempt was made by some enlightened Neomarxists to replace the totalitarian system by a new brand of "Marxism with a human face;" but it failed badly.

---

[113] I experienced this myself twice when passing the boundery between the West Berlin and the Eastern sector.

[114] Thomas J. BELKE, 1999.

V. Erosions and Collapses of the Marxist System

The ultimate failure of Communism was anticipated by inner doubts of its very founders, Marx and Lenin. They secretly had to admit that their theory didn't work.

Marx never wearied of predicting the growth of *pauperisation*- the working class' reduction to misery. He regarded it as a scientifically proved law of historic materialism. After his death Engels admitted that this had not taken place during the 19th century. On the contrary: the social situation had improved considerably. This was due to the social legislation of European governments in Germany under Chancellor Otto von Bismarck, and also in Great Britain and France. When Marx still did not stop expounding his theory, the reason was not that he was worried about the poor classes' fate. The opposite was true: he wanted the situation to get worse and worse. For only that would prepare the ground for his desired world revolution. But it did not happen spontaneously anywhere. In Russia it was enforced upon the nation by the Bolshevik Red Guards after the lost First World War; but in the "Capitalist countries" of Western Europe and North America it never could take place, in spite of continuous Marxist agitation.

Lenin died despondently. He even lost his senses. He crawled on the floor and in tears implored table and chairs to forgive him!

The doctrine of the working class's reduction to misery in capitalist countries was clearly disproved by the improvements in socio-economic conditions, to the disgust of Marx and Engels, who would have preferred crisis, starvation, uproar, and wars!

On the other hand promises of fantastic socio-economic achievements in the "workers' paradise," on their way towards perfect socialism and finally Communism, proved to be illusionary. They were contradicted empirically by the dismal conditions in the countries of "real-existing Communism:" queuing for hours in front of half-empty food shops, narrow housing often without heating, and technical breakdowns. Instead of the expected "classless society," a new privileged class, the "nomenclatura" established itself out of the top party officials. Ordinary women, however, saw themselves forced to work in order to be able to feed their hungry children. Moreover, repeated abortions became the rule in order to avoid unemployment. This resulted in the de-humanization of the females. A Russian friend of mine, *Tatjana*

Goritscheva,[115] a former member of the *Komsomolcz* youth organization, got extremely concerned about that. She became a dissenter and eventually a Christian. She founded a Christian feminist movement, called "League of Mary." Soon she was expelled from the Sovjet Union.

Many people outside who had believed in the Soviet system and tried it became disappointed. A former French Communist by the name of *Ignace Lepp*, an agent of CPF, escaped from a German prison to Russia. Deeply disillusioned he returned to France; he was converted to Christianity and became a priest.

Towards the end of the post-Stalinist era a growing disillusion was sensed all over the Soviet Union. The exiled Russian dissident *Alexander Maximov* told me in 1980: "Not even the children of Brezhnev[116] believe in it! In West Germany there are more Marxists than in the Soviet Union."

What was the most important reason for this? The answer is: the promises of a truly socialist society, and finally a Communist, classless society were not fulfilled, because they simply *could not* be fulfilled; it was a mere utopia! The basic error of Marxism is that it builds on a *wrong concept of man.* It neglects the sinfulness of our human nature and its inherent selfishness. The distinction between master and servant could not be replaced by an egalitarian structure of comradeship.[117] For the innate social sins of pride, greed, envy, deceit, lust for power cannot be eradicated simply by changes in the socio-economical structure. They will always appear again even under new external conditions.

Sinful human beings need a real redemption from within! And this can only be accomplished by a new birth in the power of the Holy Spirit, on account of our atonement with God and our neighbours by the self-sacrifice of Jesus Christ. The young Karl Marx himself had already understood this, but he frivolously rejected his own spiritual birth-right by turning from Christ to Satan!

Marxists promised an earthly paradise; when the Soviets tried to implement it, the result was an inferno! They could not meet criticism of their system and opposition to it by improvements or arguments.

---

[115] Tatjana GORITSCHEWA, 1997.

[116] Leonid Breschnew, from 1964 until 1982 General-Secretary of the Communist Party and head of state of the Sovjet Union.

[117] The word "socialism" is derived from the Latin word *socius* = companion.

Their only answer was increased intimidation. This could work for for a certain period, but I could not prevent the final collapse of the system.

Three historic attempts of non-Russian peoples were made to rid themselves of the socialist system: on 17 June 1953, the workers' uprising in the German Democratic Republic could be quenched only by Soviet tanks. The same happened in November 1956 in Hungary and in August 1968 in Czechoslovakia ("Prague Spring").

An important explanation of the turn in the Soviet Union was the *spiritual vacuum* in the hearts of the Russians, who are a deeply religious people: atheistic philosophy and socialist utopia could not meet the deepest questions in life! What consolation does it give to a cancer ridden person, or to a young student who cannot find employment and is forsaken by all her friends? Some disillusioned Marxists observed Christians' lives. Admittedly, theirs was not perfect; but it was better and more attractive than the lives of those brought up to hate and despise!

In 1985 the last governing General-Secretary of the CPSU, *Mikhail Gorbatchev* came to power. He was clear-sighted enough to realise the incurable failure of the economic system. Hence he tried to reform it by his policy of *Perestroika* (reconstruction) and *Glasnost* (transparency). But even that could not stop the Soviet Empire from falling into bankruptcy. He had to allow far bigger changes both in internal and foreign politics. Upon this, he dropped his former Communist allies in Eastern Europe and sought rapproachement with Western powers.

With the fall of the Berlin Wall in November 1989 and the collapse of the former Soviet Union during the following years the most visible attempts to implement the agenda of Marxism were exposed to dismal failure.

VI. The Christian Answer to Marxist Ideology

1. Marxism and Marxists

At the conclusion of this chapter we now ask: What should be the Christian response to Marxism? Before answering this question we must make a clear distinction between the ideology of Marxism and the persons who call themselves Marxists. Here we apply the famous saying of St. Augustine: "Hate the error, but love the erring people!" After having expounded both the theory and the practice of Marxism, it should be clear that we have to reject it without compromise. Individual Marxists, however, are human beings whom God loves for Christ's sake, no matter how much they have sinned against him. Moreover there are many people today – e.g. in Latin America – who sympathize with Marxism because of its seeming concern for the poor. But they do not know the real roots of Marxism. Nor do they share Marx' hatred against God or the brutal spirit of the Communist revolution. But they must be convicted that they are on a dangerous road from which they should turn to the Gospel.

2. The Ideology of Marxism must be Nejected without Compromise

That the Marxist ideology is stridently opposed to the Gospel was always clear to all who studied its anti-Christian tenets and experienced its dreadful consequences. Pope *Pius IX* wrote in an Instruction about Communism[118] that its doctrine is to be abhorred, since it contradicts the Christian faith and even natural law.[119] Many Christian authors refuted it because of their own experience: The famous Russian author *Alexander Solzhenitsyn* wrote the 3 volumes of "The Gulag Archipelago" (network of concentration camps in the Sovjet Union). *Richard Wurmbrand* having been a prisoner in Rumania for 14 years wrote his biographical book "Tortured for Christ." In other books he urged Christians not to be duped by Marxism's benevolent disguise as a mere political or economic theory. Even former top insiders like Stalin's daughter Swetlana Alliluyeva, who became a Christian, exposed the intrinsic evil of the system and its representatives in twenty letters, comprised in a book.

Thus it is unconceivable that leading theologians and churchmen after so much evidence are pleading for a fresh, sympathetic approach to Marxism!

3. The Contribution of Christians to Overcome the Marxist System Peacefully

It is not always realized how much the collapse of the Communist domination is partly due to the fearless witness and action of Christians. This had already started during the period of open persecution:

---

[118] Encycle "Qui pluribus."

[119] Pius XII forced Italian Communists to choose between membership in Church or in CPI.

A. The defences of Russian Christians in court trials[120]

From the study of church history we know that the Christian conquest of the pagan Roman Empire is largely the achievement of the martyrs. We still can read their pleas before their judges in the records written down by fellow Christians, which were widely circulated as a source of encouragement. The same happened also during the Communist persecution. From the defences of those Christians we can learn much how to encounter the threats of Marxist atheists. The following elements can be discerned:

1. They impressed the court by their frank appearance like Peter and John in Acts 4:13. They were even thankful for the opportunity to testify to their faith. They felt so united with Christ that they drew a parallel between their trial and that of Jesus by the Sanhedrin and by Pontius Pilate.

2. They insisted upon public justice. Thus they were able to refute the false and illegal accusations by showing that the Soviet constitution formally guaranteed religious liberty.

3. They exposed the cruel methods of persecution: the brutal treatment of Christian citizens, their exclusion from work, the shutting down of their self-built churches.

4. At the same time they were ready to face imprisonment and even execution. They pointed out that suffering is an important mark of the faithful Church.

5. Finally they turned from self-defence to a biblical testimony to the Gospel and eschatological hope: "In our worship services we do not preach against the law of the state. We preach the Word of God that says that everybody should repent and accept the kingdom of God. In my sermons I have spoken about the love of God, as Christ also loved the people: He loved them until his death at the cross, so that everyone who believes in Him should have everlasting life. This I have preached this I preach today and this I shall continue to preach."[121]

---

[120] Documentation: The Odessa Trial. Judicial Hearings of Gospel-Christians-Baptists in Odessa, 2nd-7th Febr. 1967.

[121] Baptist preacher W. T. Timtshak in his speech for defense at Odessa Trial.

A similar apology, cast in poetry, is recorded from the trial of the well known Russian preacher *Georgij Vins*. He recited it when in 1966 he was sentenced to imprisonment for 10 years, followed by deportation:

Neither for robbery, nor for gold	**We call upon the Church of Christ**
Do we stand before you	To tread the path of thorns
today, here, as in Pilate's day	we summon to a heavenly goal
Christ our Savior is being judged.	we challenge perfidy and lies.

No! You cannot kill the freedom of belief	Fresh trials now and persecution
or imprison Christ in gaol!	will serve alone to strengthen faith
The examples of his triumphs	and witness God's eternal truth
will live in hearts He's saved.	before the generations still to come.

Such undaunted confession could not fail to penetrate to the conscience of their Marxist persecutors. Often it could not save the Christian preachers from severe punishment, sometimes 10 years of imprisonment in Siberian labour camps. But morally *they* were the real victors, and that was the beginning of the Marxist ideology's breakdown.

B. Christians involved in the peaceful revolution

It is not generally known that Christians played an important role at the overthrow of Communist system both in Poland and East Germany. They did not use violence against their oppressors but used peaceful means.

In the late 1970's in **Poland** the Communist government made itself increasingly unpopular amongst the labourers by its strict demands to work harder for an increased production. The official state-controlled trade union conformed, and lost the confidence of its members. Then *Lech Walesa*, a simple electrician working at the shipyard of Gdansk, called upon his fellow workers to resist the exploitation. He formed an alternative trade union, called *"Solidarnocz."* This respected human dignity and cared truly for the welfare of its members. Through the charismatic leadership shown by Walesa it found general support and dared to stage a successful general strike. Thus the government was forced to yield to the workers' just demands. That was the start of the democratisation process in Poland, which became the first liberated country amongst the East Bloc states. Walesa, a devout Catholic, was guided by Christian principles. After the definite collapse of the Marxist system he was elected as the first non-Communist state president.

About the same time an anti-Communist opposition was emerging in **East Germany**. It was not organized but spread itself as a popular movement through small discussion groups. There was also the officially favoured *Peace Movement*, but it soon emancipated itself from Communist oversight. Some peace demonstrations were led by Christians. Most significant was a small group of eighteen young people in *Leipzig*. It was started at the height of the Cold War by a Lutheran pastor, Christian Fuehrer. They assembled every Monday in his *Nikolai Church* to pray for peace. Prayer was followed by discussion about the dissatisfactory situation in the GDR (German Democratic Republic). They also went out on the street to demonstrate for "Peace without Weapons." The prayers attracted more and more people from all parts of East Germany; thus the number grew from 18 to 1,800. The government tried to stop it by controlling all roads leading to Nikolai Church, but in vain. Large peace demonstrations were conducted in other cities as well. They grew weekly in numbers, finally attracting several hundred thousands of people. When the Communist government sensed a threat to its own existence, it sent the police to brutally shatter the demonstrations. But pastors showed their sympathy to the movement. They announced in their Sunday services the names of those who were mishandled or arrested.

On October 9th, 1989 Nikolai Church was so crowded that many attendees had to wait outside. The first ones to occupy seats in the church were 600 secret policemen. They were sent to keep the meeting under control and even to disband it by force. "This counter-revolution must be stopped now," Communist leaders shouted. But the policemen did not witness any political provocation. The atmosphere was most dignified and spirit-controlled. The young Christians simply prayed together and sang hymns. Deeply moved they listened to the words of Jesus Christ, which the policemen had never heard in their lives: *"Blessed are the peacemakers for they shall be called sons of God ..."* Finally the Christians lit their candles and peacefully stepped out, wearing orange scarves with the inscription: "NO VIOLENCE!" They passed on burning candles to the waiting crowds outside. This happened at the sight of heavy armoured police, ready to shoot at them at any moment. But there was no reason for it. Instead more then 10,000 people peacefully marched through the streets of Leipzig; not even a window was smashed. The Communists were amazed and were unable to interfere.

A high ranking member of the politbureau remarked: "We had been prepared for anything, but not for candles and prayers!" One month later, on November 9th, the Berlin Wall was broken down.

I still remember that elderly man who climbed up the wall and blew his trumpet, tuning in the hymn: *"Now thank ye all our God!"*

C. Four advices for a missionary dialogue with Marxists

1. Be clear, truthful, courageous and uncompromising. Point out the alternatives between Christian faith and Marxist ideology: Amazement at God's working vs. contempt for everything that exists; adoration vs. destruction; love vs. hatred.

2. Behave humbly, wisely, act kindly: We do not hate Marxists, for they are human beings, too. But we abhor Marxism as an anti-God doctrine, strategy, and system. Give convincing proof of that.

3. Let your witness be borne by the firm conviction: the ultimate triumph will belong to Jesus! For He has won the decisive victory already by His Cross and Resurrection. This has already led to many remarkable consequences in history!

4. Rely on the power of earnest prayer as a weapon for battle. Apply the *Jericho prayer*: by that weapon demons can be bound, bulwarks can be destroyed, even the fortresses of Marxist ideology.[122]

Conclusion: The Decisive Answer to the Korean Issue

During my year in Korea at guest professor at Yonsei University I was asked several times to state my personal view of the way in which the tragic division of the Korean people and country could be ended. I had to humbly admit that this is an extremely difficult and delicate question for a foreigner to answer. My advice can only be given in humility, trying to make use of our experience with the division and reunification between West- and East Germany. In a short statement which I read to a meeting of the Korean Peaceforum in November 2003, I said the following:

I agree with all other considerate people that the conflict between the democratic South and the Communist North can not be solved by a

---

[122] The Ukrainian Metropolitan of Catholic Church, Andrew Sheptytsky, requested that Rome order **prayers of exorcism** against the Communists, whose "regime cannot be explained except by a massive possession of the Devil." (R. Wurmbrand, 1995, p. 114).

new war. For that would ruin the whole country. Neither can it be solved by diplomacy alone nor new treaties following an optimistic, but naïve "Sunshine politics." Communists respect treaties only as long as they suit their present strategy. Kim Il-Sung and Kim Yong-Il never gave up their dream of "liberating" the entire peninsula in their way, as they had tried before 1945 and in the Korean war of 1950-53. The consequence may be a new invasion as soon as the international political situation seems to allow it.

South Koreans should never forget the dreadful experiences of earlier confrontations with the North Korean Communists and their underground sympathizers here.

Particularly Korean Christians should keep alive the memory of their fellow believers who became martyrs under Communism. If we refuse to learn from history, we shall be forced to re-live it!

But that does not mean that South Koreans should simply acquiesce with the present unhappy state of division. Germany did not. It is good and right that they should continue to hope and work for the re-unification of their common mother country. But it should be a re-unification in which the principles of liberty, justice and democracy are safeguarded for all. North Korea's first credible step towards that end is that she grants the basic human rights for all her citizens. All non-criminal prisoners must be released immediately, especially the 100,000 Christians who are suffering in cruel labour camps. It is obvious that the Kim Jong-Il regime will not consent to such proposal as long as it still clings to its Juche ideology. The demonic spell of Marxism has to be broken first.

But this will not be accomplished by diplomatic deliberations. However it can and will be broken by a secrete weapon of spiritual nature. Jesus said to his disciples: *"This kind [of evil spirits] never comes out except by prayer and fasting"* (Matthew 17:21). Korean Christians have a long experience with the use of this secret weapon. Do not cease to use it. God at His appointed time will hear you!

Chapter 5

Neo-Marxism and Its Influence on Contemporary Christianity

Introduction

During the Spring Term of 1969 at Tubingen University I had a unique experience. It confronted me personally, and in a drastic way, with the reality of the neo-Marxist inspired Student Rebellion in the late 1960's. On a Wednesday afternoon in May 1968 I went to my Institute of Missiology to conduct my seminar. I was accompanied by my assistant and my wife. But what a strange surprise! We found the stairs leading up to the seminar room crowded with noisy students. Most of them were theologians, but they were not among the members of my seminar. Having finally forced the way to my table, I found my place already occupied by the leader of that crowd. Bluntly he declared to me that today I was not to moderate this session. For it had been appointed to be "trans-functioned" into an "autonomous seminar," conducted by the students themselves. The theme would be the role of the established churches in upholding the capitalist systems that exploit the Third World. We were, however, permitted to participate in the discussion, in which, of course, I was not interested under such circumstances. I soon realised that it was impossible to enforce my right as director of this Institute; so we simply agreed that he might read his prepared statement and then leave. The group obviously still planned to stage similar "go-ins" into lectures of other professors. That was just one show case of the desired take-over of our entire "Eberhard Karls-University."[123] To that end the leftist students had re-named it *"Ernst Bloch-University,"* after a leading neo-Marxist professor who was an emeritus of our high school.

---

[123] The Duke of Württemberg *Eberhard Karl* was the founder of our university in 1477. – *Ernst Bloch* formerly had been an orthodox Marxist and admirer of Stalin, teaching at Leipzig University. Later his concept of socialism changed and he was expelled from East Germany. Tubingen University offered him a chair in the philosophical faculty. He died in 1975 at an age of 90 years.

I. The Neo-Marxist Metamorphosis (Transformation) of Marxism-Leninism

1. The Emergence of Neo-Marxism

The ideology of Marxism, as I stated in my previous chapter, has undergone several changes and regional adaptations. During the 1960's a new brand made its public appearance, generally known as "Neo-Marxism." What was meant by this term? Somebody jokingly called it "Marxism for the refined people." The *"Neo-"* indicates that, in any case, it distinguished itself from classical and established Marxism. For that had addressed itself to the proletariat; but it had degenerated into totalitarianism and finally failed to lead the people into the "workers' paradise." Neo-Marxists were quite aware of that failure. They also were aware that in Western Europe the general socio-economic conditions had improved considerably. Thus a class of ordinary manual labourers did not exist anymore; neither did the remaining ones show any interest in a major revolution.

Therefore in modern Marxist circles the question emerged: Since the "agents of revolution" cannot be found among the labourers, where do we find the new "revolutionary subject?" The surprising answer was: we must seek it amongst the liberal intellectuals, who are influential in society and might be open to new ideas. Thus the *students* were chosen to become the recipients of modernised Marxist thought, and the universities became the first subjects of daring revolutionary experiments. This took place by the "Student Revolution," which started in at Berkely University, California, jumped over the Atlantic Ocean to France and West Germany and soon spread to many other countries, and even as far as Japan.

The master minds of Neo-Marxism were German social philosophers of Jewish descent: *Theodor Adorno, Max Horkheimer, Jürgen Habermas* (the profoundest scholar amongst them), and *Herbert Marcuse*, the popular father of the students' rebellion. Originally they had been attached to the *Institute of Social Research* at Frankfurt University, founded in 1929. It concentrated on Marxist cultural criticism. They initiated their *"Frankfurt School of Thought"* and called their philosophical approach *"Critical Theory."*[124] Thereby they indicated

---

[124] Max HORKHEIMER, 1968. – The most fundamental criticism of this theory was given by the German philosopher Günther ROHRMOSER, [4]1976.

that their concern was to apply radical criticism to all established traditions and institutions. When in 1933 Hitler came to power and started his anti-Semitic persecution, they emmigrated to the United States. They settled down in New York where they established the "Institute of Social Research" at Columbia University. After the war Marcuse stayed in America, teaching at the University of California in San Diego (from 1965), whilst his three colleagues returned to Germany and – by their books – became very famous and influential. In 1966 Marcuse, too, returned to Germany and became an honorary professor at the Free University in West Berlin. His Essay on "Repressive Tolerance" (1967)[125] became the blue print of the Marxist student movement in Berlin and elsewhere.

In the United States the Neo-Marxist Frankfurt scholars had devoted their research to the root causes of Anti-Semitism, Fascism and National-Socialism. According to their theory these roots were to be found in the authoritarian character of Western, Christian culture, which ultimately originated in the biblical concept of God as Lord over nature and human history. The Ten Commandments were regarded as expressions of God's authoritarian rule, which at the same time legitimised the authority of human beings over other human beings. This is established in the ruling relationship of parents and children, husbands and wives, masters and servants, royal rulers and citizens. Even our languages were, they observed, shaped by such "authoritarian" thinking: the terms and images they use, and also their grammatical structure in which the subject governs the whole sentence. This authoritarian thought pattern, they claimed, had produced the Prussian authoritarian monarchy in Germany and logically led to Arian racism, Anti-Semitism and finally even to the horror of the "Holocaust" of Jews in Auschwitz. Therefore, the Neo-Marxist founders of the "Critical Theory" concluded, Germans should be subjected to a thorough re-education after World War II. All traditional concepts, including ethical norms and cultural values, should radically putinto question. All social structures that were based on the principle of authority should be critically analysed and be changed in favour of equality. This was applied also to the academical institutions. These were to eliminate the established authority of professors to define the content, as well as the methods, of their own research. In this way the professors' position of respect amongst their students was denounced as well. My experience which I related in

---

[125] In: R. Wolff et al. (eds), 1967.

the introduction to this chapter was a typical outcome of that Neo-Marxist ideology.

Another field for applying the "Critical Theory" was the primary and secondary schools. According to the traditional pattern teachers commanded the respect of their pupils – rather similar to the Confucian tradition in Korea! Now instead the system of "anti-authoritarian education" was introduced in our German schools, particularly in provinces ruled by Social-Democratic governments. But "anti-authoritarian education" started already in the kindergarten, and some leftist inclined parents tried it out in their families. Between 1970 and 1980 the guiding rules for our German system of education were shaped by the "emancipatory didactics," and accordingly all textbooks were written in the subject's mother tongue, History and Religion were re-written from a Neo-Marxist point of view, and a new generation grew up which was thoroughly shaped by this ideology. This meant a radical disruption in the cultural tradition especially in Germany, but also in some other West European countries.

2. Basic Doctrinal Tenets of Neo-Marxism

What did the representatives of the Frankfurt School teach?

My space limit does not allow me to go into details. Its shifting theory is unfolded in hundreds of books and many thousands of articles in magazines which appeared during the period from 1963 until 1980.[126] Moreover the four founders of the Frankfurt School do not agree amongst themselves in every aspect, and the diversity is even wider amongst their adherents. But some major trends can be analysed.

a. Criticism of Structural Dominion

The starting point is a fundamental criticism of all socio-political structures and also of the undergirding philosophies that legitimise their authoritarian character. The human being is – so goes the argument – destined to live in perfect freedom in accordance with its inner cravings, in equality with its fellow human beings and in harmony with nature. This was the pattern in which the *primal horde* of semi-animal people lived. The primal evil or "falling into sin" was the craving for dominance on other human beings and on nature. In order to avert the

---

[126] Most of these around 1000 books were published by Suhrkamp Verlag in Frankfurt; the total edition amounted to a million copies! They were read mainly by teachers, students and pupils and became official text books. Cf. Rudolf WILLEKE, 2000.

perils of nature humans invented techniques and engines to control it. But soon this progress turned against the inventors. Nature was exploited and human life started to be controlled by engines. Moreover better skilled human beings imposed their dominance over other human beings. Thus by and by structures of ruling were introduced to the social organizations of tribes and peoples. The world views, too, reflected the system of dominance, producing such evils as capitalism, racism and sexism. All social, economic and political organizations ossified the selfish pattern of domination. Ethics, religions and educational principles reflected and legitimised them. Such historical perspective obviously demonstrates the basic identity of Marxist and Neo-Marxist ideology.

The *difference*, however, lies in the *therapy* that is suggested for overcoming the misery of Western civilization. The classical Marxist approach was clearly *economic*, seeking the solution in an overthrow of the system of private property. The Neo-Marxists see the root cause psychologically in the human *craving for rule*. This is codified in cultural patterns which are perpetuated by the traditions of socialization and education at all levels: family, crèche, primary school and universities. The latter ones provide a system of culture which primarily legitimises the rule of the post-capitalist system. Moreover, in its sophisticated speculations, it is irrelevant for solving the real problems of our socio-political world. In consequence of such evaluation the radical reform of the universities became the first target of the Neo-Marxist revolution in 1968. But the same perspective is applied by them to all other public institutions as well, including the churches. Even the democratic order that epitomises civil liberty was exposed to radical criticism, since it also guarantees the right of private ownership. Therefore it should be replaced by a s.c. "basis democracy," a system in which all privileges are abolished and which in all its actions is supervised by the electorate.

b. The New Humanity

Like any other ideology Neo-Marxism has its *utopian vision* as it's the inspiring motive for all political action: It is the *"rule-less society,"* i.e. an entirely new social order without any dominance. The aim set forth is to work for a state of things in which no human being is ruled by another human being. Then the "new man" or the "new humanity" will make its appearance, which – liberated from all oppression – will realise its true selfhood. This hope is cherished with burning intensity; it bears an eschatological character. The "new humanity" in Neo-

Marxism is the secular equivalent to the return of Jesus Christ, the "Son of Man coming on the clouds of the sky" (Matthew 24:30 b) to set up his visible reign in power. I remember a conversation with my Tubingen colleague Jürgen Moltmann during the early 1970's. Wanting him to clarify his eschatology, I asked him whether he believed in the visible return of Jesus Christ. He paused a little moment before answering, but then he stated: "Yes, and this will be evident by all human beings peacefully living together without any mutual oppression." To me it dawned that my colleague had interpreted the *Parousia* (return) of Christ in Neo-Marxist terms. How could Moltmann arrive at such way of thinking? That will become understandable when we look at a particular line within Neo-Marxism, called "Messianic Marxism."

II. The Goals of "Messianic Marxism"

Amongst the neo-Marxists there is one school of thought which has been called "Messianic Marxism." Its representatives were the first Marxist-Communists who were willing to open up a constructive dialogue with Christian theologians.[127] This Marxist-Christian conversation reached its climax during the sixties. It suffered a great setback when it was condemned by the mouthpieces of established "orthodox Marxism" – i.e. by the Communist parties. The hopes set on this dialogue were almost shattered by the invasion of the Soviet Union's Red Army into Czechoslovakia in August 1968. Yet the talk continued, especially through the *Paulus Society*. At least for the Christian side its significance was steadily growing, and in Latin America it has given birth to the "Theology of Liberation"[128] as the dominant school of thought.

The importance of the concept of the messianic Marxists[129] for our theme is this: although they do cling to the premises of philosophic materialism, they received decisive new impulses from studying the Bible. In the O.T. prophets and in the preaching of Jesus about the Kingdom, they discovered a peculiarly ardent hope for the future, which they saw as intimately related to the whole of revolutionary his-

---

[127] Literature: A Christian's Handbook on Communism. New York: National Council of the Churches of Christ in the U.S.A. Committee on World Literacy and Christian Literature: New York ³1962. – Dale VREE: On Synthesizing Marxism and Christinity, John Wiley& Sons, New York 1976.

[128] Josè MIGUEZ-BONINO, 1976. – Gustavo GUTIÉRREZ, ¹1972.

[129] Peter P. J. BEYERHAUS, 1992: pp. 42-45.

tory and to the basic concerns of Socialism. *Ernst Bloch*[130] has called this emotional force the *"warm current"* of Marxism. Its complementary parallel is the *"cold current,"* consisting in socio-economic analyses and prognoses of Dialectic Materialism. Both currents need each other in order to preserve the psychological dynamics as well as the critical realism in Marxism. For this synthesis between reflection and enthusiasm Bloch coined the term *"Realutopie"* (concrete utopia), thereby giving recognized status to the word "utopia" in Marxist ideology. This "warm current" or "warm red" is the indestructible hope for a new and better life, hope for a coming transformation of all things and a Golden Age on earth. It is the specific concern of "esoteric Marxism" and of the Christian-Marxist dialogue in particular to regain those humanistic dynamics.

The most important representatives of Messianic Marxism were the late Tubingen professor *Ernst Bloch*, the two Czechs *Vitezslav Gardavsky* (*1923) and *Milan Machovec* (1925-2002),[131] as well as the Frenchman *Roger Garaudy* (*1914), former chief ideologist of the Communist Party of France (who in 1968 because of his conversion to Catholicism was excluded from the PCF[132] and finally, in 1982, turned to Islam because of its futuristic orientation!).

Ernst Bloch was the profoundest philosophical thinker amongst them. In three volumes he presented his "Principle of Hope"[133] as the decisive drive in human history. Bloch also inspired Jürgen Moltmann to write his "Theology of Hope,"[134] and thereby indirectly gained penetrating influence on ecumenical thought. ***Roger Garaudy***, however, became the more important dialogue partner for the WCC during the seventies.[135] In his writings the new "Christomarxism," which is spreading with contagious vehemence, has found its classical expression.

What are the main thoughts of "Messianic Marxism?" The starting point is dissatisfaction with the present state of the world. Garaudy sees contemporary society engulfed by a total crisis: "Our society is a process of dissolution. It calls for a radical change not only of property

---

[130] Ernst BLOCH,1962b.

[131] M. MACHOVEC, 1972. – Idem, 2000.

[132] R. GARAUDY, 1968.

[133] Ernst Bloch: Das Prinzip Hoffnung, 1954-59. – Idem, 1962a.

[134] Jürgen MOLTMANN, 1972. – Idem, 1968: pp. 42-60.

[135] Ans J. van der BENT, 1980.

rights and power structures, but also of our culture and education, of religion and faith, of life and its meaning." Our task is defined by the subtitle of Garaudy's main work "Change the World and Change Life." This desperately needed total change can and must take place only on this earth, within our human history. "Human history is the only place where God's Kingdom is to be established," says Garaudy. This implies the rejection of metaphysical transcendence.

The existence of God is rejected, too. Bloch categorically states as basic presupposition "that no God remains in the height, since no God is there at all or ever has been." Atheism is stressed emphatically in order to secure man's responsibility for ushering in the new age. In as much as it is a protest against the Christian disinterest in social affairs, this atheism is justified even by Moltmann.

Paradoxically enough, the Bible is not rejected within such atheism. On the contrary, it is praised as an unparalleled source document of hope, which really carries the force of change. Bloch tries to solve that contradiction by an incredible manoeuvre; in his book "Atheismus im Christentum"[136] (atheism in Christianity) (1968)[137] he develops the strange thesis that man's emancipation towards the complete denial of God is the secret theme of the Bible itself! The tempting insinuation of the snake: *"You shall be like God,"* is revaluated into the first promise given to man. This promise, Bloch proposes, was fulfilled by Jesus: *"He who sees me, sees the Father."* At this point the reinterpretation of the Biblical message to annex it to a messianic Marxism reveals its *blasphemous* nature: "Christ is the symbol of emancipated mankind. ... In him man for the first time invaded the transcendence and set himself in the place of God, a Messiah against God and for man ... Man becomes God, and the greatest sin henceforth is not willing to be like God!"

With the help of such de-mythologising (or rather *re*-mythologising) hermeneutics the Bible becomes one of the most important textbooks of revolution for Marxist readers. Any passage related to God's intervention in history to bring about doom and new creation is read as a challenge to man to follow the example of the "angry Jesus" by siding with the poor and overturning the present power systems of oppression. This

---

[136] Ernst BLOCH, 1969.
[137] Ernst BLOCH, 1970.

approach was taken over and developed by some theologians as a new hermeneutical key under the name "materialistic exegesis."[138]

Statements of biblical faith are increasingly filled with a new ideological content. In particular, the *resurrection of Christ* is reinterpreted by Garaudy. It becomes the symbol of the new, *horizontal transcendence* which in neo-Marxist thinking has taken the place of the metaphysical, vertical transcendence. "There is no Beyond, no divine reality above us. But there is the historic reality of the future, which lies ahead of us as a possibility to be audaciously seized." Garaudy here speaks of the "eschatological postulate of hope." "Man is a task to be realised; society is a task to be realised; this postulate is congruent with the faith in the resurrection of Christ." Faith in the resurrection, accordingly, is a mental attitude which by courageous actions makes possible what appeared to be impossible. In this attitude one has to undertake decisive steps into the revolutionary tomorrow. Thus Garaudy recognises his own conviction in the slogan of the Parisian student rebellion in March 1968: "Let us be reasonable, let us demand the impossible!"

Thus we see that in messianic Marxism the Kingdom of God has become clearly an entity within history, to be realised my man himself. Nothing can prevent mankind from opening the gate into the "Kingdom of Liberty" by revolutionary action. The future lies open before us, and reality contains unlimited possibilities which man has to grasp in responsible ventures.

III. The Cultural Revolution of the "New Left"

Since the 1960's the term "New Left"[139] came more and more into usage. The word was coined by an American sociologist by the name of *C. W. Mills* (1916-62).[140] In contrast to the traditional political Left its adherents did not come from the lower, working classes but from the sons and daughters of the higher, educated and often wealthy middle class. Some were children of professors and pastors. Basically they

---

[138] Representatives of „Materialistic Exegesis are: Kuno Füssel, Fernando Belo, Walter A. Brueggemann; N.C. Gottwald, Wolfgang Stegemann and Luise Schottroff. (See P. BEYERHAUS, 1996b: pp. 214 f.).

[139] Reimar Lenz, 1969.

[140] C.W. Mills, 1960.

were inspired by the neo-Marxist Frankfurt School, especially by *Herbert Marcuse.*[141]

1. Ideological Tenets

The leftist students refused to see the meaning of life in consumption. They doubted progress achieved by technology. They found a new meaning in the concern for the poor masses in the "Third World," whose miserable conditions they found properly analyzed by Lenin's theory of Imperialism. The modern capitalist system, he had said, had exported the proletariat to the colonized peoples in Africa, Asia and Latin America. This socio-political concern gave an ethical pathos to the New Left, although its followers expressed themselves in a crude, rather obscene language. A respected inner circle even turned into terrorism as a legitimate means to get a hearing from the public. The notorious "Bader-Meinhoff-Gang" specialized in the assassination of leading politicians and industrialists.[142]

Such extremes had not been advocated by Marcuse; he believed in a strategy of modified non-violence,[143] which however, included "resistance against objects" like turning over cars, sitting blockages of railways and streets as well as occupation of buildings. But in principle Marcuse justified getting rough in opposition as a visible protest against an affluent society. Thereby he paved the way for terrorism.

The New Left directed its protest against the patriarchal society with its moral values and aesthetic ideal of beauty. For these, they argued, covered the cruelty innate in the ruling system. Thus they accused their parent's generation of hypocrisy.

2. The Cultural Revolution

The major aim of the New Left was to work for a "Cultural Revolution" in the West. The most fatal historical event was the **Students' rebellion in 1968**. We still speak about the "1968-generation," whose members have matured since then and occupy influential positions in political, cultural and ecclesiastical life. Many have changed their radi-

---

[141] Marcuse's books: One-Dimensional Man (1967) and "Triebstruktur und Gesellschaft" (1966) belong to the standard works of reference in the Marxist student movement of the late sixties both in the U.S.A. and in Germany.

[142] Ulrike Meinhoff was the granddaughter of a German missionary linguist, Gudrun Ensslin the daughter of a Württemberg pastor; both committed suicide in prison.

[143] H. MARCUSE, 1966.

cal opinions, but others still uphold them in a less offensive way. Thus the strategy once advocated by the revolutionary student leader *Rudi Dutschke* (1940 – 1979) proved to be successful at last. He had advised his fellows not to try seizing political power at once – which in view of the strength of the state proved to be impossible. Rather they should embark on "the long march through the institutions," in analogy to Mao's strategy to conquer China.

The Cultural Revolution spread incredibly fast, like a wild fire. Its communicators were young professors, teachers, sociologists, social workers and theologians. These were very dogmatic about their new "scientific insights," and rather intolerant in their behavior. Politeness and etiquette gave way for rough behavior and provocative manners of dress and hair (and beard!) style. It became risky to criticize the world view of the young leftists. People who dared to express conservative thoughts were branded as "crypto fascists" or "racists." The leftists' mouth pieces were the mass media, school books, theatres, peace demonstrations and also panels at smaller and larger church meetings. Here radical actions were justified or even bluntly proposed.

The provocative behavior of the rebellious students made a traumatic impression on the public mind in Western Europe. That cultural revolution of 1968 brought about major changes, some of which have never been reversed. The ethical and philosophical foundations of our occidental-Christian culture were damaged. The devastating effects of the Neo-Marxist revolution and its less ostentatious follow-up are felt by our European society today. They are: a general fading away of authority in all realms of life – starting with parental indulgence and disrespect for teachers; an erosion of ethical and aesthetical values; dominance of the ugly, absurd and shocking in theater, films and literature; breach with cultural tradition; a rift between the older and younger generation; moral permissiveness; inability of governments and institutions to defend their legitimacy; disregard for the sacredness of human life from its inception to its expiry.

Pope John Paul II. was right when he branded the Western emancipated lifestyle at the end of the second millennium as a "culture of death."

In 1998 the champions of the New Left were democratically elected as the ruling *red-green coalition* in Germany. This does not act so radically as its leaders had demanded in their youth; but some main elements of the Neo-Marxist ideology are now introduced by legal reform.

This is seen particularly with regard to the liberalization of sexual norms and the devaluation of the family.

3. Impact of the Leftist Movement on Young Christians

During the later sixties neo-Marxist thought captured the minds of many Christian students, particularly theologians. The writings of the Frankfurt School were read eagerly in study groups within the Student Christian Union and the theological faculties. Some called themselves *"red cells."* The writings of Marx and Lenin were read side by side with the Bible; "Historic Materialism" and the "Critical Theory" served as hermeneutical key for a new understanding of the biblical authors.

At the peak of the Students' rebellion the effects upon the attitude of young theologians to their studies and their future role in the pastoral ministry became devastating. The Bible was treated with contempt, as was devotional practices.

The avowed aim was to disrupt and restructure the institutions of the church and theological education from within. Young ministers wanted to act as social workers or even revolutionaries. Every reference to the transcendent orientation of Christianity was sneered at.

When trying to recall my personal experiences during the hottest phase of the student revolution between 1968 an 1972, I remember **two incidents** in particular.

The *first* one was the appearance of a flood of provocative pamphlets, highly contemptuous for the content and form of our theological studies.[144] Some of my colleagues were ridiculed for their compliance with the established tradition. All of us professors were accused of upholding the capitalist system by the very theological terminology we still used. In replying to this charge my colleague *Ernst Käsemann* had maintained that there is a limit to criticizing the substance of our faith. Particularly the NT affirmation of the Lordship of Jesus should be sacrosanct. Two days later an extremely radical, even blasphemous pamphlet was spread under the title: "Partisan Käsemann – *'Jesus the Lord.'"*[145] The authors claimed that the Church's christological confession was simply motivated by the desire to uphold authoritarian systems of ruling, from which clergy and professors benefited materially.

---

[144] Theologiestudenten 1969. Dokumente einer revolutionären Generation. Ev. Verlagswerk: Stuttgart, 1969.

[145] Ibid., p. 49 f.

But in reality, the pamphlet stated cynically: "The New Testament is a product of neurotic bourgeois, a manifest of brutal inhumanity, a grand deception of the masses!"

The majority of my colleagues preferred to keep silent in view of such a blasphemy. Only two of us attended an urgent meeting of our theological students. We tried to persuade them to dissociate themselves from that open insult to our Lord and Savior Jesus Christ. But when the vote was taken, only a small minority followed our plea. The others argued that they first wanted to find out themselves how much truth was contained in the accusations of the pamphlet! This made us realize how far the process of spiritual dissolution had already affected the bulk of our future pastors!

A few weeks later the *second* incident took place: The student chaplains had invited bishop Eichele, head of our large Württemberg Church, to preach a sermon in the central sanctuary of Tubingen, the cathedral-like *Stiftskirche*. It was a time when many students were angry with the governing board of our church. For it had refused to ordain a female candidate, since in her examination sermon she had denied the reality of eternal life. The radical student organization decided to punish the bishop by disturbing his sermon. So they did. When he had started preaching, a crowd of leftist students forced their way to the altar and unrolled a placard with the inscription: *"Be first reconciled to your sister!"* The bishop's sermon was drowned by the noisy agitation from a megaphone. He therefore had no other option but to step down from the pulpit and the worship service was changed into a political demonstration. This caused great startling amongst the concerned church members. They became really frightened about the threatened collapse of spiritual reverence in their beloved church. Would the new intellectual Marxists really accomplish their aim to capture the church from inside and make it an instrument for realizing the goals of their revolutionary ideology?

IV. The Christian Answer to Neo-Marxism

1. Confessing Christians' Reaction to the Neo-Marxist Intrusion

a. The Confusion of Church Members

At the height of the student rebellion our Christian community was deeply shaken by the unprecedented storms. This was the case at all levels, from the congregational grass roots up to the top of the Church's leadership, and also in the academic ranks of our theological faculties. Bishop Eichele, whose sermon in the ancient Collegiate Church was so rudely disturbed, resigned a few months afterwards. One of my colleagues in Marburg, an authority on Reformation Theology, was so brutally treated in his lectures and seminars that he had to be treated for clinical depression. His mental health was never restored completely. The Church Council in Stuttgart held consultations with our Tubingen Faculty, but they ended without conclusion. The "people in the pew," i.e. ordinary church members, were even worse off. Young people infected by the neo-Marxist epidemic, turned against their own Christian parents. These felt that they were left alone with their anxieties. For pastors, bishops and professors were sometimes divided amongst themselves and provided no clear answer.

There was also the collective guilt problem: The German National-Socialist government had committed horrible atrocities against the Jews, parts of the German army had maltreated the occupied neighbour countries, and the majority of the people had remained passive, if they did not even sympathize with such acts. Was the neo-Marxist accusation perhaps true that it was the authoritarian stream in German culture which was to be blamed for these dreadful eruptions? Was it not right that children were guided to emancipate themselves from their elders? Should parents and teachers agree to this and refrain from using authority in their educational responsibility? But if children and young adults never were disciplined in their development, would that not lead to disorder and finally complete anarchy?

b. Maintaining the Biblical Concept of Authority

Fortunately there were mature Christians both amongst the laity and the clergy, who did not lose their senses. They turned to the Scriptures and found that here the term *"exousia,"*[146] meaning "power" in the sense of bestowed authority, is not a negative concept. On the contrary: God Himself is described both in the Old and the New Testament as the one, who commands over supreme authority as Lord, King, Shepherd, Father. God's fatherhood, from which all human fatherhood is derived (Eph 3:14-15), shows to us that His ruling is not exercised in a repressive way, but rather in loving concern for His creatures. It is by this authority He rules as sovereign over His universal Kingdom both in heavens and on earth. Everything that happens in the realm of history

---

[146] Roger R. NICOLE, 1973: p. 47 f.

and of nature is following His command or admission. Thus the Ten Commandments given on Mt. Sinai reveal Him as the supreme Law Maker who is entitled to the obedience of His people. These commandments are not to be regarded as harsh demands, but rather as a reliable guidance on the path of life (cf. Psalm 119!).

It is by fulfilling His good commands they will live in peace and prosperity.

But God does not retain his authority for Himself. He does not rule in a lonely position. No, He does so by conferring some of His own authority to His heavenly and earthly ministers to let them share in His benevolent rule. Thus political governors are acting on behalf of God. They are invested with authority, which is to be respected by all citizens; Christians included (Rom 13:1-5).

The saving work of Jesus Christ, too, is enhanced by the authority the Father has given to Him. The Risen One tells His apostles: *"All authority in heaven and on earth is given to me."* That means that no created angelic or human force can obstruct the completion of His work of redemption. Again, Christ, the King of kings, does not rule alone. His reign both over His Church and over the cosmos is executed by ministers whom He has invested with authority. It is the same authority in which He Himself during his earthly days preached, taught, performed miracles and exorcized evil spirits. Thus we read in Matthew 10:1 that Jesus after having called His 12 apostles he *"gave them authority ... "*. It is by that authority the Church is able to complete the work of redemption which fundamentally Jesus had wrought on the Cross of Calvary.

Thus *authority is a most positive reality*, absolutely essential for the maintenance of God's creation and for the fulfillment of His plan of salvation. There is nothing tyrannical or inhumane in the concept of authority. Both governors, officials, teachers and parents should not be ashamed of claiming their God-given authority, if they do it in accordance with the constructive purpose for which it was given to them. The renouncement of all authority, however, would necessarily lead into anarchy and chaos in all realms of life.

But like every good gift coming from God, *authority, too, can be abused*. This happens when office bearers administer their authority in a haughty attitude and for a selfish or even pernicious purpose. The first created being that abused its high authority by perverting it into an instrument of rebellion against God was *Satan*. It is he who tries to seduce God's human servants to turn their God-given authority against Him and their fellow human beings. This has, indeed, happened many times in history, and it is still taking place today, for example in countries with a totalitarian kind of government. In this case the good gift of God which was meant for edification is turned into a means of destruction. It is quite true that the tragedy of German history in the twentieth century was basically caused by the abuse of authority. We have realized this with shame, and German governments and churches have publicly asked the victims to forgive us for such brutal perversion of power.

In conclusion we found that the neo-Marxist denouncement of the concept of authority as such is an illegitimate generalization of a partial truth. This partial element of truth makes their ideology so tempting, – especially in our post-war situation in Germany. But the New Left "threw out the baby with the bath water" and made a terrible mess of our once Christian culture and of our public mentality. That is why responsible people, confessing Christians particularly, soon realized that we had to reject Neo-Marxism by all means and warn our people of its demonic roots and its ruinous consequences for the life of families, schools, churches and moreover the very ethical foundations of our national culture.[147]

c. Concrete Counteractions

We also had to find concrete ways by which we could build up fortresses of resistance against the spiritual threats to the ministry of our churches and to the ethical foundations of our culture. I mention just *two new institutions* in the organization of which I was involved myself.

One was the founding of *Albrecht-Bengel-Haus*, a center for Bible oriented theological studies in Tubingen.[148] It was meant as an orthodox alternative to the ancient "Evangelical Stift" (= college) which had been infiltrated by Marxist students and even tutors. Here the radical activities of the leaders of the Left had found a basis of operation. In constructive opposition to this a new college was founded by representatives of the *Pietist movement* in Württemberg and accordingly named after the famous pietist Bible expositor *Johann Albrecht Bengel* (1687 – 1752). Here theological students who wanted to become faithful pas-

---

[147] Peter BEYERHAUS / Joachim HEUBACH (eds.), 1979.

[148] 25 Jahre alternatives Theologiestudium. Special issue of DIAKRISIS vol. 17 (1/1996).

tors and missionaries would find a place where they could enjoy true spiritual fellowship in Bible reading, prayer and evangelistic outreach. The courses offered by the tutors and by professors sympathetic to our aims would deepen their exegetical insights and fortify them against the heretical influence of historic-critical and socio-critical lectures at the university. The "Bengels," as they soon were called, also joined the public debates at radical student meetings and defended an authentic evangelical position, based upon the Bible and the documents of the Reformation. We also had (and still have) guest scholars from other countries, including Korea.

The other venture in stemming the neo-Marxist tide was the founding of the *"Theological Convention"* in March 1969.[149] This was – and continues to be – an association of confessing evangelical theologians, both university professors, scholarly authors and leaders of confessing evangelical movements that wanted to uphold true Christian standards in Church and State. We decided to meet twice a year and keep in close cooperation in order to strengthen our theological testimony and to foster fraternal relations. The second aspect was very essential, too; for confessing theologians find themselves often in a rather isolated situation, in which they need comfort and encouragement. The Theological Convention conducted many internal and public meetings during the 36 years of its history. We raised our voice by issuing manifestos in which the true Christian position was maintained against the neo-Marxist and other ideological encroachments. We also publish literature in which contemporary currents are thoroughly analyzed and readers are helped given to counter them appropriately. Our aims are epitomized in our logo. It is an open Bible with the sword of the Spirit, underlined by our watchword: *"Pro fide defendenda"* (= for the defense of the faith).

2. *"Christo-Marxism – an Ideological Compromise without Promise*

Some Christians still think it is possible to cooperate with Marxists and to select some single elements of Marxism without buying the entire ideology. They want for instance to use the "social analysis" of Marxism as a scientifically established objective instrument whilst leaving aside the dogmatic elements of dialectical materialism and atheism.

---

[149] Walter REISSINGER, 1980: pp. 30-35.

But this is not possible, since the system of Marxism constitutes an indivisible organic unity.[150] All parts of it are rooted in the axiomatic foundation of atheistic materialism.[151] Consequently all different modifications of Marxism, including Maoism and Messianic Marxism, had an anti-Christian edge. This is clearly pointed out especially in the Vatican Instruction about *Liberation Theology,* written by Joseph Cardinal Ratzinger.[152]

It is not only its atheism which makes Marxism unacceptable to Christians. It is the entire system as an ideology of human self-assertion and self-redemption. When Neo-Marxists deny the existence of God, they primarily refuse His Fatherhood and Lordship. That intentionally deprives mankind of His eternal law on which a stable code of ethics and a viable culture can be established.

Finally Marxism and Biblical faith differ sharply were they appear to resemble each other most closely: in its *eschatology.* For in Marxism the classless society or "Kingdom of Liberty" is conceived as a state which is brought into being by the activities of man within secular history; according to the Bible it is a transcendental reality created by the intervention of God Himself through His returning Son Jesus Christ. Christians who have attempted to create a synthesis between the two will always end up in being absorbed by the realities of this present world and losing their spiritual orientation.

3. Testifying to the Reality of the "New Man" in Christ

It is remarkable: all modern ideologies have in common the aim to create a "new man." Even the WCC at its Uppsala assembly in 1968 redefined the goal of world mission to be "Humanization."[153] The basically mistaken idea of neo-Marxists is that new man should create himself by fighting for his dignity and emancipation. He tries to realize his "true humanity" by his own works. Man is seen as a victim of external or self-imposed suppression.

In the final instance man endeavors to fulfil his destiny as a human being by assuming the place of God, as we saw in our quotations from Ernst Bloch.

---

[150] Dale VREE, 1975. – Raymond C. HUNDLEY, 1987.

[151] Konrad LÖW, 2001.

[152] Instruktion der Kongregation für die Glaubenslehre über einige Aspekte der "Theologie der Befreiung," 6. August 1984, Verlautbarungen des Apostolischen Stuhls No. 57.

[153] Peter BEYERHAUS, [2]1972b.

In the NT, the "new man" is an important theme as well: Romans 5:12-19; Eph 4:24, Col 3:10. His true humanity, however, is not self-attained but the free gift from God through Jesus Christ, in the Holy Spirit. It is the restoration of the image of God in which we were created. Jesus Himself is the real new man in contrast to Adam, the fallen "old man." He is what God wanted man to become in his creation: God's own image. Jesus is the authentic image of God. We have to look at him: He showed his authentic humanity as God's image by His perfect obedience to His Father (Hebr. 5:8)

The character of this was manifested in His inner freedom and his loving concern for each person whom he met in her spiritual and physical need.

We are invited to become new men by being born again of water and the Spirit (John 3:5). That means: We have to die to our old nature in order be freed from the captivity of sin. And we are invited to rise with Christ to a new, eternal life as God's children, in likeness and fellowship with His first born Son (Col. 3:3) Jesus, who calls us to be his brethren (Hebr. 2:11).

Conclusion: Marxism: Dead or Alive?

After the downfall of established Communism many people think that Marxism, once having been disproved spectacularly, does not need an elaborate refutation. But this is far from reality. As we did already point in Chapter IV, Marxism is still the dominating ideology in several influential states.

Marxism is alive also in some sections of the Russian population, even in the "intelligentsia." Recently, in April 2003, it was revealed that the state committee responsible for the selection of text books in schools and required reading in the academical study of literature has eliminated some classic authors and famous dissident writers like *Alexander Solshenizyn*;[154] in their place, they reintroduced Marxist authors.

In West Germany some leading churchmen who collaborated with East Germany's socialism edited a book under the title: *"But the Hope Remains."* That implies that they regarded at least the ideals behind the Marxist experiment in the GDR as justified and still valid!

---

[154] Alexander SOLSHENIZYN (*1918) was awarded the Nobel Prize on Literature in 1970 on account of his magnificent trilogy "The Gulag Archipelago."

Influential thoughts can never be suppressed by external force, or simply disappear. They survive underground and wait for their resuscitation at a given moment. The central ideas of Marxism have remained stable throughout all political changes, and ideological alterations and modifications. Ideologies can, as stated in our chapter IV, be compared with viral epidemics. Initially the virus breeds secretly. Suddenly the disease breaks out virulently, until it slows down and recedes, but still waiting for a new emergence.

Marxism shares these characteristics. The reason why it cannot be extinguished completely is that it is not simply the product of human thought. Both in its appearance and origin it is demonic, for the main tenets of it are identical with the plan of Satan when he rebelled against God and when the Snake seduced Eve in the Garden of Eden.

Seen in this perspective, Marxism must be fought against on three levels: firstly the political one, secondly the intellectual one and finally – most important! – the spiritual one. Therefore Christians when facing the challenge of Marxist ideology must keep in mind the injunction of Paul (Ephesians 6:12 f.):

"For we are not contending against flesh and blood, but against principalities, ... against the world rulers of the present darkness .... Therefore take the whole armor of God that you shall be able to withstand in the evil day."

Chapter 6
Syncretistic Tendencies in Feminist Theology

Towards the end of the 1970's the modern, ecumenical movement of *theological feminism* touched the Korean churches. It gained ground when some Korean feminists came to the conclusion that "the situation of women in the Korean churches was still far from satisfactory." This was, allegedly, particularly the case in the Presbyterian Church of Korea – in spite of its decision in 1992 to introduce the ordination of women.[155] It was complained that "attitudes towards women in the church are still strongly controlled by traditional ideas. They are expected to be satisfied with a subordinate role as second class citizens."[156] This was and still is the typical language of the modern feminist movement.

Within the churches in general, however, the aims of feminist theologians went far beyond securing equal rights for women in the ecclesiastical organization. They proceeded to demand that the very faith of the Church should be re-examined from a feminist point of view. This request, which originated in the USA, was soon taken up even in Korea. In fact one extreme type of Feminist Theology has been shaped by a Korean feminst theologian, *Dr. Chung Hyun-Kyung*. She became far.famed after having demonstrated her syncretistic vision in a ritual performed at the WCC's 8th Assembly in Canberra in 1991.[157] In her homeland similar ideas were taken up by the *Association of Korean Feminist Theologians*, founded in 1982.[158]

But what exactly is "Feminist Theology?" Let me characterize its aims by venturing my own definition:

Feminist Theology is the attempt to provide a theological basis, shape and goal for the movement of female emancipation.

Giving such a definition makes it is necessary – before entering into our subject proper – Feminist Theology – to say a few words about "Feminism" as such.

---

[155] Sung Choon OH et. al., 1992: p. 79.
[156] Ibid.
[157] Walter Müller-Römheld (ed.), 1991.
[158] Association of Korean Christian Family (ed.), 1983, p. 39.

I. The Roots of the Women's Liberation Movement

In the middle of the 19th century, progressive women in Great Britain and other European countries started an early feminist movement.[159] Its ideological and historical background was partly Christian humanism, partly enlightened liberalism.[160] Those ladies openly complained about the limited political rights and the inferior social position of women in general. In England they were nicknamed "suffragettes" (from *suffrage* = the right to vote), because they agitated for the democratic right of women to participate in political elections.

By that time women had limited rights in other sectors of public life as well.[161] Since the appropriate place for them was regarded to be in the kitchen and in the nursery, they were excluded from many professions. In particular they were shut out from higher education. For males had fostered an attitude of superiority, claiming that females had a lower IQ.

In agriculture, however, women took a major share, and through the Industrial Revolution they were needed in many jobs. But they received lower wages on account of their alleged physical weakness.

Against such gender discrimination and apparent injustice the first women's liberation movement waged growing protests. On the whole these were justified, and by and by the demands of the early feminists were fulfilled.[162] They did receive the voting right, and female applicants were matriculated at universities. More and more professional careers were opened to them as well, except those which could dehumanize them, in particular military service. But even these restrictions have now been removed in all Western countries – in Communist states even earlier, for better or worse!

---

[159] Lutz E. von PADBERG, 1985, pp. 42-48.

[160] Op.cit. pp. 59-67.

[161] Ingeborg HAUSCHILDT, 1983, p. 11 f.

[162] In Britain, the First World War is thought to have given a major impetus to early feminism. Before it, the suffragettes had been unsuccessful: their fanaticism (one even committed suicide by leaping in front of a race horse owned by the king, as an act of protest) had alienated politicians like Winston Churchill who had some sympathy for them. After the war, women got the vote very quickly because, with most men in the army and navy, women had to take over their work in factories, especially of course in arms factories. This broke the tradition of what women could do, and after the war it was felt that women had earned the vote.

In the former Soviet Union the demand for "equal *rights* to women" was reinterpreted to mean "equal *duties* for women."[163] That led to their de facto reduction to the state of labor slaves.

In the West social and cultural reforms have considerably improved the position of women. Thus by now the fight of the classical women's liberation movement has achieved its original purpose.

Yet the movement did not simply go to rest. On the contrary, after some decades a new women's lib movement emerged, building on the older tradition, but much more radical in its appearance and goals.

II. The Emergence of Ideological Feminism and Feminist Theology during the 1970's

1. The Female Protest against the "Patriarchate"

The beginnings of ideological feminism are hard to trace back. Some of its ideas appeared already during the epoch of Romanticism early in the 19th century amongst emancipated women in the upper class. These received new content and quality in the 20th century through Marxism[164] and the philosophy of existentialism. The new goal was not so much fighting for improved rights, but rather absolute equalization of the sexes. The dependency of women on the male sex was to be shaken off in all social institutions: in marriage and family to start with, in government, and also in the church.

Moreover, modern feminists are fighting for their *complete independence*. They want to develop their own lives as free persons, either as singles or even in marriage, in order to reach their full "self-realization." They declare the age old paternal order to be their arch-enemy, the order in which the family lives under the *"pater familias,"* i.e. the male as the head of the household. Both ethnological, Marxist sociological and Freudian psychological theories are utilized. These are to prove that the social order of the patriarchate was not the primal one. Rather, feminists say, it was introduced at a later stage of history to secure private property and the male craving for domination and sexual monopoly.

---

[163] Tatiana GORITSCHEWA, [16]1984, pp. 107-112.

[164] Herbert MARCUSE, 1974: p. 86.

This socio-economic change opened up the tragedy down the ages of discrimination against, and the suppression and exploitation of, women. The Judeo-Christian tradition in particular is accused of having introduced and sanctified male superiority in family, society and church, and of still upholding it by the exclusion of women from the ordained ministry. This is why modern feminism acquired a stronghold in Western churches, particularly the Roman Catholic Church.

Like any other ideology that seeks to legitimate its claims, Feminism overstates its cause by untenable historical constructions, by sweeping statements and by unfairly generalizing judgments. But here, too, an element of truth is undeniable. It is, indeed, possible to observe an age-old faulty development in the mutual relationship between the sexes, – not particularly in Christianity, but in almost all human cultures. *Confucianism* is a striking example of this.

Behind the feminist rebellion there is an understandable protest against an ancient, deep-rooted discrimination against and even abuse of the weaker sex by men. That is a special aspect of original sin that specifically affects the male sex. In many cultures we can observe a growing deterioration in the diversification of the two genders' specific roles.[165] Often husbands suppressed their wives. It can be studied in non-Christian cultures how women have been humiliated to such a degree that they even have developed an inbuilt inferiority complex: they doubt their own full humanity! Thus, to a certain degree, a feminine reaction against materialized chauvinist male attitudes (*Macho* in Spanish) is defendable.

But such reaction on the female side now becomes the bridgehead for *ideological feminism*. What do I mean by the term "ideological?" Ideologies are secular ways of salvation that rival the biblical plan of human redemption. Man on his own, without God and His Son, undertakes to liberate himself from suffering under unbearable captivity. In the final stage he also wants to be free from all established order, free even from traditional ethical values, which consequently are abrogated. But man wants to realize his/her "true humaneness," and not only in

---

[165] In Korea the historical period when the position of women decisively deteriorated was during the Koryo dynasty and the Chosun dynasty. The Confucian Etiqette of Matrimoney caused women to be brought up to cultivate the ideal of submission and obedience. An ideology developed in which women were attributed less value as human beings. Cf. "Modern Society and Women." Asian Social Welfare Foundation (ed.), 1986: pp. 22 f.

private. The target is widened to envisage the world wide "new humanity" in the coming "world community."

Feminist ideology fights against female dependency from masculine domination and for living one's life fully, especially in the sexual sphere. At the extreme even *lesbian lifestyle* is practiced and propagated publicly as a legitimate female right.[166] The ultimate motive for this is not so much a plea for sympathy with the homosexual disposition of some individuals. It is rather the desire to get rid even of that aspect of female dependency where a woman by her very biological constitution is tied to her male counterpart (cf. Gen 3:16 *"your desire will be for your husband"*). The far-reaching goal is to feminize society and thereby lay the foundation of an alternative world order.

2. The Feminist Intrusion into the Churches

This second, ideological feminist wave has entered into the churches as well. This happened in the middle of the 1970's and made its first ecumenical appearance at the WCC's Fifth Assembly at Nairobi in 1975.[167] What motivated the feminist champions to choose the churches as their favorite area for experiment? There were two reasons for it:

Positively they wanted to bring home that which was taught already about women within the churches. Here they appealed to the example of Jesus[168] who was the pioneer of restoring that dignity to women which God himself had invested in them. He called women to be his followers, and they proved to be even more faithful to Him than his male disciples.

Negatively they wanted to bring to an end that error which, in their opinion, had been practiced in the churches. For these were accused of having acted and still acting as main bulwarks of intolerable paternalism.

Therefore, Feminist Theology has set its mind on conquering the churches to make them instruments for the demonstrating and obtaining complete equalization of the genders. In that way they would, as it is hoped, finally become capable of fulfilling their humanizing role in society.

---

[166] The American feminist author Ti Grace ATKINSON coined the slogan: *"Feminism is the theory – Lesbianism is the practice,"* (quoted by L. E. von. PADBERG, 1985, p. 98. – Carter HEYWARD, 1986, p. 17. – Ingeborg HAUSCHILDT, 1989, pp. 93-95: "Lesbische Liebe." – I was shocked when during the Spring Term 2003 at Ewha University a meeting propagating Lesbianism was publicly advertised!

[167] Hanfried Krüger (ed.), 1976: pp. 61-74.

[168] Elisabeth MOLTMANN-WENDEL, 1980.

III. The Program and Emotional Appeal of Theological Feminism

1. A Threefold Expression of Feminist Theology

Feminist Theology appears in **three forms**, closely related to each other: one – but not the primary - is the academic: teaching and researching. Another one is activism, publicly fighting for female rights. A third one is regarded as the most important and specific one: it expresses itself in playful, highly emotional experiments, making intensive use of *group dynamics*.[169] Elements of it are creative workshops, dances, songs, and colorful festivals. This is demonstrated at larger or smaller ecclesial gatherings. Here it attracts many young women and girls who then spread it in their domestic settings. Feminist theologians maintain that dry rational thinking does not really fit the female nature. The supreme capacity of a woman does not lie – they say – in her intellect but in her feeling, her fancy, dreaming, playing, enjoying pleasures. *Elisabeth Moltmann-Wendel* suggests that women should replace rational theology by practicing *"theo-phantasy"*[170] This involves a new relation to her own body: women are to discover it as an "instrument of lust" per se, not only for the sake of conception. Anything that stimulates sexual enjoyment is regarded as legitimate.[171]

The **basic element** common to all forms of Feminist Theology is its protest against male paternalizing, against the "male church." This movement can be observed in all denominations, even – albeit in a hidden way – evangelical ones. However the strongest and primary feminist protest was waged in the Roman Catholic Church, where the priesthood, indeed, is limited to men. Quite a number of convents in North America were captured by theological feminism, and the Vatican was at a loss how to stem the tide.

2. Two Schools of Thought

It is important to notice that Feminist Theology appears in two **schools of thought** which, however, cannot be distinguished sharply. For they influence each other.

---

[169] Ingeborg HAUSCHILDT, 1983, pp. 21f.

[170] Elisabeth MOLTMANN-WENDEL, 198,: p. 17 f.

[171] Cf. Ingeborg HAUSCHILDT, 198,: pp. 86-94: "Sexuelle Freiheit – Mut zu Ehe und Familie."

1. One school of thought claims to retain a **biblical orientation**. Therefore it seeks to justify its teachings exegetically both from the Old and the New Testaments. One renowned representative is the aforementioned *Elisabeth Moltmann-Wendel*, the wife of Jürgen Moltmann.

2. The other school of thought breaks with the biblical tradition and has a wider, pan-**religious outlook**. *Mary Daly*[172] in America may be regarded as its most radical speaker.

The former thought school still feels some obligation to the biblical tradition, although not in an orthodox, but rather in a critical sense. The same applies, by the way, to all other present *"contextual theologies,"* e.g. *Liberation Theology* and *Minjung Theology*. Here selected biblical texts are taken as a basis or starting point. But the Scriptures are, however, "re-read." They are read with "female eyes," that is seen from the perspective of women's emancipation.

The starting hermeneutical principle is *"ideological suspicion."* At the outset stands, thus, the question: could it be that all previous interpretations of the Bible were influenced by an ideological prejudice, i. e. a paternalistic one? Or – to put the question more radically: could it be that even the biblical authors themselves were guided by the paternalistic principle? Did they possibly falsify the liberating message of the Gospel acordingly, to the disadvantage of women? This is the particular charge directed against St. Paul, who wrote in Ephesians 5:22: *"Wives, be subject to your husbands as to the Lord ..."* Therefore, this Apostle has become the main whipping boy in feminist exegesis. Consequently his writings and all other scripture passages implying female subordination become subject to being eliminated by biblical criticism.

Positively Bible oriented feminists make it their specific aim to discover and re-evaluate the important role which women like the prophetess Hulda, Mary and Phoebe have played in the biblical history of God's people. Occasionally one finds a tendency towards overstatements or even speculative interpretation. Yet apart from that, some emphases in such contributions can enrich our general picture of women who lived and acted in biblical times. Christ's sympathetic dealing with them is especially noteworthy.

---

[172] Mary DALY, 1968a. – Idem, 1968b, German edition ²198,: p. 8.

IV. Feminism's Enmity against the Biblical God and Its Syncretization of the Gospel

1. The Feminist Perversion of the Biblical Concept of Salvation

The distinction between the two schools of feminist theologians with regard to the use of the Bible and their attitudes to radical biblical criticism of is not as clear as the former group claims. For even most of them openly attack central scriptural concepts. I shall give some examples for this:

How do feminist theologians understand *salvation*? Here we can trace an obvious affinity to Marxist thought. Both Marxists[173] and feminists claim that paternal dominance was historically introduced in connection with private property. Originally, they affirm, there had been a free harmonious relationship between both male and female members of the community. But by the introduction of the "possessive" institutions of monogamy and patriarchate, wives became the property of their husbands. That alienated them from their own nature. The historical process of liberation, consequently, must lead to the freedom of women so that they realize their true nature.

But what is the "real nature of women?" Here we meet a rather optimistic self-evaluation. It is maintained that the essence of females is good in itself. It is, feminists maintain, much closer to nature than the essence of males. Women should daily assure themselves by the auto-suggestion: "I am good, I am whole, I am beautiful!"[174] Therefore women, it is suggested, radiate harmony, which is so important for our time when we struggle to maintenance the ecological balance that has been disrupted by technology.

At the same time, feminists believe that women possess a *deeper spirituality*. That makes them receptive for such impulses. Woman as such, they teach, is a receptive organ for spiritual impulses. Her spirituality has an affinity to the working of the Holy Spirit.

Yet feminists also stress the *bodily* nature of women with its longing for sensual pleasure. This is impeded, they deplore, when they are confined to maternity. Therefore such restraints should be cast off.

---

[173] Friedrich ENGELS, ⁵1975, vol. 2,: pp. 152-173.
[174] E. Moltmann-Wendel, 1985, pp. 155-169.

How then do feminists view the biblical concept of salvation as release from sin and guilt before God? Here several of them bluntly declare that women do not need such a type of salvation originating in the redemption by the sacrificial death of Jesus Christ. For their nature is good as such. If a woman needs to be released from guilt, it is the guilt of their husbands who oppress her. Or it might be the wives' own guilt of having endured such oppression far too long. This is how feminists interpret e.g. the *Magnificat*, the triumphant song of Mary: *"He who is mighty has done great things for me ... he has scattered the proud in the imagination of their hearts, he has put down the mighty from their thrones and exalted those of low degree ..."* (Luke 1:49,51-52). Accordingly, a woman must fight for her liberation. She should repent that she had accept a lot which was not meant for her. But men will benefit as well by the emancipation of women: Peaceful conditions will prevail in human society; by the unfolding of women's natural disposition cosmic harmony will be restituted.

The penetrating transformation of the biblical faith also affects *sacramental theology.* Theological feminists unashamedly compare the blood of Jesus Christ shed for us with the blood that women loose monthly. This is seen in the following quotation from a text read at a course conducted in a Protestant Lay Academy in Bad Boll, Southern Germany:[175]

"It is quite consequent that in the Communion shed blood is offered. Now suddenly it is regarded as pure. Why actually do men need blood, streaming from a wound of the crucified One? Why not the blood that women shed constantly? The blood of a woman contains something particular and mysterious that signifies connection with the earth."

3. Total Breach with Biblical Theology

As stated before, there is another line of feminist thought which resolutely and completely leaves the common biblical basis. The reason is this: these authors have concluded that the entire biblical tradition is hopelessly written from a male perspective. The Bible, they say, cannot be freed from its paternalist ensnarement. This does not only apply to social relations, but even to the very **concept of God** itself. Thus you better dissociate yourselves entirely from biblical thinking, radical spokeswomen advise their readers.

---

[175] Susanne KAHL et al., 1981, p. 139 f. – Cf. Mary DALE, 1981, pp. 104 f.

Theological feminists are offended by the patriarchal structures which they find both in the present churches and in the social order presupposed in the Old and the New Testament. But they are in fact correct at one point: they rightly realize that this biblical affirmation of the authority both of the *pater familias* (the father acting as head of the family) and that of political rulers are derived from the authority of God Himself (see Eph. 3:15; Rom 13:1-5). For He has invested them with part of his authority. Accordingly, the Bible speaks of God predominantly in male terms, describing Him as Lord, King, Father, Shepherd. So it was not the ancient and medieval church theologians who conceived a masculine idea of God in order to strengthen the contemporary socio-political order. It is the Bible itself which communicates us this picture, although God stands above the natural sex distinctions. . Therefore it is impossible to remove the male features from the Christian concept of God without destroying the biblical world view as such.

4. The Androgynous Ideal Projected on God

One line of feminists would like to get rid of the entire polarity of sexes which they find in nature and culture. They want to replace the bi-polar constitution of the human race by an "androgynous" concept:[176] Every human being is a composition of both sexes, male and female. Therefore we should equally develop both elements of ourselves. To give metaphysical sanction to such androgynous[177] anthropology, feminist theologians eagerly try to develop an *androgynous concept of God* as him/herself. They could find it only in other ancient religions; nevertheless they try to trace it in the Bible itself. Some think it could be hidden in the plural name for God *"elohim,"*[178] which, of course, is a mere hypothesis. This is widened into the theory that behind the Old Testament's male concepts of God an older source could be hidden that belonged to an original matriarchal tradition of divinity.[179] This, they claim, has been purposely eliminated by the biblical authors and been replaced by patriarchal images of God. No wonder, they say, for those authors were all men!

---

[176] Rosemary RADFORD RUETHER, 1975; German edition, 1979, p. 228 f. – Urda NONNENGASS, 1970. – Herrad SCHENK, ²1981, p. 204 f.

[177] The term *"androgynous"* is composed out of the two Greek words for "male" and "female."

[178] R. T. BARNHOUSE, 1976, p. 284.

[179] Heide GÖTTNER-ABENDROTH, ⁴1984, pp. 201 f.

Now theological feminists reverse that alleged process. With the help of extra-biblical mythologies, they construct a new concept of a female goddess or an androgynous godhead. At the same time, they radically fight against all biblical statements that present God in masculine expressions. *Kurt Lüthi,* an Austrian (male) champion of Feminist Theology writes:[180]

"In connection with the death of the masculine imagery of the Bible even such ideas die which imagine God as Lord, Father, King, Patriarch, Shepherd. New names and images of God should be found. These should support and stimulate an ... erotically mature coexistence of man and woman."

Masculine names of God are replaced by feminine ones. One of them is taken from the Bible itself: *"Sophia"* = divine wisdom. *Hildegunde Woeller* in Hamburg writes:

"Jesus is the son of Sophia. He is her messenger, her representative. Through him salvation streams into the world, that salvation which is provided by Sophia. To know Sophia means nothing less but to confess that she is the mother even of God the creator."[181]

In some cases feminist criticism of God assumes even blasphemous features. *Christa Mulack* writes:[182]

"In my perspective Yahweh, the OT God, is the real seducer, who abducted man to sin, i.e. to miss his target."

Rosemary Radford-Ruether, an American feminist, wants to combine the values of *Yahweh* with those of *Baal.*[183] The former one transcends the world, the latter one renews it. Such unification of gods, Ruether suggests, could serve to bring about our post-technological reconciliation with the earth.

However, as every Bible reader knows, *Baal* was, according to the OT Scriptures, that pagan god of nature against which Israel's prophets directed their fiercest counterattacks. Just think of the confrontation between Elijah and the priests of Baal on Mt. Carmel. He challenged the people of Israel to make a clear option:

---

[180] Kurt LÜTHIE, 1978, p. 202 f.

[181] H. WOELLER, 198,: p. 17 f.

[182] C. MULACK, 1983, p. 156.

[183] Rosemary RADFORD RUETHER, [3]1982, S. 201 f.

"How long will you waver between two opinions? If the LORD (Jahweh) is God, follow him; but if Baal is God, follow him!" (1 Kings 18:21)

For it was just such a mixing of Israel's faith and Canaanite religion which constituted the most serious temptation to the people when they had entered the Promised Land.

Now modern feminist theologians advocate openly reconciliation between those two incompatible divinities. For they are not at all afraid of syncretism and getting entangled in non-Christian mythologies. On the contrary, they seek to appropriate to themselves mythological tales of gods and goddesses. They find especially useful those divinities which deal with creation, destruction, renewal and redemption. For these contain, they suggest, humanizing and healing elements which can help to solve our ecological problems. Following that tendency, such authors turn diametrically against the prophetical mainline of the Old Testament. For this is rooted in the First Commandment:

"I am the Lord, your God. You shall not have other gods besides me!"

To accomplish their program, feminist theologians have to reverse the multi-millennial process of biblical revelation. Since the Bible itself does not provide them with material helpful enough for their purposes, they have to look out for alternative sources. One of them, even the primary one, is for them the female essence as such. Women, when doing theology, are to use their own nature and experience, and make it the hermeneutical key for exegesis. This is bluntly exhibited by *Peggy Anway*:[184]

"Those of you who are interested in methodology may have observed that I am using my human way of experiencing as a valid source of theology. I claim that the female way of experiencing be regarded as a legitimate source of theology."

Catharina Halkes, the Dutch pioneer of Feminist Theology, promotes the establishment of women's churches. She says that rebelling women are the theme and subject of Feminist Theology. They lift up their relationship with God and the divine as central object of their theology.[185]

---

[184] P. ANWAY, ³1982, p. 176.
[185] C. J. M. HALKES, ³1982, p. 32.

What is the **result of this venture?** It is a **complete transformation (or even perversion!) of the Christian faith.**

The doctrine of God is radically changed, – both by the critical elimination of basic biblical concepts and by their substitution with alien religious elements. This logically leads to a fundamental alteration of all other doctrinal articles as well.

That starts with the *doctrine of creation.* The biblical assertion that God by His word created the world out of nothing is rejected as "naïve."[186] It is taken to express a patriarchal ideology of creation. The male concept of "creation" is substituted by the female concept of nature, in which woman shares herself. Creation means to give birth and to be born by a woman, a mother, a goddess. This applies to ancient times as much as to ours. "Creation is nature, who is female and maternal; she is the life of the goddess," says *Uwe Gerber.*[187]

A radical re-modeling is applied to the doctrines of Christ, *Christology*, and the Holy Spirit, *Pneumatology*. When the ancient Church in its worship glorified Christ, feminists say, it actually strengthened political power structures. Governing authorities were sacralised and thereby guaranteed forever. That sovereign Christ, therefore, should be replaced by a mild one, sympathetic with women. *Chung Hyun-Kyung,* a graduate of Ewha-University, proposed in Canberra 1991 that the Buddhist bodhisattva *Kwan In*, an enlightened divine being, should serve as an Asian picture of a female Christ:[188]

"It would be a woman, the first begotten amongst us, who leads the way for us and takes along others."

The *Holy Spirit* is treated likewise. Feminist theologians claim to discover "*her*" as a goddess already on the first page of the Bible. She is the female *ruach* who soars over the primal waters and initiates the creation. "The first day of the world begins with *Sophia.* What we are longing for is the sacred marriage between Christ and Sophia," writes *Erika Godel.*[189]

---

[186] "A naive belief in the first creation is no more possible for us," states Dorothee SÖLLE, 1985.

[187] U. GERBER, 1987, p. 61.

[188] Hyun Kyung CHUNG, 199,: pp. 47-55, esp. pp. 54f.

[189] E. GODEL, 1989.

We have already pointed out what feminist theologians are doing with the biblical concepts of *sin, salvation* and with the sacrament of *Holy Communion.*

Let me mention, finally, two additional fatal examples:

Firstly Christian **ethics** are transformed or rather radically perverted. Formerly, feminists deplore, ethics were upheld by the concept of a sovereign God who rules our moral life by severe commandments and prohibitions. But the feminist godhead is far more sympathetic with human nature. Thus *Elga Sorge* in Germany changes the Ten Commandments into *"ten permissions."*[190] Whilst the Bible says in the Seventh Commandment: "You shall not commit adultery!," Sorge claims that the intention is to say: "You are allowed to commit adultery, but you need not do it."

Secondly a logical consequence of the changed understanding of God is the feminist concept of *"spirituality."* This is a neutral term which practically replaces the personal concept of the Holy Spirit and his work in us. We heard about the removal of the personal polarity between man and woman in favor of an androgynous anthropology. In analogy with this, three other basic distinctions in the biblical world view are removed as well. These are, to start with, those between *Creator and creation* and then the one which exists between *nature and man* as the crown of creation. In a third step, the distinction between *God and man* is blurred likewise. Feminists feel that human beings, particularly women, directly participate in the divine nature. They sense that they are filled with divine life. Thus they share in the divine capacity to create, or rather to give birth. This line of thought leads theological feminists to sympathize with such non-Christian religions which basically believe in the **identity between God, nature and human beings.** They sympathize with the cult of "Mother Earth" of the American Indians' *nature religion,* but also with *Hinduism*. This indicates a similarity between Feminist Theology and the **"New Age"-movement**.[191] All of them represent a world view which is basically *monistic*. That means that a basic biblical duality is absent: the duality between the eternal, uncreated God and man as a created being, affected by sin.

This leads us to the most fatal consequence of Feminist Theology: at first it seduces women to discover their spiritual nature; on account of

---

190 E. SORGE, ³1987, p. 97 f.
191 Lutz von PADBERG, 1987. – Uli OLVEDI, 1985, p. 988.

this, secondly, they should consider themselves as divine. Women are told to achieve their self-realization by approaching goddesses; in this way they would eventually become goddesses themselves. In feminist prayers goddesses are invoked as symbols of spiritual realities. They serve as symbols for women's strength, for their intimate relationship with "Mother Earth" and for spiritual communion amongst women.

To start with, women should accept their roles as *witches,*[192] benevolent witches who radiate healing forces to remedy our torn society and disturbed ecology. In doing so, women should refuse to recognize the ruling norms for good and bad, for healthy and insane.

Thus we see that *radical theological feminism consequently leads to a modern paganism with an anti-Christian tendency.* It dares to confront the biblical faith by the cult of feminist self-deification. Swiss author *Ursa Krattiger*[193] writes:

"The old God has died to me. The Church of doctrine and stoned has tumbled. The borders between confessions and religions, between true faith and false disbelief, have been wiped out to me. Having left the paternal world of faith through feminist theology, I discover myself immediately as god. Religiously I am supplied out of my own self."

V. The Christian Answer to Theological Feminism

It should be evident by now that Feminist Theology in its radical, syncretistic shape is one of the greatest counter-revolutions in the history of the Christian faith. For it does not only falsify important aspects of it; it is a rebellion against God himself and leads to a complete distortion of His biblical self-manifestation. It endangers God's plan of human redemption; for our destination is not to submerge into a diffuse maternal spirituality. It is to share the divine life by being received into a personal fellowship with God the Father, the Son and the Holy Spirit.

Feminist Theology, by now, is no longer limited to be one distinct modern school of thought. Is is pervading Christian theology in general by persuading it to make accomodations to its tenets. This also applies to the churches' liturgical language, especially with regard to the invo-

---

[192] L. v. PADBERG, op. cit. pp. 66-77. – Mary DALY, 1968b, p. 84.
[193] U. KRATTIGER, 1987, p. 16.

cation of God, where "male" connotations like "Lord" or "King" are avoided. The holiness of God becomes weakened by being feminised.

Our earthly life in general is greatly disturbed likewise, for by female self-assertion the relationship between husbands and wives, as much as that between mothers and children, is undermined. It is a fact that many feminists act out of frustration about their own unhappy relationship with their parents or/and their husbands.

The cultural crisis which is both articulated nd deepened by ideological feminism can only be overcome by a return to a truly Christian view of man. This includes a thorough reflection about the biblical concept of the relationship between the two sexes. What does Scripture teach us about the correlation between man and woman? What is true subordination, as it is expected from wives with regard to their husbands, and how does a woman find fulfilment in life without pushing her "self-realization," but rather by realizing God's plan with her?

Here we have to differentiate between the three subsequent orders of creation, preservation, and redemption.

1. The Order of Creation

In Gen 1:27 we read that God decided to create man in His own image. Immediately it is added that He created them male and female. This indicates that it belongs to our human nature as images of God that we are not uniform, androgynous beings but exist in the polarity of two distinct genders. These stand in close correspondence with each other.

At the same time, the verse indicates in a somewhat mysterious way that even in God himself such a correspondence between distinct persons exists: it is the personal fellowship between God the Father, the Son and to the Holy Spirit. Human beings are to live not as individuals but in a fellowship of such personalities who are distinct from each other. But at the same time, they enrich each other by their mutual communication in their difference as men and women. This presupposes equality in worth and rank. But it does not necessarily imply equality in position and uniformity in function. For even in the triune communion of God Himself there is a structure of primacy and subordination between the Father and the Son within the bond of the Holy Spirit (1 Cor 11:3b; 15:28). This divine subordination is absolutely voluntary. It secures the harmonious working together in the work of creation and salvation. Likewise husband and wife are equal in dignity, but wives are called to be an aid to their husbands (Gen 2:20) to let them fulfill their specific responsibility. This subordination is not suppressive. For it is steered by perfect mutual love and respect.

2. The Order of Preservation

The original harmony between the two sexes was severely disturbed by the Fall, in which both Adam and Eve participated. It disrupted man's primal intimate relationship with God. But the relationship between husbands and wives was disturbed likewise. Adam puts the blame for his sin on Eve: *"The woman whom you gave to me to be with me: she gave me fruit of the (forbidden) tree, and I ate"* (Gen 3:12). In this moment, mutual confidence between the spouses breaks up. Now the fatal fight between the genders starts. In order to prevent complete chaos, God replaces Adam into the position of headship over Eve. But this new form of subordination receives an authoritarian character. God punishes the woman by telling her: *"... Your desire shall be for your husband, and he shall rule over you"* (Gen 3:16 b). Marriage and motherhood become a hard yoke for the woman; but only by her accepting it in spite of pain, human social life can be sustained during the order of preservation. This does not entitle husbands to torment their wives or suppress them tyrannically. For they should realize that only a moderate way of ruling can prevent female rebellion and the disruption of the family.

3. The Order of Redemption

By the reconciling work of Jesus Christ and by the gift of the Holy Spirit the relationship between husbands and wives is restored from its previous tension into a new fellowship of mutual love. The marriage of regenerate Christians can fulfill God's original purpose for it: i.e. to present itself as a joyful communion between two persons who use their distinct constitution and gifts for mutual assistance. Thereby they can foster a new generation of God's children. Moreover they can jointly exercise their dominion over creation as representatives of God. *In Christ men and women are completely equal both in worth and in their relationship to God (Gal 3:28).*

But even Christian matrimony is characterized by a principle of voluntary subordination. Christian wives should not emancipate themselves so that they can enjoy their liberty in a selfish way. They should be subject to their husbands as to the Lord and fear them (Eph 5:22). This means they ought to respect their husbands' distinct role of headship in regulating the life of the family.

But Christian husbands have to exercise their role in a responsible, caring way. Their specific duty is even harder to fulfill than their wives' is. For they are told to love them "as Christ has loved His Church by giving himself to her" (Eph 5:25). That means that the husbands' love for their wives should not be merely erotic, but sacrificial. Wherever these specific assignments to men and to women are fulfilled, there is no more reason for moaning, suspicion or rebellion. God's wonderful purpose for harmonious relations between the sexes is approaching its fulfillment.

This is the authentic answer to Feminist theology.

> "When two become one in order to serve their Lord together, a new bridgehead is established for the heavenly host in this present world that is still hostile to Him."
> *Georg Spoerri, Swiss theologian*

Chapter 7

Affirming Christ's Uniqueness in the Face of Religious Pluralism and Syncretism

Introduction

In 1991 at the WCC's Canberra Assembly the Korean feminist theologian Dr. *Chung-Hyun Kyung* delivered the keynote lecture on the Holy Spirit. She used it to present to the ecumenical delegates a modern kind of Shamanist ritual.[194] She said that today the Holy Spirit speaks to us through the voices of the "*han*" spirits who cannot find peace because of their tragic fate. This was an event of historic significance. For the fact was that she had been invited officially by the General Secretariat. Moreover her theatrical performance was hailed by a standing ovation of the ecumenical dignitaries from all confessional traditions – except the Eastern Orthodox.[195] This signalised that by now a syncretistic contextualization of theology was fully accepted in large sections of established Christianity. It also signalised a resolute breach with the entire tradition of biblical faith since the days of the Prophets and the Apostles.

Some months later Chung-Hyun Kyung was also invited to address the large rally of German Protestantism, the "Kirchentag" (Church Day), in Munich. Feminist theologian *Mrs. Elisabeth Moltmann-Wendel* commented on both events by saying: "Chung-Hyun Kyung has emerged as a bearer of hope for all women on earth!"

These events are no eccentric episodes. They are characteristic of the spiritual climate both in theology and the church in which we have to live today. They also show the extreme importance of theologians and church leaders who have a sense of responsibility towards the Bible, taking up the themes of *"syncretism"* and religious pluralism. They should regard it as the most crucial challenge to biblically orthodox Christianity today. It is not accidental that many theological meetings

---

[194] Hyun-Kyung CHUNG 1991, pp. 48-50. – Critical reports: John MILLHEIM 1991. – Odd Sverre HOVE 1991, pp. 68-70.

[195] "Überlegungen orthodoxer Teilnehmer, gerichtet an die Siebte Vollversammlung," in: Bericht aus Canberra (see Note 1), pp. 280-282.

and publications[196] treat the uniqueness of Christ in view of other religions as their central theme. This was also the case at the meeting of the Japanese-Korean section of the *Asia Theological Association* held in Seoul on November 7th, 2003. On a personal note, I may add that syncretism and religious pluralism have had a lion's share in my own theological thinking during the last decades. This was reflected by the title of a "Festschrift" dedicated to me on my 70th birthday: "**No other Name**. The Dialogue with non-Christian Religions."[197] Under the same title in the same year our Theological Convention of Confessing Fellowships in Germany issued a weighty statement[198] which was welcomed by many as a decisive help.

I. Biblical Affirmation of Christ's Uniqueness

Before we enter into the treatment of *religious syncretism and pluralism* it is essential to be reassured about the theological contrast to it. We should remember how the Christian Church from New Testament times until the present age of theological modernism has been eager to maintain the absolutely sovereign position of Jesus Christ as the supreme Lord and only Saviour of the world over against all other claims of divine lordship.

Let us start with the famous confession of Simon Peter in response to Jesus' question concerning His true identity. When Peter replied: *"You are the Christ, the Son of the living God,"* he acknowledged Him as the messianic Saviour of Israel as well as the One in whom God Himself is present.[199] At once Jesus reacted by stating that on this rock he would build His Church. Thereby He made it clear that the Christian Church finds her very identity in upholding the faith in Christ's divinity and destiny of being the universal mediator of salvation. After Christ's ascension, Peter affirmed this in his fearless assertion before the Sanhedrin (Acts 4:12): *"Salvation is found in no-one else, for there is no other name under heaven given to men by which we must be saved."*

---

[196] Bruce J.NICHOLLS (ed.) 1995. – Ajith FERNANDEZ 1995.

[197] Thomas SCHIRRMACHER (ed.) 1999

[198] No Other Name! (Acts 4:12). Theological Declaration Concerning the Assessment of the Religions in the Light of the Gospel, (separate print); the German original is published in: DIAKRISIS 1/2000.

[199] Gerhard MAIER 1987, S. 171-191. – Carsten Peter THIEDE 2000, pp. 49-64. – Oskar CULLMANN ³1970.

Here, Peter did not simply state his private conviction. He spoke by the commission of his heavenly Lord Himself and on behalf of the entire apostolic Church. This becomes evident in many similar affirmations made by other Apostles, especially John and Paul. John in his Gospel records the famous self-assertion of Jesus (John 14:6): *"I am the way, the truth and the life. No one comes to the Father except by me."* Paul affirms (in 1 Cor 1:22f.): *"Jews demand miraculous signs and Greeks ask for wisdom, but we preach Christ crucified, a stumbling block to Jews and folly to Gentiles, but to those who are called ... the power of God and the wisdom of God."*

This divinely inspired elevation of Christ was upheld and dogmatically expanded in the writings of the ancient Church Fathers and the ecumenical Creeds. Let me quote from the Nicene Creed which in hymnological language adores Jesus Christ: *"God of God, light of light, true God of true God, begotten not created, of one substance with the Father ..."*

In accordance with the biblical witness the universal Church of all confessional traditions affirms the magnificence of Jesus Christ by using a number of terms: Sovereignty, superiority, centrality, absoluteness, universality, exclusiveness etc. Today it has become common to speak about the *"uniqueness"* of Jesus Christ. By this it is meant not just that Jesus is rather different and singular compared with other great religious figures. The term "uniqueness" is meant to affirm that Jesus Christ holds a position so extraordinarily high and significant that He cannot be **reached** by any other being in the history of religions. No other religion can make a similar claim with regard to its founder or saviour figure, whether it be Krishna, Buddha, Confucius or Mohammed.

With regard to Jesus Christ we can speak of a *threefold uniqueness* that pertains firstly to his **person**, secondly to his **work** and thirdly to his **relationship** to his believers.

A. Uniqueness of Christ's P e r s o n

Jesus Christ is not just a human being. He is that man in whom the eternal Son of God, the third person of the divine Trinity, has become incarnate so that he is equally God and man. He was pre-existent, i.e. from all eternity he lived in a close relationship with God the Father. He became the Mediator both in the acts of creation and salvation. He became man not by a biological act of begetting but by the Holy Spirit overshadowing his virgin mother. Even during Jesus' earthly days the fulness of God dwelt in him (Col 2:9). After his resurrection all authority in heaven and on earth was given to the God-man Jesus Christ. As the King of kings He became seated on the heavenly throne at the right hand of the Father. At the end of history Christ will be the universal Judge of all people who ever lived on earth. Then he will rule over God's fully established kingdom for ever.

B. Uniqueness of Christ's w o r k

Even before the creation of the world the pre-existent Christ was destined to be the *one Mediator of salvation* (1 Tim 2:5). This he became in a unique way: He was to be sacrificed as the Lamb of God who takes away the sin of the world (John 1:29). No other religion has a similar belief in a redemption freely given to man. Redemption is not wrought by man acting himself under the assistance of a religious saviour; no, it comes by the Saviour giving his own life for it. Neither does any other religion know of a bodily resurrection of a saviour who thereby is able to impart eternal life upon all who believe in him. The redemption wrought by Jesus is a comprehensive one: It liberates lost human beings from the bondage of sin and demonic captivity and from the power of death. It does so, on the basis of reconciling abject men with the Holy God. As a loving Father He now receives them into His fellowship as beloved children. Moreover this redemption will eventually also restore the entire distorted cosmos (Acts 3:21).

C. Uniqueness of Christ's R e l a t i o n to Believers

Jesus Christ is a unique Saviour by being not just a person of the past and the future. He is not a moral teacher to be followed nor an abstract ideal to be imitated. Neither is he a completely transcendent godhead, unreachably removed from his followers on earth. No, he promised to his disciples that he would always be with them in their life and ministry. He would be so by sending to them the Holy Spirit, His own Spirit, who dwells in them and creates a tie of intimate relationship with him (John 14:16f). Jesus became united with his believers both individually and corporately. He is so by being identified with them in the community of the Church which is his body, he being the head, we the members. In Holy Communion, he feeds us spiritually with His Body and Blood, thus becoming mysteriously joined with us. He continues his saving work on earth through the ministry of his Church, investing his messengers with his own authority. He comforts us in our anxieties and assures us of our eternal communion with him in the Kingdom of the Father.

No other religion gives such centrality to its founder as the Church does to Jesus Christ, so that apart from him it would be dissolved. Hinduism could exist without Krishna, who after all is only a myth; Buddhism could practise the way to illumination without Gautama Buddha. Islam could maintain its central affirmation of Allah being the only God apart from Mohammed who claimed only to confirm the message of the historic prophets before him. Moreover, no other religion ascribes such a comprehensive work of salvation to its founder than that which we Christians owe to Jesus. No religion experiences such a realistic communion with its pioneer as Christianity does with Jesus Christ. Even if certain similarities might appear, no religion can verify its claims concerning its founder by a historically experienced and proven reality such as the incarnation of God in Christ and his bodily resurrection. His resurrection was a unique event in history. Its evidence is given not only by the credibility of its apostolic witnesses. We find this verification in the entire history of Christ's Church in which He has manifested himself alive and powerful.

Yet this uniqueness of Christ appears not so evident to the world that it would easily approve of it once the claim has been presented. On the contrary, it has always been doubted and disputed. Peter compares Christ to the *corner-stone* of a building which is precious to those who believe. But it becomes a *stumbling-stone* to those who disobey the Word (1 Pet 2:7f.). Thus right from the beginning, the central significance of Christ has been contested and so it is today. But in contrast to apostolic times, His uniqueness is contested not only by outsiders. This happens even within the church and this at so many places that those who still adhere to it, will find themselves in a minority position.

II. The Threefold Contest of Christ's Uniqueness

A. Blunt Denial

The most ostentatious way of refusing to bow before Christ's authority is plainly to deny it. This was the response which Jesus received from most of the Jewish religious leaders in his time. Jesus radically challenged their own theological convictions on which they based their authority. That made them hostile to him. Consequently they sentenced him to death.

A similar hostile resistance to the universal claim of Christ in modern times is shown by totalitarian ideologies. They do so by persecuting his stauch confessors. Jesus had predicted this outcome already during his earthly days (Mt 16:2; John 15:20f.).

B. Pluralistic Relativization

Another more polite way of relativizing the uniqueness of Christ is to concede a *relative dignity* to him but at the same time to maintain that there are other impressive figures beside him in the history of religions. In this case *Jesus becomes one religious genius amongst many others*, perhaps one of the greatest. Thus the way to salvation taught by him may be viable to those who follow him, especially when they come from a Christian tradition. But others are entitled to make their alternative option and find peace and happiness with their objects of adoration. We ought to respect them, it is said, and seek mutual understanding and cooperation with them.

Today this is virtually the position of those Christian scholars who are advocating a "Pluralist Theology of Religions,"[200] *John Hick*[201] being their outstanding representative.

Today there are three models of theologies of religions.[202] These are the exclusive, the inclusive and the pluralist. It appears that the third one is gaining the ascendency since it seems to meet both reason and the demands of our time for peaceful coexistence.

C. Syncretistic Undermining

The third way of evading the uniqueness of Christ is post-Christian or *pseudo-Christian syncretism*. What is meant by the term *"syncretism?"*[203] In general understanding it means a *mixing*[204] *of different religions*, which is unavoidable wherever different religious cultures come to overlap. The underlying attitude is the assumption that all religions and spiritual experiences derive from the same invisible sources. Names and forms may be different but they denote the same.

---

[200] John HICK (ed.) 1987. – P. SCHMIDT-LEUKEL 1993, pp. 354-360.

[201] John HICK (ed.) 1977.

[202] Peter BEYERHAUS 1996c, pp. 134-140.

[203] S. HARTMAN 1969. – A. Scott MOREAU in EDWM 2000, pp. 924 f.

[204] The word may derive from Greek *"synkerannymi"* = to mix. Others deduce it from the island *Crete*, thinking of the habit of Cretans to forget their tribal fights and to unite temporarily for repelling an external common enemy.

Thus they can be transferred freely from one religion to the other. That happened in the Roman Empire between the gods and goddesses of the Greek and Roman pantheons: Zeus became Jupiter, Poseidon became Neptune and Hera became Juno.[205] Likewise in Latin American syncretistic cults like Umbanda,[206] Jesus is identified with the most powerful figure in the Indian and African spirit world. This is the spontaneous or naïve form of practised *syncretism*.

In distinction to the form just described, there is another sophisticated type which is consciously planned. It is the attempt to merge different, heterogeneous religions and ideologies with a concrete purpose. This is being done with the aim of making them the spiritual basis for a wider unity, often of a socio-political character. In this way the Macedonian king and conqueror *Alexander the Great* (356-323 B.C.) tried to create a synthesis of the various national religions in his conquered territories to knit a spiritual and moral bond for his multi-cultural empire. We may call this *planned syncretism*.

Planned syncretism can also appear as a *strategy of* one religion *infiltrating* another one in order to conquer it from inside. It does so by assimilating select elements of that rival religion to itself. This happened in New Testament times when the religious philosophy of Gnosis infiltrated the early Church. It claimed allegiance to Christ but changed his true nature into that of a mythical revealer of gnostic wisdom.[207] Thus the threat was to change the Gospel into a pseudo-Christian heresy. Here the uniqueness of Christ is betrayed by misusing his name for another concept. Present day syncretism is largely following a *neo-gnostic* pattern.

III. The Biblical Struggle with Pluralism and Syncretism

A. The Fight of the OT Prophets

The pluralistic struggle between the self-revelation of Yahweh as the supreme, only true God and pagan polytheism begins with the exodus of Israel out of Egypt. God wanted Israel to become His witness to

---

[205] Nathan SÖDERBLOM (ed.) 1931, pp. 300-302. – Hans CANCIC et. al. (ed.) 2001: p. 210.

[206] L. WEINGÄRTNER 1969.

[207] F. BORSCH 1970. – R. M. GRANT ²1969. – Hans JONAS ²1963.

the nations, proclaiming that He is the Creator of heaven and earth as well as the sovereign Lord who rules the destiny of all peoples. This is enshrined in the First Commandment of the Decalogue *"I am Yahweh, your God ...,"* and in Israel's central confession (Deuteronomy 6:4): *"Hear O Israel: The Lord our God, the Lord is one: Love the Lord your God with all your heart and with all your soul and with all your strength."* The entire history of the ancient people of God as told in the historical and prophetical writings of the OT has one main theme. It is the record of how God again and again tried to impress this truth in their hearts both by reminding them and punishing them. Israel failed fatally to fulfil this important commission.

God wanted to manifest Himself as a God who is motivated by "holy jealousy."[208] His entire plan of creation and salvation was based upon His eternal decree that mankind could attain its true life only by being restored to absolute loyalty to the one God as its maker, protector and redeemer. But Israel – with a few occasional exceptions – did not really heed her commission. Instead she fell into a two-fold temptation. During the first centuries after entering into the promised land, the people sought additional support from pagan deities of the Canaanites such as the god of fertility *Baal* and the sexual goddess *Asherah.* Sometimes this was plain polytheism and sometimes it showed the features of syncretism.[209] Yahweh assumed the features of Baal. Although His name was retained, Yahweh was worshipped in a crude naturalistic way, whilst His holy, ethical character fell into oblivion. During the later period the country was invaded by the powerful nations of Assyria and Babylon – occasionally Egypt as well. Now even Israel's kings and priests bowed to the pressure to install the worship of their imperial gods in the Temple at Jerusalem. Considering the apparent weakness of Yahweh to protect His people, many Israelites voluntarily indulged in the cult of oriental divinities. The people did not heed the constant warnings of Yahweh's faithful prophets. Accordingly, the prophets interpreted the final national disaster of both the Northern kingdom Samaria and the Southern kingdom Judah, as their deserved divine punishment (e.g. Jer 29:16-19; 2 Chron 36:11-21).

It was only by the Babylonian captivity that the Jews eventually grasped their historic lesson. *Judaism* then became mankind's *first really monotheistic religion.*

---

[208] G. von RAD [5]1969: Vol. II, pp. 216-225: "The First Commandment and Jahweh's holy jealousy."

[209] Otto PROKSCH 1950, pp. 212-216.

B. The Apostolic Warrant for Monotheism and Christological Uniqueness

In NT times the biblical struggle against religious pluralism and syncretism no longer addressed itself to the Jewish people. The former error became the primary target of the missionary *message to the gentiles*. This happened in view of the widely prevalent polytheism. The first charge directed to pagan listeners, therefore, is to "turn to God from the idols and to serve him as the living and true God." (1 Thess 1:9). Those heathen objects of cult are identified as dark expressions of the power of Satan (Acts 26:18; 1 Cor 10:20). For that reason, Paul warned the Corinthians sharply about bringing Jesus Christ into association with idol-worship, lest they provoke the Lord to jealousy (1 Cor 10:21 f; 2 Cor 6:14-18). We see that the Apostles consistently follow the anti-syncretistic prophetical line of the OT.

Other recipients of such NT warnings against syncretism include some *young churches*. They were those who were tempted by the gnostic heresy to distort the faith in Jesus Christ as the incarnation of God Himself. We have already mentioned it in this chapter. But it should be added that Paul, too, was alerted to syncretistic tactics. He warned against the misuse of the very name of Jesus Christ by introducing a completely different concept of saviour and salvation. In 2 Cor 11:2-4 he "jealously" warns the congregation of its inclination to be trapped in syncretism. He sees in it an actual repetition of Eve's primal seduction by the snake. At this place he mentions three main doctrinal points in which pseudo-Christian syncretism is characterised: *another Jesus* – a *different Spirit* – a *different Gospel* (cf. Gal 1:6-9). This shows that the NT Apostles anticipated the entire history of the Church's permanent syncretistic temptation. It is a mortal threat that affects all central points of the Christian faith: Christology, Pneumatology and Soteriology (the doctrines of Christ, the Holy Spirit and Salvation). This temptation has hardly ever been so extensive and intensive as it is today!

IV. Contemporary Appearances of Pluralism and Syncretism

A. Pluralistic Theology of Religions

We have already mentioned that some influential theologians in the West are pleading for a new Christian concept. This should place all religions of mankind on an equal footing with Christianity. We also heard the name of its pioneer, the British systematic theologian *John Hick*. He and his friends assume that beyond the variety of particular religions there is an ultimate common ground in the depth of the human soul. Here the devotees of all belief- systems could meet in analogous mystic experiences. Their dogmatic articulations may differ but in nature they are one. The presuppositions of such pluralistic thinking exclude any attempt to voice normative claims for the person of Jesus Christ. He may be regarded as one amongst many religious figures who had some kind of transcendental vision. As with all of them, Jesus, too, could still render a spiritual contribution to improve the harmony of the human race. Since all religions are regarded as equally valid, it makes no difference which religion we choose. In 1986 Hick invited a group of like-minded friends to a consultation at Claremont in California. The papers read there were published under the title: *"The Myth of Christian Uniqueness: Towards a Pluralistic Theology of Religions."*[210] The participants left under the impression that a Copernican Revolution had just taken place. They had, to use their own expression, "crossed the Rubicon." By this symbol they referred to the borderline that up until that time, had separated biblical Christianity as the evident subject of Christian theology from religions in general.

B. Pluralistic Prayer for Peace

On October 26th 1987, *Pope John Paul II* convened a large meeting of the heads not only of all major Christian confessions but also of all other religions.[211] They assembled in the ancient town of *Assisi*, where, historically, St. Francis had founded his order of preaching monks. Through that meeting John Paul wanted to promote peace amongst all divided nations. His method was to let the representatives of all religions pray for peace at one and the same time and place. Conservative Christians of different confessions, traditionalist Catholics as well,[212] were shocked by that bold move, for they warned the Pope that this would lead to syncretism. I myself also sent a warning letter to him[213] through the mediation of my former Tuebingen colleague Cardinal Ratzinger, now Pope Benedict XVI. To this charge the Pope replied with the assertion, that no syncretism was intended. The representatives of the different religions would not pray together, but they would come

---

[210] Orbis Books, Maryknoll, NY, 1987.
[211] Johannes DÖRMANN 1988. – Idem 1990-1998.
[212] Manfred JACOBS 1989. – Louis-Marie de BLIGNIÈRES 2003, pp. 3-29.
[213] The Christian Herald, Nov. 11th 1986: p. 1.

together in order to pray. By that rather hair-splitting distinction he meant that they would not join in a common liturgy of prayer, read together by all of them.

Yet this explanation could not remove our misgivings. For after all the Pope was chairing a religious ceremony in which one religious leader after the other stepped forward to offer his prayer to the deity worshipped in his own religion: Brahma, Allah, Jahweh, Manitu, the Bodhisattvas. Did not this imply, we asked, that at the final instance all these prayers were effective? Do all of those different gods have the power to answer them; or were these gods considered to be proper representatives of the one supreme God? Still, Pope John Paul II was determined to continue the spiritual venture of the first inter-religious prayer-meeting at Assisi 1987. He allowed only one adjustment to be made. During the following meetings the spiritual leaders of the different religions did not pray on the same stage; they now did it separately in the specific venues allocated to them.

Nevertheless, "Assisi I" meant a historic break-through towards religious pluralism or even syncretism. Christians world-wide henceforth became inclined to think that all religions are ways to the one true God. Now it has become quite common that inter-religious meetings are held where ministers of different religions are united in prayer and listen to readings from their sacred books.

C. WCC's Programme on Dialogue

In May 1970 the General-Secretariat of the World Council of Churches endorsed the plan to stage a "pilot project" starting in the Lebanese town *Ajaltoun*.[214] This eventually led to the installation of a new Department in Geneva which became responsible for the *Programme on Dialogue with Adherents of Living Faiths [i.e. non-Christian religions] and Ideologies*. At Ajaltoun, for the first time, representatives from various Christian traditions met on an equal basis with those of non-Christian religions. They entered into a so-called dialogue in order to discuss common concerns. They also learned which specific contributions particular religions could make to solve human problems.

The revolutionary new feature at Ajaltoun was that the participants partook in the morning devotions performed in accordance with the

---

[214] H.-J. Margull and St. J. Samartha (ed.) 1972, pp. 17-31; pp. 74-89.

different faith-systems represented there. Christian theologians did not hesitate to join in ceremonies of other religions held in their temples. Rather they felt deeply enriched. To that experience a new name was given: *"sharing in spirituality."* From then on such trans-religious venturing became an integral feature of the ecumenical Programme on Dialogue and at other ecumenical events as well. We remember the erection of an Indian totem pole by WCC'S leaders at the VI. Assembly at Vancouver in 1983[215] and the inclusion of the Shamanist ritual performed by Chung-Hyun Kyung in Canberra 1991. Those were consistent steps forward on the syncretistic avenue opened up in Ajaltoun in 1970. In Canberra a report was received from an inter-religious consultation in Hong Kong, convened on behalf of the WCC Department on Dialogue.[216] The participants of the Hong Kong consultation called on the Canberra Assembly to promote a "pooling of spiritual resources" of all human religions. Only on this basis political leaders could, they argued, receive the inner strength to cope with the global problems facing them in social, ecological and other realms.

D. "New Age" Religiosity

One striking phenomenon of our time is the fact that in Western countries a new quest for transcendental experiences has emerged.[217] For centuries they had been dominated by a rationalistic world view. In one aspect the era of modernism is being undermined by a new era of *post-modernism*. Particularly in the younger generation many people are tired of a civilization which puts its highest value upon consuming material goods. Youngsters show a new interest in that which may mysteriously be hidden beyond our three-dimensional world. Simpler minds may try to make ecstatic encounters, "peak experiences" by enjoying hard rock music, engaging in sexual orgies or taking drugs. Others use parapsychological channels and participate in spiritistic séances. More serious minds choose spiritual ways offered by Eastern religions in their various methods of Yoga techniques or transcendental meditation, preferably Zen. Indian gurus,[218] Buddhist *bikhus* and Islamic *sufis*

---

[215] W. Müller-Römheld (ed.) 1983, pp. 23. 25. 35.

[216] Konrad Raiser & Matthias Sens (eds.) 1991, pp. 125-128.

[217] Harvey COX 1977. – Dave HUNT / T.A. McMAHON 1985. – Reinhard HEMPELMANN et.al. (eds.) 2001.

[218] Rabindranath R. MAHARAJ 1977. – Ronald ENROTH & others (eds.) 1983. – Reinhart HUMMEL 1980.

direct their mission to Western countries and gather their own benches of followers.

Various names are given to this movement. Some call it the *"new religiosity,"* others the *"quest for spirituality."* Yet another term is *"esoteric religion."* People of such inclination flock together, conduct workshops or organise larger events and expositions where the various offers are demonstrated and can easily be acquired. Some of this emerges rather spontaneously. There are also leaders who are busily knitting a world-wide network between groups and individuals. They also supply a common religious ideology for it.

During the 1980s this movement became famous under the ominous name *"New Age."*[219] Its spokes-persons developed an ingenious strategy calling it the "soft revolution." The sources can be traced to "theosophy" and "anthroposophy." These originated during the first decades of the 20th century; they tried to mediate main tenets of Hinduism and Buddhism to Western culture. The New Age movement shares with Hinduism a monistic world view. According to that all reality is basically spiritual, emanating and returning into an all-embracing oneness. If mankind started to realise its spiritual nature, all contradictions and tensions would be removed. Then, finally, a cosmic harmony will guarantee abiding peace.

The proponents of this movement claim that mankind and all beings are entering the **new age of *Aquarius***. This, by an astrological law, will succeed the previous **old age of Pisces**, – a hint at the fish as the symbol of Christianity. Thus a modern system of syncretism is promoted which is basically anti-Christian. But New-Age prophets do not frankly admit that. On the contrary: they try to appease Christians by maintaining that they are presenting true Christianity at a deeper level. It is that spiritual insight which was concealed under the surface of the church's external forms and transmitted by esoteric circles. Consequently some outstanding New Age pioneers like *Alice B. Bailey*[220] (1880-1949) offer a gnostic re-interpretation of the Christian faith. That renders a new type of Christianity which is fully compatible with the New Age philosophy.

---

[219] Alice BAILEY 1944.

[220] Idem 1945. All 24 books of Alice B. Bailey were republished by Lucis Trust 1997-2002. [The original name of Lucis Trust was "Lucifer's Trust," which indicates the demonic background of Theosophy and New Age thinking.] – Marilyn FERGUSON 1982. – J. MELTON 1990.

V. The Increasing Quest for a One-World Religion

A. The Popular Level

The Danish missiologist *Johannes Aagaard*[221] has proposed the thesis that a new world religion is in the process of emerging. It has its roots in the classic religions but it has no preference for any of them. Rather, its agents select some elements out of them which appear to fit their purposes: Mediums, gurus, prophets, immortality, reincarnation, aura, spiritual masters, Yoga, karma, new birth, bio-rhythm, tarot cards and astrology. The new spirituality does not come about by a return to one of the classic religions nor by a Christian revival. It happens by mixing elements of heterogeneous world-views, religions and even esotericism, magic and occultism. Some experts call this "city religion:" You go out shopping and buy whatever pleases you from the various stores. I think that Aagaard is partly right but he does not realise that the process which he observes is moving on *two different levels*. He takes notice of the private level, where individuals pick up what appears useful to them, sometimes also jointly in religious interest groups. All this is moving towards a great, seemingly chaotic mixture. Apart from it there is a movement on a higher level, even more threatening.

B. The "Syncretistic Project"

In his book, "Where is the Swedish Church Going?" (1995)[222] the Uppsala scholar *Folke Olofsson* introduced a new term into our theological vocabulary which he calls "The Syncretistic Project." This concept confirms what *W. A. Visser 't Hooft*, the first general-secretary of the WCC had discussed in his famous book "No Other Name." There, the Dutch churchman had pointed out the necessity of *distinguishing* between a *spontaneous* and a systematically *planned* kind of *syncretism*. I have referred already to this. Olofsson writes about ideologies in general: "Out of his own mind, man projects his thoughts, dreams, hopes, his ideology into time and space." Likewise in the "syncretistic project" individual persons, ideological groups, but even political, cultural and religious organizations attempt to shape the future state of mankind according to their own visionary models. Therefore, they include religions as building-stones for that utopian architecture.

---

[221] Johannes AAGAARD 1993.

[222] F. OLOFSSON 1995, pp. 112-129.

Olofsson regards the syncretistic project as the most recent in history which is just about to emerge. Indeed, earlier investigations have uncovered the fact that a similar plan has existed for two centuries already. It was forged at the end of the 18th century, contemporary with the French Revolution (1789-92). Its ideological supporters are to be found in Masonic Lodges, particularly in the *Order of Illuminates* that was founded on May 1st 1776 by the Bavarian professor *Adam Weishaupt* (1748-1830).[223] The aim from the beginning was to create a new universal order for mankind. Its spiritual basis was to be a common unified religion. It should be ruled by a World Government, controlled by leading members of that secret movement, the "Illuminates."

In recent decades a vast literature about the "conspiracy theory" has appeared, either to support or to deny it. Personally I do not belong to those who suspect the activities of Masons wherever a similar idea is proposed. Therefore I am careful not to propagate that theory but I know that appealing visions, ideas and utopian concepts can gain a strong influence in penetrating culture and motivating political programmes. Marxism and Fascism are typical examples of it. Once a visionary concept has been presented with a certain degree of plausibility, it is going to find supporters who will attempt to translate it into concrete policies. When the historic situation is favourable, it will find far-reaching support. A universal movement can emerge that either puts theory into practice or will end in historic disaster.

In such perspective, the "Syncretistic Project" appears to be extremely relevant in meeting mankind's main contemporary problems for it contains the promise to solve the present cultural crisis of meaning. It may even help us to overcome the growing problems of social misery, wars, terrorism and ecological disaster. Therefore it is not astonishing to find that especially philosophers, theologians, churches, Christian movements and even ecumenical organizations promote syncretistic projects. These might either be of their own conception or offered to them by other influential bodies. Those international figures who promote such prospects are hailed as bearers of hope, sent by God Himself.

This is one unavoidable consequence of the loss of biblical authority in Christianity. Authentic Biblical prophecies concerning the forthcoming Messianic Kingdom are transformed into a semi-religious, basically

---

[223] A. WEISHAUPT 1787 – John R. HINNELS (ed.) 1984, p. 161. – John ROBINSON ³1798.

secular utopia. I will mention only a few notorious examples: 1. The jubilant reception of the Dalai Lama at German "Kirchentage" (ecclesial mass rallies); 2. the "Project World Ethos" proposed by my Tuebingen colleague Hans Küng as a basis for a forthcoming order for world peace; 3: The programmes on dialogue both of the WCC and the Vatican; 4. the prayer for world peace in the wake of Assisi 1987; 5. the Conciliar Process for Justice, Peace and Sustenance of Creation, during which a major congress was staged in Seoul March 6-12, 1990;[224] 6. the Shamanist ritual performed in Canberra 1991 by Dr. Chung-Hyun Kyung; since then she has been busily engaged in promoting the acceptance of syncretism focussed on survival and liberation;[225] 7. The World Conference of Religions for Peace which has regularly been staging meetings in several parts of the earth. Finally I want to mention (8) the **"United Religions Initiative"** (URI).[226] It was solemnly promulgated on June 25, 2000 at a meeting in Pittsburgh in the presence of religious and political leaders from 40 countries. Amongst its founders are *Mikhail Gorbatchow*, UN general-secretary *Kofi Annan*, and Archbishop *Desmond Tutu*.

The aim of the new movement was characterised by its vice-president William Ranklin: "URI has been founded to bring together people from all religions and to create a world in which nobody needs to die by God or for God. It shall be open for all spiritual expressions. The emblem of the movement is a wreath of 15 religious symbols arranged around the letters URI. One of them is the occult Pentagram, another the empty circle, which shall be filled by all faiths which are going to join us." *Hans Küng*, who supported the initiative, explained to me in a letter (29th September 2003) the name *"United Religions Initiative:"* It indicates that it is meant to be a parallel to the *United Nations* with which it wants to cooperate closely. The Vatican had also been invited in 1996 by the American Anglican bishop *William Swing* to join URI.[227] On behalf of Pope John Paul II, Cardinal Francis Arinze declined, because it promoted "religious syncretism." This impression is confirmed by Bishop Swing, the main initiator of URI, himself. He

---

[224] Bericht aus Canberra 1991, pp. 135-137.

[225] Hyun-Kyung CHUNG: "The Contribution and the Future of Asian Women's' theology in: Hanna STENSTRÖM (ed.) 1992, p. 201.

[226] William E. SWING 1998.

[227] Lee PENN 1998 and 1999.

demanded that evangelism and mission should be outlawed world-wide, since it was a work of "fundamentalists."[228]

The examples listed here, I agree, are different in character, acceptability and seriousness. Neither do I suggest that they are all part of a single system, organisationally connected with each other and centrally controlled. Yet there is much overlapping concerning the persons involved and the sequence of events in the development of each of them. Moreover there is a great similarity between the promoted ideas. I shall try to point this out this by stating a number of observations made by myself and others.

VI. Evaluation

A. Six Essential Observations

My *first* observation is the astonishing *convergence of aims* between the endeavours of all these proposals and organizations, in spite of their confusing variety. Everywhere the target is to get a grasp on the future of mankind by imposing a multi-religious project to coordinate the corresponding efforts.

My *second* observation is that the assumed religious *"pluralism"* is *not really pluralistic but only allegedly so.* For pluralism means an uncoordinated variety and contrast of ideas and practices – each one being tolerated. But in reality the tendency is always to harmonise the various expressions of particular religions. This is done by tracing a common origin, an inner *affinity* and predisposition for the same ultimate goal in them. The *common root* is found in the mystic subconsciousness of the human race. In view of the assumed affinity, adherents of different religious traditions are encouraged to exchange their spiritual experiences. In view of the assumed *common aspiration* they are challenged to synthesize their ultimate concerns and to attach them to a universal humanitarian goal.

My *third* observation is that in all cases the *Christian faith is included* in the inter-religious project. Moreover, Christianity even plays a central role.Therefore, the religious or philosophical objects are basically secularised biblical prophecies, changed into a this-worldly utopia.

---

[228] Schwarzer Brief – Informationen aus Kirche und Politik, 34 (no.31/2000), reprinted in DIAKRISIS 24 (No.3/2003), pp. 151-154.

My *fourth* observation is that leading *representatives of church and theology,* of ecumenism and mission, *do not perceive the perversion* of the Christian faith which is imminent in the "syncretistic project." Much worse: Theological avant-gardists and church councils are taking the lead in this enterprise! To biblically orthodox Christians it appears as if a fatal blindfolding has overcome the minds of the responsible persons.

My *fifth* observation is that the challenge to get engaged in inter-religious dialogue and cooperation is issued in a mood of *growing urgency.* This is achieved by pointing out the importance of securing the threatened survival of mankind. If world peace and the sustenance of nature are at stake, these treasures of mankind must be protected by all means. Therefore it is necessary to set aside the particular doctrines and to pull down the dogmatic fences between cultures, religions and ideologies. I vividly remember the favourite song repeated over and over again and danced to during the WCC's Fifth Assembly at Nairobi in 1975: "Pull down the walls that separate us and unite us in a single body!"[229]

My *sixth* observation comes as a combination of the former five. It is the most important for our theme: As we have seen, the syncretistic project is promoted with great urgency. Its chief ideologists insist that all churches and religious communities should participate. Consequently the demand for solidarity is presented with *radical force.* Conscientious objectors to such a request cannot hope for a sympathetic understanding; rather they are met with growing impatience. Thus the *principle of tolerance* is turning into one of *intolerance.* It addresses itself particularly to those who uphold the uniqueness of Jesus Christ. It criticises those who are not prepared to relativize the Gospel as one way of salvation amongst others.

Such intolerance may appear in different degrees and various forms. It starts with deriding Bible-minded Christians as "old-fashioned." It moves on to exclude them from the established Christian community and to prevent them from receiving responsible tasks and positions of authority in the ecclesial hierarchy and in theological faculties. The next step is to denounce conservative believers as fanatical fundamentalists like Islamist Ayatollahs. Their theological convictions are claimed to be politically motivated. They are scolded as "racists." Consequently they will be declared to be enemies of human progress, a

---

[229] David M. Paton (ed.) 1976, p. 31.

menace to peace and human survival. From here only one final step is left, i.e. violent persecution. This no doubt will break out when religious intolerance is combined with political tyranny.

I do not want to create the impression that these predictions reveal an alarmist mentality that does not shun grotesque exaggeration. I am quite aware that it is illegitimate to generalise apparent tendencies and occurrences into an established fact or a universal plan shortly to be fully realised. Conditions vary regionally, and processes can be retarded or come to a temporary standstill. Some schemes may dissolve themselves for lack of substance, internal unity and support.

Moreover, there are still *counterforces* at work. One of them is secularist rationalism and materialism that is alien to religious proposals. Neither is it possible to offer a time-table for the syncretistic project, not even by those who are involved in it. One of the main counterforces to religious pluralism is *fundamentalist movements* that occur in all main religions, even in Hinduism and Buddhism. The fiercest enemy to a peaceful co-existence and melting of religions is *Islam*, whose main agents still believe in and work for the universal submission to its *"Sharia,"* the theocratic rule of the Koran's Law.

Yet my six observations as presented right now are still valid as such. There is such a syncretistic movement of convergence, no matter at what speed it moves. Moreover – and this is my main argument – *it corresponds with biblical prophecy.*

B. The Syncretistic Project in the Light of Biblical Prophecy

In his eschatological speech on the Mount of Olives (Matthew 24), Jesus makes one point perfectly clear. In this present age, world history does not move towards a state of universal peace and social harmony in obedience to the rule of God. Rather the approaching end is characterised by dismal signs of the times: Wars and rumours of war, nations rising against other nations, natural disasters such as famines and earthquakes in various places. This is accompanied or even caused by spiritual disintegration. Seduced by false prophets and christs, many professing Christians will fall away from the true faith and betray one another. Moral decadence will cause their love to grow cold. Disobedient mankind, including apostate Christianity, will move towards its ruin. By all this mankind will grow mature for the Day of Judgment, executed by the returning Christ.

But as both Paul and John – the latter in his book of Revelation – point out: The return of Christ will be preceded by a penultimate stage of salvation history: There will emerge a powerful conglomeration of human self-assertion and craving for power. This will show both political and religious features at the same time. The personification of that trend will occur in the emergence of the two apocalyptical beasts, symbols of the expected Antichrist and his False Prophet as taught in Rev 13-19. The reign of the coming Antichrist will be characterised by a unity, a *one-world system*, which is both fascinating and frightening. It will be a unification of all political, socio-economical and cultural endeavours, including religion as the integrating element. This will become acceptable to mankind on account of two polar aspects: Threatening global disaster on the one side and the fulfilment of mankind's perennial dreams about a golden age of happiness, justice and peace on the other.

The basic condition that must be achieved to fulfil this prophecy is that mankind is prepared to accept a unity which supersedes all former cultural and religious divisions. In John's prophecy, the ten kings of the last time will be of *one mind* (Greek: *mia gnomee*; NIV: "they will have *one purpose*"). Therefore, they will be ready to submit their political authority to the Antichrist (Rev 17:13). Some evangelical Bible teachers suggest that this will happen in the EU (European Union); but there are other theories as well, e.g. that the whole earth will be divided up in 10 supra-national regions and be controlled by a central global authority.

One additional part of that apocalyptic scenario is played by the Woman who rides on the beast, the *Babylonian Harlot* (Rev 17-19:10). The interpretation of that figure has always been controversial. Personally, I am persuaded by the arguments of those who regard her as a symbolic representation of apostate Christianity. For some, that would be composed of one large historical confession, traditionally seen in Roman Catholicism.[230] Yet that would be too one-sided. Rather we are to think of a conglomeration of the apostate sections of all existing churches. They will be enriched by mystical and ritual elements of other religions. Thus that ecclesial conglomeration would be widened to an anti-Christian World Church or even a One-World Religion. She will be *"drunk with the blood of the saints, the blood of those who bear the testimony of Jesus"* (Rev 17:6). That indicates that she – the "Har-

---

[230] Michael de SEMLYEN [2]1993.

lot" Church – in close alliance with the antichristian world government, will become the direct persecutor of the faithful Church, the eschatological Bride of Christ.

Before the Bridegroom will return to lift her up out of her earthly distress there will be many martyrs in her. They will be killed because they have ventured their lives on account of their undaunted confession of the uniqueness of Christ. But in reality their external defeat will be their victory in the eschatological struggle against Satan and his dark angels (Rev 12:11). *"For they have conquered him by the blood of the Lamb and by the testimony of their mouth."*

Conclusion

When we apply that vision to our present situation it admonishes us not to fall into resignation in spite of the continuous spread of the spirit of religious pluralism. We have to discern the signs of the times, even in the "Syncretistic Project" and resist it. It does not matter if eventually it might be successful and accepted by the majority of mankind in general and of Christianity in particular. Rather we should become firm in our biblical insight and not give in one inch. Yet mere resistance by shutting ourselves off is not enough. Faithful confessors are also motivated at the same time by the *love of Jesus*. He loved even a world that hated Him. Filled by His Holy Spirit we want to testify to our fellow men about that new life which we have received from Him. In contrast to the presentation of treacherous utopias, we are to win as many wavering souls as possible to the One who is the real and only hope for the world: Jesus Christ, the universal Lord and Saviour!

Chapter 8

The Christian Encounter with Islam

Introduction
The Timeliness of Our Theme

1. The Shock of September 11, 2001

The terrible event of Al Qaida's suicidal attack on the World Trade Centre on September 11th 2001 made many people, for the first time, sensitive to the challenge of Islam. They realized that Islam is the world's second largest religion, virtually spinning its network over the entire surface of our six continents. Islam with its 1.4 billion members constitutes 20 % of the earth's population. As such it is the only world-wide rival of Christianity. Westerners also began to perceive that this attack could only be understood in connection with the Muslims' vision of a world entirely controlled by the law of Allah, the *sharia*, in the religious, political and economic realms. Now they discovered that this is not only a faint wish of theirs. No, it is a concrete historical goal for which its zealous followers are ready to fight and even sacrifice their lives. That raised the question:

2. Islam – a Religion of Peace or of Terror?

The main question arising from the 9/11 event was: Should terrorist assaults like the destruction of the twin towers be regarded as isolated acts of some extremist groups? Or are they backed by the world-wide Moslem community as such? True enough: Most Islamic governments dissociated themselves from the attack. On the other hand, people like *Osama Bin Laden* defended it bluntly. They were supported on the popular level in various countries: Palestinian people in the Gaza strip danced hilariously upon receiving the news! In German villages even Turkish school children did not conceal their triumphant smile. No wonder when many Western people started to suspect every Moslem of being a potential terrorist.

But how should attacks of fundamentalist movements really be assessed within the framework of the Islamic religion? This question was and still is answered differently by experts in Oriental culture, and also by Christian theologians who followed their own distinct thought- patterns concerning the Islamic religion.

3. Divided Views

1. Many people felt confirmed in their general misgivings about Islam as a violent religion. They were supported by those experts who deduced the fundamentalist strategy from Mohammed's own concept of *"jihad"*[231] = fighting Allah's war. This view was presented by – to name one outstanding expert – the German orientalist *Hans-Peter Raddatz* in his book: "From Allah to Terror" (2002).[232]

2. Others insisted on the need to distinguish between authentic Islam as a religion of peace on the one hand and radical Islamism, "fundamentalism," on the other hand. This was the official position of the Bush administration. The American president favoured it as a basis for his plan to forge a world-wide political alliance for combating terrorism where the support of moderate Muslim governments was essential. A similar view was advanced by the Pope. He sharply condemned any hatred and terrorism covered by the cloak of religion. At the same time he stated, thus putting forth the traditional Roman Catholic attitude:[233] "The Catholic Church highly respects Islam, referring to authentic Islam, that Islam that prays and is solitary with the poor." This, in fact, became the view which generally prevails and which is propagated by most newspapers which supported the self-recommendation of Islam as a "religion of peace."

3. Another view was taken by those theologians who interpreted the event as a challenge to perceive the encounter between Islam and Christianity as the most important spiritual struggle of the new century.

---

[231] Sura 2:186f.212 ff; 3:103 ff. 4:76 ff.; 47:4 ff. – H.-P. RADDATZ, (see following note): pp. 46-67. – Louis GARDET 1968, p. 112. 115. 157. 234. – Eberhard TROEGER 199,: pp. 59-64.

[232] Hans-Peter RADDATZ 2002.

[233] The II. Vaticanum's "Declaration on the Relationship of the Church to Non-Christian Religions" states: "Upon the Moslems, too, the Church looks with esteem. They adore one God, living and enduring, merciful and all-powerful, Maker of heaven and earth and Speaker to men ..." (The Documents of Vatican II, ed. by. Walter M. Abbot / Geoffrey Chapman 1966: p. 663. In a footnote, reference is made to a graceful letter by pope Gregory VII (1020-1085) to *Anzir*, king of Mauritania. Pope John Paul II was much concerned to foster friendly relations with the Muslim world, which became particularly evident in his pastoral journeys to countries with a substantial Islamic population, cf. JOHANNES PAUL II 1994: pp. 119-122.

4. A final grouping, while agreeing with the view just mentioned, went
    on to point to the need for placing increased weight on *Muslim
    evangelism*. Americans deplored the fact that merely 2 % of their
    missionaries were engaged in it!

In fact, what we are witnessing today could be the beginning of a
new era of Christian mission to the Muslim world.[234] That presupposes,
of course, a proper knowledge of Islam: its history, doctrines, goals,
and present condition.

I. The Basic Tenets of Islam

1. The Emergence of Islam in History

Islam is a religion that suddenly emerged in Arabia during the first
third of the 7th century. After the death of its founder (632 AD), Islam
spread, under his successors, by military conquest in all geographical
directions. A century after Mohammed's death the Muslim empire had
reached its widest extension. Having lost its monolithic political organization it continued to spread by conquest, by demographic fluctua-
tions and by religious propaganda – both organized and spontaneous.

Original Islam as a religion contained elements of Christianity, Judaism, and Arabian animism. It arose in a period of crisis when Arabs
felt challenged from outside cultures and when the Byzantine Church
had lost its grip over Oriental peoples. Through the agency of Mohammed Islam developed around the *Ka'aba*, an ancient sanctuary in the
Arabian city of Mecca.[235] It had a long religious lineage which was
traced down to Abraham and his sons, especially the eldest, Ishmael.
The cult had become highly polytheistic and merchandized; but there
was also the concept of a supreme divinity by the name of *Allah*. Remains of an old Christian church of Syrian orthodox style were
archaeologically discovered under the foundations of the Ka'aba. That
would support the Arabian legend that the Ka'aba was the first sanctuary on the Arabian peninsula, built by none less than Abraham and
helped by Ishmael. Now the new religion of Islam, too, was going to
become centred around the Ka'aba cult, having undergone a new interpretation. Mohammed conceived as his first religious mission the task

---

[234] Dieter KUHL 2002, pp. 202-211.
[235] Sura 2:138 f., 144f. 214; 5:2f.9:18f. 22:25-27; 48:25-27. – G.R. HAWTING: "The
Origins of the Muslim Sanctuary at Mecca," in: G.H. Joynbull (ed.) 1982, pp. 23-47. –
Günter LÜLING 1977.

of purging the Ka'ba from all idolatrous defilement. Today the Ka'aba is the spiritual centre of the world-wide *umma* (community) and the highly desired goal of the Moslem *hajj* (pilgrimage).

2. The Vocation Experience of Mohammed

Islam owes its birth to one person and his sense of vocation.[236] Young Mohammed (*570 AD) had a highly sensitive soul, shaped by tragic experiences in his childhood as an early orphan. He had a deeply religious mind, the sensitivity even of a medium. As a merchant, he had travelled to Syria and had come into contact with monastic spirituality. There he was deeply impressed by the missionary preaching about the one God and His imminent judgment. This made him worried about the crude paganism practised around the Ka'aba, and he went into the wilderness to meditate. There, in 607 AD, he had that visionary or rather auditory experience which revolutionized his life.[237] According to Sura 96:15, he felt called to become the prophetic messenger of the highest divinity – Allah – to the Arabian tribes.[238]

The source of that inspiration is debated. Some interpret it mainly psychologically; others (including Hans Küng)[239] evaluate it as a genuine prophetic calling; others again believe that the appearance was of a spiritistic kind.[240] Mohammed himself was not sure at the beginning but his wife *Khadidja* persuaded him to accept it as being genuine.

Personally, I tend to adopt a synthesis of the 1st and the 3rd interpretations, which means a mixture of psychological and occult elements. At the same time it should be taken into account that Mohammed's messages contain some elements of Biblical truth. These include the basic concept of one almighty, omniscient God who is our creator, ruler and future judge. But even Mohammed's doctrine of God; – let alone his Christology and Soteriology! – is heretically distorted. Occasionally it assumes demonic features. Today the cruel actions of the fundamentalist *Hisb'ollah*, the Shiite "army of Allah," are executed on his presumed commission. That makes Islam such an ambivalent phenome-

---

[236] Tor ANDRAE 1932/1977. – Ibn ISHAQ 1976.

[237] Rudi PARET ⁵1980, pp. 47-57.

[238] Emanuel KELLERHALS 19, pp. 23 f.

[239] Hans KÜNG, Josef van ESS et. al. 1984, pp. 55-60.

[240] Sura 25:8; 52:29.

non; I call it a ***tripolar religion***.[241] It contains contradictory elements: merely human, but also divine and – alas – even satanic ones. Nearly all of them present obstacles to a Christian approach, yet some of the former ones can serve as stepping stones.[242] A wise missionary policy would be one which re-claims the Biblical elements in the Koran for Christ and in this way leads Muslim readers to Him!

3. One God – Apocalyptic Judgment

The first *suras* especially, which Mohammed recited at Mecca, were shaped by two elements: the strictly monotheistic doctrine of God and the eschatological ardour. They present an extremely transcendent monotheism[243] and severe warnings about an imminent judgement.[244] Both doctrinal issues called for a radical transformation of the Arabian nature-religion.

4. Mohammed the Final "Rasul" in the Prophetic Tradition

Mohammed did not claim to be the founder of a new religion. On the contrary, he wanted to renew the ancient true religion. He placed himself into the succession of four major Biblical prophets (***rasul***), starting from Noah and going over Abraham and Moses to Jesus.[245] He thought that he had the same mission which Moses had to the Jews and Jesus to the Christians. The task committed to him was then, as he thought, to call people to repentance and to reinstall the monotheistic religion. The extraordinary feature was that he regarded himself as the final and, as such, greatest prophet, the **seal** upon the entire history of Allah's prophetic revelations!

5. Articles of Faith

Mohammed did not dictate a dogmatic textbook. The main tenets of his belief were gathered and systematized later by Islamic theologians. They were summarised in five (or six) elements which appear as basically Biblical: *One God* – The *Angels* (including dark angels and Satan,

---

[241] "By this I mean that in our theological analysis of human religions we have to distinguish clearly among *three* constitutive elements or sources of origin: the human, the divine and the demonic." Peter BEYERHAUS 1996c: p. 142.

[242] Phil PARSHALL 1983.

[243] Sura 112. – Louis GARDET 1968, pp. 48-58.

[244] Ibid. pp. 82-92. Sura **11**:105 ff.; **50**:19 ff., 40 ff.

[245] GARDET, op. cit, pp. 62-66

iblis) – The *Prophets* – The *Scriptures*: Thora – Gospel – Koran. Amongst these revealed books the former ones were, thus goes their theory, handed over in distorted shape by Jews and Christians ... Therefore they had to be corrected by the final one. The fifth article of faith became that of an ultimate *Judgment*. Later on *predestination* was added as a sixth article of faith. This shaped the fatalistic mentality of Muslim people.

6. Five Pillars of Duty

Islam is a **legalistic religion** strongly based upon the demands of Allah. Keeping them consistently qualifies for admission to Paradise. The Aramaic names of the duties indicate their Jewish origin: *Shahada* (invocation of the one God), prayer(*salat*), fasting (*zakat*) almsgiving (*almuna*), pilgrimage (*hajj*) to Ka'aba and sometimes *jihad* (holy war) is added as the sixth Islamic duty.

7. Theocratic Concept

a. Islam = surrender, submission

Contrary to its modern interpretation, the name *"Islam"* does not mean peace (*salaam; sholom*). Semantically it is derived from *aslama* = to be completely surrendered to the one and holy God in heaven. The single Moslem is a person who is fully subject to the absolute will of God. His relationship to him is that of a servant to his master. From this concept two behavioural expressions emanate: fatalism and fanaticism. The latter one makes Islam so aggressive, for God's holy will, his decree, must be, in Islamic understanding, executed by all means and at any expense, both one's own and that of others.

b. Establishment of Sharia

Allah's will is codified in the theocratic legal system of *sharia*. This rules all aspects of personal and corporate life: religious, social, political, economic. Accordingly, those who hold office are not considered to be priests but rather lawyers.

Sharia regulates the life of the Islamic community, the *umma*. Virtually all people on earth should become subject to *sharia*, because this is believed to be the basic condition for a peaceful living together. Allah wants all mankind created by him to be governed by *sharia*. Therefore its imposition on all nations is the ultimate vision and target of the dedicated Muslim.

The whole earth is divided up into two realms: the house of Islam (*dar al Islam*) and the realm of war (*dar al harb*), i.e. countries which still must be subdued.

Wherever necessary, the way to establish a pacified state is *jihad*, the holy war. People who do not surrender voluntarily must be compelled to do so. The methods of jihad will depend on the resistance encountered. In accordance with this, all means that help to enforce surrender are justified, without moral inhibition. Today apologists of the Islamic religion try to give a milder interpretation to jihad. They translate it as "intense endeavour," but they cannot offer any warrant for it either from the Koran or from the Muslim tradition.

8. Legalistic Religion of Self-salvation

Unlike the major Eastern belief-systems (e.g. Hinduism and Buddhism), Islam is not a religion of salvation. It does not share Christianity's doctrine of human sinfulness. Man, assisted by Allah, can find the way to eternal bliss by keeping the basic demands of the law. The ultimate Judgment will be executed according to the balance of good and evil works in a person's life.

9. Muslims are Motivated by Hope for Paradisiacal Enjoyment

The eschatological nature of Mohammed's message is characterised by the glowing colours in which both eternal bliss and eternal punishment are painted. Therefore the legalistic nature of Islam is softened by the ardent hope and anticipation of future pleasures in paradise. These are imagined predominantly in sensual terms, particularly sexual enjoyment. This concept of a paradise is the main incentive for combatant Muslims to sacrifice their lives in the battle. It is one explanation for the fanaticism of suicidal terrorists.

II. How Does Islam Look at Christianity?

1. Mohammed's Calling a Response to the Challenge of Christianity

The experience of Mohammed in the desert at *Mt. Hira* cannot be understood as a completely autochthon event in the history of religions. It did not originate entirely from his meeting with the assumed angel

Gabriel (*gibriel*). Mohammed's conscious and subconscious mind had already been conditioned by his previous encounters with the Biblical faith. Much, perhaps even most of it, he had found in the tradition around the Ka'aba. That contained very ancient material. Other information he received from his encounters with Christians and Jews who lived in Arabia or whom he met in neighbouring countries.

Scholars still struggle with the question about what type of Christianity – e.g. Syrian orthodox or heretical – was offered to him here.[246] There is also the tradition that he had intimate conversations with a hermit living in the desert near Mecca. Mohammed's soul was, it appears, moved deeply by these Biblical thoughts, and he pondered their significance for the reformation of the pagan Arabian folk-religion and his own role as a potential reformer of the Ka'aba. Thus his passionate rejection of central Biblical doctrines cannot be excused by complete ignorance.

When Mohammed perceived the voice of the mysterious appearance, he associated himself with Biblical recipients of revelation. The question is, however, whether he was prepared to meet the authentic Gospel and accept it. Or did he rather see a specific role for himself? Did he aspire to be Allah's messianic prophet to the Arabs and finally to mankind? At this point he may have become subjected to a pseudo-Christian seduction. There is much to support this hypothesis. At least, it is clear that Mohammed's ambiguous attitude to Biblical Christianity was fatally determined during the period of his vocational experiences.

2. Biblical Material in the Koran

a. Common Themes and Persons[247]

At first glance, the Koran looks almost like a popular textbook of Biblical stories; no wonder that early Eastern Orthodox theologians treated Islam as a new Christian heresy.[248] Seventy per cent of the contents of the *suras* deal with Biblical themes like creation, fall, flood or events in the life of Jesus. Mohammed's particular interest is dedicated to the great men of God who acted as His commissioners. He regards all of them to be prophets, including Adam, Abraham, Moses and David.

---

[246] Rudi PARET [5]1980, p. 42.

[247] Siegfried RAEDER, 1997, pp. 309-331. – R.P. JOMIER 1962. – Wilhelm RUDOLPH 1922.

[248] Gottfried SIMON 1920, pp. 7-9.

b. Sectarian distortion

The parallels between Biblical and koranic traditions are, however, rather vague. This might be due to the fact that Mohammed could not distinguish between authentic and apocryphal accounts. In some cases the distortion might, however, have been deliberate. Mohammed wanted his own alleged revelations to be authenticated by the older sacred books of Jews and Christians. Soon he claimed that his version was the authentic one. Thus he accused Jews and Christians of falsifying their holy scriptures. This is still a basic theory of Islamic theologians. It is used in an attempt to refute the Christian appeal to Biblical authority. Missionaries must, therefore, familiarise themselves with it in order to be able to keep their stance in Muslim-Christian disputes.

c. Pointing to Mohammed himself

Mohammed's decisive interest when reading and interpreting both the OT and NT was to discover that they pointed either openly or mysteriously to him as the forthcoming final prophet of Allah.[249] Muslim scholars employ still rather scurrilous hermeneutical methods to follow this tradition. For them it is crucial; for only in this way can they uphold the claim of Islam to be the final and most perfect religion for all mankind. Thus, the decisive point in the present Christian-Muslim dialogue is the finality of Jesus Christ vs. the finality of the prophet Mohammed.

3. Transformation of Christology[250]

Neither Mohammed nor his followers had an aversion to the person of Jesus. On the contrary, the Koran speaks of him with high respect. It recognises both his virgin birth[251] and his miracles[252] and even his exemplary ethical life. These are not even reached by the description of Mohammed's own personality. Moreover the Koran uses without reflection some of the highest terms of dignity presented in the Christology both of the NT and the Church's creeds: Messiah, son of the virgin Mary, word of God, spirit of God.[253]

---

[249] Sura 7:157. – Hermann STIEGLECKER 1983, pp. 546-561.

[250] Samuel M. ZWEMER 1912. – Heikki RÄISÄNEN 1971.

[251] Sura 19:16-21; 21:91.

[252] Sura 3:49.

[253] Sura 3, 45; 4:169.

But all this is more than outweighed by the changes to which ortho-dox Christology is subjected by Mohammed. The very terms just men-tioned are devalued by the immediate context within which they are found in the suras. Mohammed abhors and emphatically denies the affirmations by which Christians underline the uniqueness of Jesus Christ. This applies both to His person and to His work of atonement wrought on the cross. Jesus, he protests, is not the son of Allah[254] and even less a member of a divine trinity. Neither did he die for our sins; for the Jews crucified another person instead of him[255] – an ancient gnostic heresy! Mohammed rejected the entire concept of the Cross. The true reason was that he did not want to go the way of suffering death, but the way of triumph.

Later on, the Muslims felt the apparent contrast between the holi-ness and eschatological role of Jesus and the person of Mohammed as embarrassing. Thus, in their tradition, Mohammed's figure was gradu-ally transformed by assuming elements of Christology.[256]

4. Mohammed's Divided Reaction to the Objections of Jews and Christians

Mohammed was initially convinced that Allah's revelation to him, the *Quran,* stood in perfect continuity to his former revelations both to the Jews, the *Taurat,* and to the Christians, the *Indjil.* Likewise he ex-pected that both would accept him as a new prophet, indeed the final one, in the Biblical succession. Therefore he treated them kindly as "people of the scriptures."[257] But both groups denied his claims, show-ing him the contradictions to the authentic Biblical revelation. There-fore his initial benevolence turned into indignation, even wrath. From then on he practised a differentiating approach, particularly to Chris-tians.

a. Those who submitted to his claims were accepted graciously. Even if they did not completely change their convictions; Mohammed would employ a certain degree of tolerance. This is the original mean-ing of the koranic saying: "There is no compulsion in religion." It does not imply complete tolerance of non-Islamic faiths. It means simply pedagogic patience with recent converts to Islam.

---

[254] Sura **9**:30 f.
[255] Sura **4**:156.
[256] Gottfried SIMON 1920, pp. 282-288.
[257] Sura **5**:82-83.

b. There were ethnic groups of Christians who submitted to the political rule of the Islamic conquerors. They were allowed to practise their own religion, but under strict limitations.[258] They were not permitted, however, to propagate their faith. Making converts of Muslims was treated as a criminal offence. Both Christian proselytisers and their converts were and still are threatened with execution.[259]

Moreover Christians were reduced to the state of second-class citizens. They were not granted full civil rights, neither in court nor in public affairs. They had also to pay a special tax. This was one main reason why in all conquered areas in the Middle East and in North Africa the large indigenous churches gradually shrank or disappeared completely.[260]

c. The hardest lot hit both Christians and Jews when they came to be regarded as polytheists. By a stricter interpretation of the term *shirk* (associating Allah with other gods) they were accused of committing the unforgivable sin. Even their Trinitarian concept of God was regarded as shirk. Placed on the same footing with pagan people, Christians became subject to cruel persecution. Muslims everywhere were encouraged to catch the infidels and to behead them. Several verses in the Koran can be quoted to prove this (e.g. Sura 2:291; 4:91; 8:12; 47:7).

In recent times, radical Islamist groups collectively denounced Christianity, especially the capitalist West, as having lapsed into paganism. Any act of terrorism can thus be justified as a lawful punishment for this.

III. The Expansion of Islam

1. Historic Spread

After the death of Mohammed in 632, his successors took his religion "by fire and sword" in powerful campaigns in West and East-bound directions. Having conquered Syria, Palestine, Egypt and all other North African countries they were able to cross the Mediterranean strait of Gibraltar and take control of the Iberian kingdoms of Spain and Portugal.[261] Nothing seemed able to prevent the achievement of their ulti-

---

[258] Sura 9:29-33 – Christine SCHIRRMACHER 1999, vol. I, pp. 81-83.

[259] Sura 4:89. – Chr. SCHIRRMACHER, op. cit, .vol I, pp. 250-252.

[260] Walter FREYTAG 1961, Part II, pp. 63-71.

[261] Siegfried RAEDER 2001, pp. 47-55.

mate goal: the conquest of Central Europe. In that venture the Muslim army was stopped and defeated by the Franconian commander Karl *Martell* (688-741) in the battle of Tours and Poitiers in 732. In this way, the Christian Occident was saved from Islam in the first of three historical invasions. The second was the defeat of the Turkish army in 1529 by the defenders of Vienna; and at a third instance, in 1683, this was repeated.[262]

Today we can speak of the fourth Islamic attempt to conquer Europe.[263] This time, however, it is to be accomplished by another, non-military strategy, although accompanied by occasional acts of terrorism.

Quite early Islam also spread northward to Turkey, the Balkans and into the Caucasian regions. In its expansion to the East, Persia and the North of the Indian subcontinent were conquered. Muslim merchants took their faith as propagandists as far as Indonesia, to the Southern provinces of China and to the Philippines. The conquest of Black Africa proceeded partly in the same manner and partly it came about by military subjection.[264]

2. The Historic Effect of the Crusades

The age of the Crusades contributed much to the deterioration in relations between the two great monotheistic religions, Christianity and Islam.[265] Both sides came to regard each other as the fiercest enemy and to despise each other's faith as paganism. The brutalities committed by European Crusaders against Turkish and Arabian Muslims had traumatic effects. Henceforth any attempt at Christian mission was regarded as a revival of the crusading spirit and dealt with accordingly.

This applies even today. The mediaeval past is still present in Muslim minds.[266] This greatly reduces the opportunities for Western missionaries to engage in evangelism amongst Islamic people in the Middle East. At the same time, this situation calls for an increased effort on the part of Asian churches to direct their mission activities especially to Muslim countries. For here the traditional charge is refuted that Chris-

---

[262] Hans-Peter RADDATZ 2002, pp. 142-144.

[263] Adelgunde MERTENSACKER 1998.

[264] J. Spencer TRIMINGHAM 1962, pp. 10-15.

[265] Bernard PALMER 1980.

[266] Francesco GABRIELI 1973.

tian missions, by being directed from the West, are a continuation of the historical crusades.

At the recent Eighth Triennial Convention of AMA (Asia Missions Association) held at Moscow September 9-12, 2003 this was clearly recognised. Accordingly, the Moscow Declaration stated AMA's missionary aim in these terms: The people in Muslim countries should realise "that we do not come as enemies of Islam, but as messengers of Jesus Christ, the Prince of Peace." Asian missionaries should preach love and reconciliation.

3. The New Situation: Renascent Islam

The historic defeats of the Muslim armies in 732 and 1683 not only weakened the military force of Islam but it also introduced a period of moral and cultural stagnation. During the 18th and 19th centuries, the Muslim states could not even stop the expansion of Western imperialism. In many countries, Muslims had to submit to European colonial rule. This humiliating situation was changed drastically after World War II. The colonized peoples in Africa and Asia successfully struggled for their independence. In several countries there appeared an ideological synthesis of Nationalism, Marxism and renascent Islam. This Islamic revolution was greatly assisted by the discovery of oil in the Arabian hemisphere. Indigenous hereditary or revolutionary leaders capitalised upon these new and unparalleled sources of income. They used them not only for modernization and personal comfort but also to support the propagation of the Muslim religion. On all continents mosques,[267] schools, cultural centres and publication agencies sprouted like mushrooms.

In many cases, oil multi-millionaires secretly sponsored the activities of Islamist terrorist groups. One spectacular example is *Osama Bin Laden*,[268] the prosperous son of a Saudi Arabian oil magnate.

Today, the Muslim world may be divided up into secular states giving a priority to the religion of Islam and Islamist states in which the rule of a modified *sharia* has been fully installed. But in all countries fundamentalist movements are fighting for an Islamist revolution. The most successful example was the take-over of the government of Iran

---

[267] Adelgunde MERTENSACKER 2001.
[268] Roland JAQUARD 2001.

by *Ayatollah Khomeini* (1901-1989) *in* 1979. He himself considered his political victory as an important step to an Islamist world revolution.

This would, naturally, imply the eradication of Christianity, even in its traditional Euro-American domain.

Even now, Christian churches were or still are outlawed in Islamist states like Afghanistan and Saudi Arabia. Christian mission is strictly forbidden; conversion to Christianity or influencing others to become Christians is avenged by public execution.[269]

4. Islamic Evaluation of Western Christianity Today

In modern times, Islamic believers who came to Western countries as diplomats, travellers, students or immigrants made their personal observations about the Christian religion as it is practised by its nominal adherents. They came to the conclusion that the churches have lost their controlling influence on the majority of their members. Ethical standards are rapidly declining and the entire once-Christian Occident is in a state of spiritual disarray. The prevailing values are economic materialism and sensual licentiousness. Christianity does not even protect its faith from blasphemous ridicule. Even with them, it has fallen into contempt.

Moslem leaders in Arabian countries concluded that the European states have lost their religious and ethical foundations and are about to collapse.

This assessment serves as a negative incentive to embark on a new strategy of conquest, not based on military force but on religious penetration and by the demographic outgrowth of the indigenous folk-Christian population. In Germany, the native birth-rate has shrunk to 1.2 children per family; with the Muslim immigrants it is 3.8! That means that by 2040 AD German descendants may constitute an ethnic minority in their own country! The day when the Muslims can impose their *sharia* on all European states seems to have dawned.

5. The Significance of the Middle East Conflict

In recent decades, hardly a day passed when the conflict between Israelis and their Arabian neighbours, particularly the Palestinians, did

---

[269] The penalty for apostasy from Islam according to the four schools of Islamic law ... German translation from the Arabic Original (Kairo 1987) by Ishak Ersen, Licht des Lebens: Villach, Austria 1991, pp. 18-25.

not make headlines. The tension between the Arabian native population and the Jewish immigrants started towards the end of the 19th century. The impulse of Zionism led to the *aliya*, i.e., the gradual return of Jews to the country of their forefathers.[270] This movement assumed large-scale dimensions after World War II on account of the Nazi Holocaust. In 1948, the UN agreed to the establishment of the state of Israel in a limited area of their ancient homeland. Leaders of the Palestinians protested strongly and that led to three successive wars between them and the Israelis. Arabs never accepted an abiding political settlement including the recognition of the new state. Up to now, the "peace process" attempted by international bodies has constantly been frustrated.

The conflict could have been settled long ago. However, both fundamentalist Palestinian movements and Muslim statesmen in neighbouring countries would not acquiesce with the emergence of a non-Muslim state in a territory which was claimed as belonging to the "House of Islam."

Most observers in the outside world fail to recognise that the main conflict between Israel and her Arabian neighbours is neither political nor economic. In its deepest analysis it is ethnic and religious. It is rooted in the age-old struggle concerning the two sons of Abraham. To which of them does the primary birth-right belong? Is it to *Ishmael* and his descendants or to *Isaac* and his genealogical line? That introduces the question as to whom of the two the salvation-historical promises to possess the country of Canaan applies. The Arabs started to claim it since the country was conquered by Caliph Omar I (592-644), in honour of whom the Muslims built the majestic Dome of the Rock on Mt. Zion, the very place where once King David had built the Temple of Yahweh.

Some years ago, *Ayatollah Khomeini* gave his own Islamist interpretation to the apparent defeat of Muslim monopolist hegemony:[271] Allah himself allowed Satan to create the hateful Zionist state in order to punish the Muslim for their religious sluggishness. The Islamic peace could not, therefore, be restored until the Muslim *umma* awoke to its divine mission to establish the rule of sharia all over the world. That should start with the re-conquest of *El Kuds,* which the Zionists call Jerusalem. With this prophetic utterance, (the word *ayatollah* means "pronouncement of Allah"), Khomeini supplied the basic political phi-

---

[270] Hans EISSLER / Walter NÄNNY 2001.

[271] Lance LAMBERT 1998, p. 126 f.

losophy for Islamic fundamentalist movements all over the world. It is an instigation to fight fanatically for the universal rule of *sharia*.

Up to now, all attempts of the fundamentalist Palestinians and their Muslim allies to re-conquer Jerusalem and to eradicate the "Zionist construction" have failed. They cannot recognise that this will always be impeded by the Lord's protection of His people. They ascribe it, with some truth, to the support of the State of Israel by the influential Jewry in the USA. For that reason, Islamists hate America as the "big Satan" and try to damage it. But since the USA is largely a Christian country, that hatred is extended to include Christianity in general. Thus the age of the Crusades is on again but this time in an inverted form.

6. Missiological Evaluations of the Iraq War

The new Christian-Islamic encounter assumed a wider dimension in connection with the wars in Afghanistan (2002) and Iraq (2003). President Bush would interpret them as a crusade against the "axis of evil." This, according to him, is mainly constituted by some militant Muslim states, stretching from Iran to Libya. Several mission leaders, however, warned that unilateral war instigated by Western states against Iraq might well provoke a new solidarity of all Islamic nations against the alleged Western aggression on Islam as such. That would turn out to be most dangerous both for evangelism and indigenous minority churches.

At the AMA Convention in Moscow in September 2003, a speaker, familiar with the situation in the Gulf region, recommended that missions from Asia should use the present post-war confusion for the advancement of the Gospel. The despondency of the Iraqi population creates, he believed, an opportunity for evangelism. "Today the way for missions to the Arab world goes through the open gate of Iraq," he claimed.

No matter how we assess this view, one fact can be observed positively: Many mission agencies both in the West, South and East now show an increased concern for work among Muslims.

IV. Christian Views of Islam

Right from the time of its origin and throughout the centuries, Christians differed in their basic assessment of the new religion introduced by Mohammed and forcefully spread under his successors. The various interpretations depended upon one's own theological outlook or on the general ideological climate.[272] Crucial was the empirical encounter which individual Christians, churches and countries had with Islam. In times of fierce aggression, they regarded Islam as a nearly pagan enemy; during periods of peaceful coexistence Christian attitudes softened. Today, too, we find a variety of evaluations amongst theologians, church leaders and missionaries. Especially for the latter, it is highly important that they come to a clarified religious evaluation of Islam before they conceive a strategy for approaching its adherents. This, again, will depend upon the particular brand of Islam represented by the addressees. For Islam in general is not a monolithic religion. There is the traditional cleavage between *Sunnis* and *Shiites*, whilst mystical *Sufism* has its particular spiritual character. Today, quite apart from those confessional distinctions, Muslims differ widely amongst themselves with regard to orthodoxy. The question is: How faithfully does one really observe the original precepts of the prophet Mohammed and to **sunna**, the Islamic legal tradition? In vast regions of Africa or Indonesia, the nominal Muslim masses cherish types of rather syncretistic folk- Islam, mixed with animist elements.

In countries which have been exposed to clashes with Western technocratic civilization, Muslims may have developed a rather secularised outlook and lifestyle. Therefore, evangelists to the Muslims should always keep in mind an important missiological rule: We do not address ourselves to an abstract religion, but to fellow human beings who in different degrees claim allegiance to their particular religion.

Having said this, it is still important to be mindful of the various Christian theological interpretations given to Islam as such and to seek an answer to the question as to which stance we ourselves adopt.

So what are the options? Let me present six typical ones before I present my own, rather differentiating conviction.

1. Islam: The Anti-Christian Enemy

One of the oldest and most persistent judgments was arrived at by Christians who had been exposed to the ferocious physical and spiritual attacks of Islam. In the light of their experiences, they called it an, or even *the*, antichristian religion. Some of them saw or are seeing it as that apocalyptical movement out of which Antichrist himself will emerge. Even *Martin Luther,* on account of the military threat of the

---

[272] Klaus HOCK 1986.

Turks advancing to Austria, expounded this conviction.[273] Today this view is held by many Dispensationalists. Often they refer to the Dutch author *Marius Bahr,* a student of Middle East conflict who warns urgently of the present world-wide advances of Islam.[274] He points out the Koran's opposition to central Christian doctrines and its hostility to Christians. His theological conclusion is: "There is no non-Christian religion in the world which so consistently and clearly denies the Sonship of Christ and His crucifixion as does Islam." Accordingly, he protests against the tendency to identify Allah with the Biblical God Yahweh, suggesting that in reality Allah is Satan in disguise. The consequence of this view is either a rather aggressive homiletical approach to the Muslim or - more commonly - the retreat from Muslim evangelism.

2. Islam: A similar Monotheistic Faith

The complete opposite to the view just presented is that reassessment of Islam which was advocated by the philosophy of the Enlightenment. They were wearied of any orthodox rigidity having met a rather self-sufficient Muslim culture. Thus, they evaluated the Islamic religion as one of the three classical expressions of an ethical Monotheism, besides the older sister religions of Judaism and Christianity. This view was propagated by the famous "parable of the three rings" in G. E. *Lessing's* drama "Nathan the Wise." Lessing compared those religions with three rings so similar to each other that nobody could tell which of them was the genuine one. Consistent with this, the enlighteners' plea then and now is for tolerant religious coexistence instead of mutual attempts to convert each other.

3. Muslims: People like Other Sinners in Need of the Gospel

In close connection with the great evangelical awakenings of the 18th and 19th Centuries, the Protestant missionary movement emerged. It directed its zeal to spread the Kingdom of God to all parts of the newly-opened Southern and Eastern continents. Evangelical missionaries regarded all people, irrespective of their culture and religion, as lost sinners. For their salvation Jesus Christ had shed His blood. Consequently, modern evangelical missions did not follow the advice of the enlighteners to let Muslims find their salvation in their own religion. A considerable number of evangelical societies faithfully included in their

---

[273] Martin LUTHER, 1955: vol. 30/II, pp. 107-148.

[274] Marius BAHR 1980, pp. 230 f.

world-wide programme, missions to the Moslem world. It was a sacrificial venture, in which many Christian witnesses lost their lives. In view of the hardness of this work, wise mission- leaders called Moslem missions the "acid test of our faith in Christ as universal Saviour and Lord."[275]

4. The Islamic World: The Inconvertible Block

At the end of "the Great Century in Missions" (Latourette), a statistical assessment was undertaken. The numerical results were deeply disappointing. Leading missiologists concluded that the Moslem world had proved to be the *"le block inconversible."* Muslims appeared to be immune to any attempts to present the Gospel to them. The German missiologists *Karl Hartenstein* and *Walter Freytag*[276] – while still upholding the plight of witnessing to the Muslim – showed that such immunity was the result of a historic rejection of Christ and a typical mark of a post-Christian religion turning into an antichristian one. The practical consequences varied between faithful endurance, a partial redeployment of the missionary force in favour of receptive people-groups (see the theory of *Donald McGavran*), and complete withdrawal. But other responsible missiologists regard the latter as a betrayal. They advocate a bold new venturing in Moslem evangelization.

5. Muslim Creed – a Partner of Inter-religious Dialogue

Today we observe a general tendency amongst missiologists to devalue preaching and evangelism which aim at conversion and church planting. Such preaching and evangelism are replaced by inter-religious dialogue aimed at mutual understanding and co-operation. Some missiologists do not regard Mission and Dialogue as mutually exclusive but rather as complementary. Yet in practice, the emphasis has definitely shifted to dialogue. This applies particularly to the Christian encounter with Islam. The reason given for this is partly the apparent fruitlessness of Moslem missions, partly a new version of the Enlightenment's attitude. A new element, however, is added. That is the modern categorisation of Islam as an "Abrahamic religion."

---

[275] Samuel ZWEMER 1907.

[276] Walter FREYTAG 1961, Part. II, pp. 53-62.

6. Islam: One of the Three Abrahamic Religions

Recently it has become customary to advance the view that Judaism, Christianity and Islam are historically and spiritually related to each other. This assertion relies upon more than the monotheism common to the three religions. The fact that all of them have a high esteem for the OT Patriarch Abraham is regarded as foundational. He is regarded as their spiritual or even biological father. The latter applies both to the Jews and to the Arabian Muslims, the difference being that Jews are descendants of *Isaac*; the Arabs, according to the theory best known, of *Ishmael*. Abraham, indeed, plays an important role both in the Old and New Testaments and he is frequently mentioned in the Koran.[277] Roman Catholic and Ecumenical proponents of dialogue suggest that these three contending religions should make practical use of their lineages from Abraham. They should discuss both their common and their distinct features. That, they think, might contain the key for solving the crucial problem of the Middle East conflict. The main advocates of the Abrahamic concept are Hans Küng and his disciple Karl Kuschel.[278] The late Pope John Paul II also advocated this view though with some differences regarding its concrete application.

7. A Tri-polar, Salvation-historical View of Islam

Let me now try to present my personal missiological view which I have arrived at after a long struggle with the Islamic riddle and after having considered the pros and cons of the six specific concepts presented to you. There are, to different degrees, true elements in each of them, but usually they suffer from one-sidedness and from isolating specific elements from their context.

I have already attempted an analysis of Mohammed's vocational experience by discerning three contrasting elements in it: the human, the divine and the demonic. The same diacritical analysis can be applied to the entire religion derived from that complex experience. Missionaries to the Muslim world should proceed diacritically.

First of all, they must regard and sympathize with the Moslems as fellow *human beings*. They are in need of God but go astray and even

---

[277] Abraham (*Ibrahim*) is mentioned in 25 Suras, e.g. 2:124-136; 6:74-81; 11:69-81; 15: 51-74; 19:41-58; 21:51-72; 26:69-93; 29: 16-35; 37:83-113.

[278] Karl KUSCHEL 2001. – Theologischer Konvent Bekennender Gemeinschaften: Juden, Christen und Muslime vereint für den Frieden? Der Nahostkonflikt in biblisch-heilsgeschichtlicher Sicht, in:DIAKRISIS, vol. 23 (5/6 2002).

rebel against Him. We can develop the right attitude when we are motivated by the love of Christ. This includes getting familiar with the culture of our Muslim addressees and to be empathic to their present situation.

Secondly, we must be prepared to meet with resistance and even hostility. There are several reasons for that but the deepest one is their being *blindfolded by a demonic spirit.* This excludes any harmless kind of evaluating and approaching Islam. I refer to the rationalistic, the dialogical and the current Abrahamic proposals. The three so-called "Abrahamic religions" have rather different concepts of the one God and also of the specific role of Abraham himself. Indonesian evangelists who are ex-Muslims themselves, for example, realise the occult nature of Islam. In view of this, they employ exorcism as a major form of encounter with Muslims.

Thirdly, we have to strive for a deeper, i.e. Biblical understanding of the *divine factor* in the origin and history of Islam, including the experience of its founder. One of the most controversial questions debated amongst Christian students of Islam and missionaries to the Muslim is: Who is Allah in Islam? Three strident answers are given to this question which have caused splits even within the Christian camp. The extreme answers to the left and to the right are: Allah is identical with the God of Biblical revelation. Accordingly Jews, Christians and Muslims worship the same God. The answer on the other extreme is that Allah is the Devil himself. Converts have to renounce him outright and to submit to the true God of the Bible, the Father of Jesus Christ. The latter recommendation is right but what about the former one?

I am intrigued by the title of the famous autobiography of *Bilquis Sheikh*, a noble Pakistani convert: "I Dared to Call Him Father."[279] Her conversion experience was not that she turned to an entirely different god, but that she, by the inspiration of the Holy Spirit and the testimony of Catholic nuns in the hospital, conceived the idea that Allah is not a remote, rather impersonal despot, but a loving father. Orthodox Islam has removed all traits of fatherly love from him and thereby distorted His true image. But still Muslims, Jews and Christians alike confess Him as the one holy God, maker of Heaven and earth, who sustains our life and will act as our ultimate judge. The real news of the Gospel is that we need not tremble like slaves when we approach Him, never knowing whether ultimately He will accept or condemn us. For in sac-

---

[279] Bilquis SHEIKH 1977/2002.

rificially giving His one and only Son Jesus Christ for our redemption, He has opened for us the way to come back to Him as children to their loving Father.

Thus the missing centre in Islam is exactly that Biblical revelation which Mohammed fought passionately: Jesus Christ, the beloved Son of God, who gave His life for our salvation. He died to save Muslims as well and for that reason the Christian Church cannot cease to give an authentic witness in evangelizing the Muslim world.

There is, however, one additional reason why we ought to regard the Muslims as our main object of mission. There is, indeed, some substance in the new idea of a brotherhood between the adherents of those three religions who see an important place for Abraham in God's history with mankind. It cannot be ruled out historically that the inhabitants of the Arabian Peninsula are either directly or indirectly descendants of Ishmael, the illegitimate first born son of Abraham. Oral tradition amongst oriental people can be found to be very consistent here. If, however, this could be confirmed, the religious claims of Arabian Muslims on the one hand and those of Jews and Christians on the other would still not be equal. The Bible emphatically insists that the salvation-historical promise given to Abraham and his descendants would not be inherited by Ishmael and his genealogy but by Isaac and his descendants (Romans 9:7). This applies particularly to the possession of the promised land of Israel.

Nevertheless, God did not completely neglect Ishmael in His promises given to Abraham and to Hagar. Even after his expulsion to the wilderness, Ishmael remained under the special protection of Yahweh. He was even distinguished by God's promise: "I will surely bless him; I will make him fruitful and will greatly increase his numbers. He will be the father of twelve rulers, and I will make him a great nation" (Gen 17:20).

Ishmael developed a rather wild character, and this was inherited by His descendants up to the present day. But that should not incite Jews and Christians to adopt a policy of retaliation. It should rather challenge them to overcome Muslim roughness by the gentleness of God, the Father of Jesus Christ, who wants to be recognized as the Father of the Muslim, when they accept Him by faith in the Gospel.

A Belgian missionary to Muslims in many countries wrote a book under the challenging title: "Love those Arabs."[280] In it, he calls our attention to a number of remarkable promises given by God in connection with the life -story of Ishmael. One of the special ministries to the Muslim world operating from Germany adopted as its watchword the prayer of Abraham on behalf of his elder son: *"If only Ishmael might live under your blessing!"* (Gen 17:18). This prayer had been partly answered in the past history but the complete fulfilment is still to come. Some Biblical students see such a fulfilment as a part of eschatology.

Conclusion

The Future of the Muslim World in Biblical Perspective

1. Distinguish between Islam as an Antichristian Religion and the Muslim People

In this chapter I have tried to explain the apparent tension between the missionary duty to reinforce our obligation to carry the Gospel to the Muslim world despite the increasing Islamic opposition to Christianity. There are at present two errors which are equally fatal. One is to believe in an imminent appeasement of the Muslim by joining with them in an ecumenical union of the three Abrahamic religions. The other error and consequently temptation is to retreat from evangelisation of the Muslim because of fearing them as inconvertible anti-Christian enemies.

Both errors can be avoided when we distinguish clearly between Islam as a rather complex religion and its adherents, the Muslim people. Islam as a religion asks for critical analysis, spiritual discernment and courage to resist its aggressive claims and strategies. Muslim people are erring human beings, deceived by their religion and therefore in need of the pure Gospel.

2. Share in God's Love for the Muslims

Missionaries are ambassadors for Christ. They incorporate God's own appeal to human beings who rebel against Him and who, at the

---

[280] The book by B.V. HENRY is written in Norwegian; a summary is given by him in DIAKRISIS vol. 23, (5/6 2002), pp. 197-201: " Habt diese Araber doch lieb!"

same time, are almost torn asunder amongst themselves. In empathy with this double tension, Christ's messengers cry out: *"We beseech you ... be reconciled to God!"* (2 Cor 5:20). Muslims always have been and still are in desperate need of reconciliation, both religiously and politically. They do not show this openly, because they are hindered either by pride or anxious respect of Allah and his alleged revelation in the Koran In their majority, they are blindfolded and captured by ancient prejudices. But still in the depth of their hearts they are longing for a loving God who bears concerns for them personally.

Is our theory right that the Arab nucleus of the Moslem world is descended from Abraham via Ishmael? Then we should expect that his tragic fate as recorded in Genesis is still burning in their collective subconscious mind. On the other hand, God Himself remembers His promises given about Ishmael and his descendants. On account of these, He loves them with a particular love, and we should be filled and directed by that love, no matter how resistant Muslims prove to be towards our endeavour. Our oral witness about Christ must, therefore, be substantiated by an attitude of loving concern, verified by practical deeds. It is not by chance that most Protestant and Catholic missions to the Muslims have traditionally been supported and prepared by charity work.

Today there are many instances to prove that in the long run Muslims will not remain insensitive to God's love in Christ. The first proof comes from the testimony of many contemporary converts from Islam. They confirm that formerly they had missed precisely the central dimension in the character of God- His self-giving love as our Father. If this is shown to them, it will not fail to touch the hearts of obstinate Muslims.

There are whole areas today which have become responsive to the Gospel on account of political[281] or natural disasters which made them destitute and doubtful about Allah's care for them. One country in which, presently, many conversions are taking place is *Algeria*. During the brutal massacres committed by fanatical Islamist groups, 150, 000 civilian people were murdered. That made the population abhor that type of religion and long for peace. In the province of *Kabul, as a result,* there is no village without a group of Christians. The estimated number is 20, 000.[282]

---

[281] Avery WILLIS 1997.

[282] D. KUHL, loc. cit. p. 210.

3. Be Aware that Muslim Hostility will Continue

Nevertheless, Islam as a whole is most likely to remain defiant of the Christian Gospel. We have reminded ourselves of the grand vision of Islamist leaders and fundamentalist movements of continuing and even enforcing their *jihad* until all countries on earth have accepted the *sharia* and become *dar al Islam*. Therefore the naïveté which has become so common among Western statesmen and spiritual leaders is out of place. If we do not resist, many countries will fall prey to the Islamist conquest.

4. Jerusalem the Stumbling Stone

We have spoken about the Palestinian determination, backed by Islamic leaders all over the world, to re-conquer the city of *El Kuds*/Jerusalem to make it the undivided capital of liberated Palestine. It is very likely that the present *intifada* may turn into a major war.[283] Most Arabian or Muslim nations in general would participate in it. That might become the initiation of the third world war. Such turn of events is likely to come not only in political perspective; it is also supported by Biblical prophecy. In the 12th chapter of the Book of Zechariah, it is predicted that at the end of history all nations will unite to wage an all-out attack on Jerusalem in order to crush the people of Israel. But they will not succeed for God himself will prevent this by direct intervention. *"In that day,"* says the Lord, *"I will seek to destroy all the nations that come against Jerusalem."* That means that the final *jihad* of the Muslims will end in disaster. It will spell out the end of Islam as an antichristian religion. That will involve the destruction of the united armies of many nations and result in hundreds of thousands of casualties. But it will not be the end of human history. On the contrary, it will be the beginning of an entirely new era. This will also be the era of a universal Christian mission to the Muslim nations. Zechariah (14:16) prophesies: *"Then every one that survives of all the nations that have come up against Jerusalem shall go up year after year to worship the King, the Lord of hosts ..."*

5. The Messianic Vision

The Christian encounter with Islam is, therefore, inspired by a great eschatological hope. It is a partial anticipation in faith of that time when all people will live peacefully together in the Messianic Kingdom

---

[283] Moussa AFSCHAR 2002.

of Peace. This will be centred on Mt. Zion, the capital of Israel. But the messianic vision has a special word of prophecy in view of the Middle East conflict. It is found in Isaiah 19:23-25:

> *"In that day there will be a highway from Egypt to Assyria (the present Iraq!) ... Israel will be the third with Egypt and Assyria, a blessing in the midst of the earth, whom the Lord of hosts has blessed, saying, 'Blessed be Egypt my people, and Assyria the work of my hands, and Israel my heritage'."*

At last peace will reign: Peace between the fraternal peoples in the Middle East, ecological peace in nature (Zech 8:12) and universal peace amongst all peoples on earth (Zech 14:9).

Chapter 9

Neo-Hinduistic Missions in Christian Countries

Introduction

During the summer of 1989 I went as a tourist to St. Petersburg, then called "Leningrad." It was the time of historical transition: The age of Soviet communism rapidly approached its end, whilst a new epoch of democratic liberty and opening up to the outside world was dawning. When we visited the famous art gallery "Hermitage" we looked through the window down onto the large Alexander Place. From this vantage point, we saw a curious sight: A group of young men with shaved heads, dressed in saffron vestments, clutching a kind of rosary, performed an enthusiastic dance to the playing of oriental music on Indian instruments. Loudly they shouted the names of two favourite Hindu gods: *Hare Hare, Krishna Krishna, Hare Krishna, Hare Krishna*! When we came outside to approach them, we realised that they were not travelling monks – *sanyasis* – from India, but otherwise normal Russian youngsters. Formerly they had belonged to the compulsory Bolshevik youth organization "Komsomolcz." Now they had taken advantage of their new freedom to quench their spiritual thirst. But they did not return to the Orthodox Christian faith of their forefathers; no, they had joined a Neo-Hinduistic sect!

Twenty-two years before this, an Indian friend of mine had been amazed at a similar scene in the famous Oxford Street in the heart of London; the difference was simply that those were British young men who had turned from their Anglican or Methodist background. But both groups had adopted the same brand of Eastern spirituality.

Those two experiences pointed to the same event in the modern history of religion: Hinduism, the classical national faith of the majority of Indians, had started to cross cultural boundaries and to build bridgeheads in both parts of Europe and in America as well. And it was determined not only to stay, but even to expand in many ways.

That makes it necessary to take a look at classical Hinduism itself, before we deal with its modern transformation.

I. Character and History of Hinduism

1. General Observations

Hinduism is one of the four largest living religions of mankind.[284] However, it is not one religion; it is a conglomerate of quite different religions which in the course of history have settled on the Indian subcontinent, a process which started with the invasion of the Aryans from Central and West Asia. Each newly arrived religion built on the foundation of the former one by merging with it. Thus Hinduism is essentially syncretistic; it has developed the capability of absorbing almost any other religion by reinterpreting it in its own terms.[285] Islam and Christianity were the exceptions by staying independent but Hinduism enriched itself by integrating some Christian elements, which may account for some similarities between certain types of Hinduism, particularly *Bhakti* yoga,[286] with the Biblical doctrine of grace.

2. Historical Development

After the Aryan invasion of North India, Hinduism took its philosophical shape mainly amongst the Sanskrit language groups.[287] The central concepts are expressed in the Sanskrit vocabulary. It spread southwards but left whole tribal areas virtually untouched. By migration it also spread to other Eastern countries, particularly South East Asia and some Indonesian Islands as e.g. Bali. Later on, groups of Hindu people settled in East and South Africa as well.

3. Types of Hinduism

There exists a variety of religious types in Hinduism: The first type is Philosophical Hinduism. This is based on the major schools of thought, especially the Vedanta system of *Shankara* 788-820 (AD). Religiously- reflected Hinduism can be categorised either by the various divinities worshipped - particularly *Shiva* and *Vishnu* – or according to the different ways – *"margas"* – of self-salvation through various forms of *yoga*. On a lower, more popular level there is the *polytheism* of 330 Million gods to choose or combine and finally the nearly

---

[284] Jan GONDA 1963/1978. – Pratima BOWES 1977. – J. N. FARQUHAR [2]1912. – Benjamin WALKER 1968.

[285] Helmut von GLASENAPP 1963, p. 63.

[286] A. J. APPASAMY 1970. – Rudolph OTTO 1930. – Stephen NEILL 1974.

[287] T.W. ORGAN 1974.

unaffected tribal religions of the *Adhivasis* in North India. *Tantric Hinduism*, on the other hand, produces ecstasy by sexual orgies, whilst finally many modern Indians could be called *secularised Hindus*, whilst staying within the Hindu culture. Quite ancient is the peculiar social order of the highly discriminative *caste system*. It ranges from the Brahmin elite down to the untouchable low caste or even outcasts, whom Ghandi upgraded to the spiritual rank of *Hariyans* (children of God). Historical reform- movements like *Buddhism* and later on *Neo-Hinduism* tried to break with the caste system or at least to mitigate it. Thus the castes do not form an element in those movements which propagated the Hindu religion in the West.

4. Central Concepts of Hindu Thought

It is impossible to give, in a single chapter, an adequate presentation of the religious thought- world of Hinduism with all its subtleties, varieties and interpretations. But there are some basic concepts which have emerged from the sacred literature: the ancient *Vedas*, the *Upanishads*, the classical *epics* and the shorter discourses (*sutras*), and especially from the classical philosophical system of *Vedanta*. These have penetrated the Hindu mind and are settled there as central ideas. They appear also in modern Neo-Hinduistic literature and even in Western poetry influenced by Eastern thought. Thus, we find all Indian people speak about *Brahman, atman, maya, karma, samsara* and *moksha*. I shall therefore base this short introduction mainly on these terms.

Philosophical Hinduism is expressing a monistic world-view. This means the essential oneness of the invisible reality and the visible phenomena. The ultimate, all-embracing reality is the invisible **Brahman** which is impersonal, indivisible, without attributes or quality, eternal. There is no created reality outside Brahman; there are only emanations of its own self appearing in various features, which have no reality in their distinctness. To conceive of them as real is a cognitive error; the impression that they are real is brought about by the influence of **maya**, the process of self-deception.

The human or animal self is its soul, which is spiritual and may be called a temporal individuation of the large Brahman, essentially identical with it. The most important insight for the human being is to become conscious of its oneness with the Brahman, which calls for a return of the small **atman** into the huge Brahman. But by self-deception the atman is being entangled deeper and deeper in the crude matter by which it estranges itself from its real nature. Every action, right or wrong, is setting its mark on the materialized soul, which is its *karma*.

The goal of the religious struggle is to get rid of one's bad karma and by becoming de-materialized, to be qualified for re-immersion in the Brahman. That is the Hindu concept of salvation = *mosksha* (or *murti*). But if the evil karma exceeds, atman is compelled to get reincarnated, in a long circle – called *samsara* – of birth and death until it is totally purged from its bad karma.

The way towards realising my true nature by enlightenment = *sahmadi* is to get engaged in spiritual exercises, called *yoga*.[288] There are different types of yoga, as fitting the state of the individuum: The way of cognition (*Jnana yoga*), of bodily exercise (*Hatta yoga*), of working out my duty (*Karma yoga*), of loving devotion to a favourite deva i.e. deity (*Bhakti yoga*), of repeating and chanting the sounds of a mystic formula (*Mantra yoga*) or even of sensual orgasm (*Tantra yoga*). All of these yogas have the same purpose: to lead towards self-realization of the soul, that is, its appropriation of Brahman as one's true self.

Persons who by constant yoga practice have reached that stage are considered to be holy men who can become the *Gurus*, the spiritual teachers of religious seekers. They may, however, prefer simply to remain in this state of semi-consciousness and thus become the object of admiration by unenlightened people who regard and worship them as gods. Sometimes the highest god may feel pity for the miserable, unenlightened state of people by condescending to them as a human person. These are called *avatars*, and might be taken as an analogy with the incarnation. But their apparition lasts only for a short while, and the saving work is confined to action as a super- guru. In Neo-Hinduism, as expounded by the famous philosopher *Sarvepalli Radhakrishnan* (1888-1972),[289] the title *avatar* can also be conferred on a human being who wants to transfer his own enlightenment or salvation to unenlightened fellow human beings. Radhakrishnan finds such avatars not only in Hinduism but in all higher religions, including Christianity. Therefore he is inclined to recognize Jesus Christ, too, as a great avatar.[290] This apparent generosity deprives Him, however, of His uniqueness. Here we are touching the crucial point in the Christian encounter with Neo-Hinduism.

---

[288] This Sanskrit word is related to the English "yoke" which is put on a working animal.

[289] S. RADHAKRISHNAN 1939. – Paul A. SCHILPP (ed.) 1952.

[290] S. RADHAKRISHNAN 1939, pp. 173 ff. – Cf. M. M. THOMAS 1970: pp. 156-198.

5. Christian Mission in India

Christianity has a long history in India. According to tradition the Apostle *Thomas* preached the Gospel both in Kerala at the West Coast and near Madras on the Eastern shore, where he was martyred. In the 16th century the famous Jesuit missionaries *Francis Xavier* (1506-52) and *Robert de Nobili* (1577-1656) worked with great numerical results in the South (1542-49), developing the controversial method of *accommodating*[291] Christianity to the indigenous religious culture. They dressed and behaved like Brahmins.

Under British colonial rule many Western *Protestant missions* started their work in India, unfolding their activities in the three branches of evangelism, charity and education. Thereby many Indians – even those who never joined the Church – came under the influence of Christian ideas. That made an abiding impression on modern culture in India.

Recently[292] the American missiologist *Ralph Winter* proposed that Christian missions ought to be flexible in India, giving recognition also to a new type of "churchless Christianity."[293] It should suffice, he suggested, when people choose to follow Jesus and read the Bible.

This proposal is, however, rather questionable. It could increase the danger that Christianity – like so many other religions – might be absorbed by Hindu syncretism and lose it's saving power.

In fact evangelical Christianity has planted many self-reliant local churches which have started to send and support their own evangelists to other Indian provinces.[294] Consequently the Indian church is at present producing the largest number of Two-Thirds-World missionaries, followed by Korea.

6. Emergence of Neo-Hinduism

Some decades after the arrival of the first Protestant missionaries, some sensitive Indians started to realise that their traditional religion was unable to meet the challenge of the new culture that was establishing itself in India. Educated Indians felt ashamed about many superstitious elements in traditional polytheistic Hinduism and about the lack

---

[291] George HUNDSBERGER: Art. "Accommodation," in: EDWM pp. 31 f.

[292] At the Eighth Triennial Convention of Asia Missions Association Sept., 09-12, 2003 in Moscow in an unpublished paper read in his absence.

[293] Herbert E. HOEFER 1991.

[294] Emil JEBASINGH, 2003.

of ethical impetus to take care of the masses of needy people on account of the karma belief. Temple prostitution became disgusting to them. Especially they felt guilty about some cruel practices connected with Indian funeral rites like *Sati*, the burning of widows on the pyre of their husbands. They realised the urgent need of thorough religious and social reforms. One of those concerned was *Ram Mohan Roy* (1774-1833), who for some time had worked with the Serampore missionary trio, William Carey and his companions. He adopted some Christian doctrines but he did not realise the need for personal salvation and regeneration through appropriation of the atoning sacrifice of Christ. For Roy, Christ was the preceptor of moral principles and in this function, the way to real happiness.[295] In 1828 he founded the first Neo-Hinduistic reform movement, called *"Brahmo Samaj"* (Theistic Society). It tried to accomplish a synthesis between Hinduism and Christianity. Similar movements, some of them of monastic character, were initiated by others.

The *Arya Samaj* (Society of Aryans) established by Dayananda Sarswathi in 1875, was more conservative. It supported some reforms but it opposed Christianity and claimed the superiority of the Hindu tradition in its Vedi purity.[296]

7. Neo-Hinduism – Individualistic Religiosity with a Claim to Unify all Religions

We may identify the essence of Neo-Hinduism as a renaissance of Hindu religion which tries to strip it of its crude features and to adapt it to modern culture. It incorporates many new, particularly Christian elements. But it remains within the monistic world-view of classical Hinduism. Neo-Hindus are proud of their spiritual heritage which they want to share with people of other religions. They exercise tolerance of other beliefs, whilst attempting to unite them on the basis of their own presuppositions. Neo-Hindu temples provide space for other gods and religious heroes, including Christ. But they put Him on the same level with e.g. *Mahatma Ghandi* (1869-1949),[297] the great moral reformer of modern India, or they conceive him as an avatar like one of the incarnations of Krishna.

---

[295] Ram Mohan ROY 1820. On the debate between Roy and Joshua Marshman cf. M. M. THOMAS 197, p. 1f. and Stanley J. SAMARTHA 1970: pp. 40-42.

[296] M. M. Thomas, op. cit. p. 339.

[297] M. M. THOMAS, op. cit, Chapter VIII, pp. 199-245: "Mahatma Ghandi: Jesus, the Supreme Satyagrahi."

II. The Penetration of Neo-Hinduism to the West

Rudyard Kipling, a British novelist (1865-1936), coined, in 1889, the famous saying: "East is East, West is West, and never the twain will meet!"[298] That was at the end of the 19th century. That saying was eventually disproved by the modern development towards a globalized culture in the final third of the 20th century. In the wake of *Post-Modernism* many Western people started to be attracted by Eastern spirituality. In the reverse, representatives of Eastern religions unfolded a sense of mission and went out to penetrate Western countries.

1. Swami Vivekananda's Appearance 1893 in Chicago and Western Fascination

a. The Ramakrishna Movement

One of the most famous modern Hindu mystics was a man who called himself *"Ramakrishna"*[299] (1834-86), feeling that he was the incarnation of the two supreme deities, *Rama* and *Krishna*. In his meditation he also tried to identify himself with the founders and saints of other religions. He was deeply attracted to the person of Jesus, visualizing him and identifying himself with the central events of His life story. Soon he attracted young men to become his spiritual adepts and he imparted his spiritual experiences to them. Before his death he celebrated the nativity of Jesus with his disciples and commissioned them to take their message out to the spiritually starving masses of India and other parts of the world. That eventually, in 1897, gave birth to the *Ramakrishna Mission*. Formed after the model of a Catholic order of monks, it still seeks to advance Hindu social and religious concerns through its many monastic settlements in India and throughout the world. Ramakrishna's favourite disciple, *Swami Vivekananda*[300] (1862-1902) became his sussessor and was the actual founder of the Ramakrishna-Mission.[301]

---

[298] R. KIPLING 192, p. 231.

[299] His family name was Paramahamsa.

[300] Family name: Narendranath Datta.

[301] Swami VIVEKANANDA [7]1946/47.

b. Vivekananda's Message

In 1893 Vivekananda went to America and played a dominant role at the first *World Parliament of Religions*[302] staged in connection with the World Exposition in Chicago. He delivered a series of messages that thrilled his Western audience. For he, cleverly enough, presented to them his Hindu beliefs which he then identified with the essence of all true religion. He scolded the West for having wasted its spiritual heritage by adopting a philosophy of rationalist materialism. Thereby Westerners had, he reprimanded, become forgetful about man's true nature, which is essentially divine. Even Christian doctrine had a fatal share in this, he claimed, because it kept to the humiliating doctrine of man's sinfulness. To this he objected: It is a sin to call men sinners, for in reality you are gods! As a way to realise one's divine nature, he proposed Hindu meditation practices.

c. Birth of a "Vedanta Society"

Immediately after the Chicago event Vivekananda accepted a number of invitations to speak in several European countries. The Theosophical Society of Madame *Helena Petrowna Blavatzky* (1831-91) had prepared this climate of interest. In many places the new *Vedanta Society* was established. It spread Neo-Hindu thought and provided centres for meditation and yoga practices. The Vedanta Society was the first of several similar groups that were founded during the second phase of Neo-Hinduistic expansion to the West in the latter part of the 20th century.

2. Contemporary Hindu-Gurus Proselytizing in the West

a. General Features

In the early 1970s the world-wide student rebellion started to lose its fanaticising force. Many observers were astonished by a sudden awakening of religious interest in the younger generation whose thirst for intense experience could be satisfied neither by consumerist nor by Marxist materialism. Here the Indian *Guru movement*[303] discovered a fertile soil to spread its religious seed. It invaded to popularize its Hinduistic ideas by adapting them to Western psychological categories and

---

[302] In commemoration of it the second World Parliament of Religions was convened a century later in Chicago again. At that occasion Hans Küng presented his "Project World Ethos."

[303] Reinhart HUMMEL 1984.

selling them as a mental remedy against stress, frustration and loss of meaning. By simplifying Vedanta thought they made it easy to comprehend. Gurus posed as *avatars*, perfected spiritual masters who were able to transmit their experience of enlightenment to their followers. They taught easy methods of various yoga systems, which at home, however, were regarded as a fraudulent simplification of true Hindu asceticism.

The Gurus exhibited tolerant attitudes to other religions and ideologies. They adapted themselves particularly to Christianity as a still prevalent religion in the USA. At the same time they re-interpreted Christian ideas and the person of Jesus himself in Hinduistic terms. Like Swami Vivekananda, they criticized Western churches for having adapted themselves to materialism and having become void of genuine spirituality. Some of their adherents were fascinated by them. They worshipped them like gods and followed their invitations to visit them in their *ashrams*[304] in India. Even the *Beatles* gave an example of this.

The Gurus were attractive also because they did not make strict demands on their disciples' morals nor ask them to practise ascetic rigour. In other words, they presented a "Hinduism made easy for Westerners."

b. Three Examples:

1. The Hare Krishna Movement

In our Introduction we met one of the most popular and mission-minded groups, widely known as "Hare Krishna Movement."[305] The official name is "International Society for Krishna Consciousness" (ISK-CON). It was founded in 1933 by the Indian *Swami Bhaktivedanta Prabhupada* who believed himself to have become an incarnation of Krishna by having attained to his consciousness of universal oneness. His Hinduistic teaching is relatively orthodox. He also recognizes the Bible and the Koran as sacred scriptures but he declares them to be distorted in order to make them compatible with Hindu thought. His method is a kind of *Mantra meditation* in which the chanted sound-vibrations lead to rapture. Therefore his disciples spend most of their time in chanting the names of Hare and Krishna ten thousand times a day.

---

[304] An *ashram* (derived form Sanskrit *shrama*=endeavour) is an Indian hermitage, where single Hindu monks or small cells dedicate their lives to meditation and ascetic exercises. P. CHENCHIAH/V: CHAKKARAI/A. N. SUNDARISANAM 1941. – Friso MELZER 1976.

[305] A. C. Bhaktivedanta Swami PRABHUPADA 1971. 3. – Reinhart HUMMEL 1980: 134-137.

2. The Divine Light Mission (DLM)

DLM is the movement led by *Guru Maharaj Ji*,[306] who regards himself as the incarnation of a god. The name of his group indicates his missionary ambition to lead people towards the mystical experience of enlightenment. He recognizes other famous religious figures including Christ as "enlightened masters" or *avatars*. But his own position, he assures us, is not really exceptional, for he promises that his faithful members will reach the rank of avatar as well. The mystical state arrived at by meditation is characterized by a glazed expression on the face. The enlightened one loses his sense of being a distinct personality. He becomes insensitive to all external proceedings and is unreachable by people around him. If this becomes habitual, the god-consciousness has been attained.

3. Transcendental *Meditation* (Society for Creative Intelligence)

TM was founded by Maharishi (the great seer) *Mahesh Yogi*,[307] who posed as a super-guru. He, too, builds on the principle of Mantra yoga. By reciting a secret word or syllable, confided to the adept in the rite of initiation, the sound-waves penetrate deeply into the sub-conscious mind. Then the movement goes upwards. Carried by a mystical elevator, the soul ascends until it reaches the highest state of consciousness. TM is not presented as a religion. Rather it is acclaimed as a scientifically-approved psychological method, compatible with any world view. It is said to have the effect of removing stress and making the mind harmonious and receptive. TM, therefore, is offered as a remedy not only for depression but also as a clue to solve all socio-political problems. Its proponents claim that criminality would disappear from a city or country, if only 25% of the population practised TM. On a global level peace becomes feasible through a radio and TV network sponsored by TM world. In the USA several states have taken such self-recommendation seriously. For some time at least they granted the introduction of TM into Universities and schools as a teaching subject.

---

[306] Reinhart HUMMEL, op. cit. pp. 73-79.

[307] Aleyamma ZACHARIAH 1990: pp. 249-256. – David HADDON 1983: pp. 135-150. – "TM's Secret Texts," in: UPDATE: A Quarterly Journal on New Religious Movements, vol. III, issue 3-4, Dec. 1979, pp. 20-48.

3. Hinduistic Features of the New Age Movement[308]

We have already described the New Age movement as a modern form of all-embracing syncretism. Now it is important to be aware of its Hinduistic fountains, mediated originally by pioneers like *Alice B. Bailey*.[309] Philosophically, New Age is based on monism. It stresses the unity of divinity, human beings and nature. We should realize, it says, this essential oneness as well as the spiritual essence of the universe. The New Age movement provides the means and personal contacts through which our alleged spirituality can be enhanced.

There is a mighty force of individuals and groups linked in a worldwide network to transport these Eastern concepts to the West. New Age also claims the common essence of all religions, including Christianity. The latter is consequently interpreted according to a Hinduistic pattern. Christ becomes a symbol of man having fully realized his spirituality.[310] The eschatological hope for the return of Christ is transformed into mankind achieving its ultimate goal. It means to become fully united amongst themselves and united with the Universe in a spiritual communion. There will be peace on earth in the forthcoming Age of Aquarius.

New Age has many communicators. One highly influential means is psychedelic music, in which both sounds and texts show a Hindu background. New Age is propagated by musicals like "Aquarius" and by famous films like "Star Wars," produced by actress *Shirley MacLaine*. New Age has also developed its own school of psychology: "Transpersonal Psychology." It traces links to former incarnations of the patient or to "ascended spiritual masters" in *Shambala*, a mythological city in the Himalayas.

We may call New Age a multi-facetted movement of syncretistic Hinduism, being open to all other types of religion, magic and spiritism as well. It has been able to penetrate into all levels of society, even to centres of nuclear science (*Fritjof Capra,*[311] *Carl Friedrich von Weizsäcker*),[312] to international politics and big business. Thus it pur-

---

[308] Douglas GROOTHUIS: Art. "New Age" in: EDWM pp. 677 f. – Marilyn FERGUSON 1980. **Critics**: Constance CUMBEY 1983. – Caryl MATRISCIANA 1985.

[309] Lit. see VII Chapter.

[310] Alice B. BAILEY 1922. – Lévy DOWLING 1964. – David SPANGLER 1978.

[311] Fritjof CAPRA 1983.

[312] Carl Friedrich von WEIZSÄCKER 1988.

sues its ultimate goal by a "gentle revolution" (*Marilyn Ferguson*). It prepares Western culture to go Eastwards.

4. The Occult Dimension

The most dangerous aspect of Hinduistic yoga practices is that they lead into transcendental experiences of an occult nature. This is a consequence of Hindu monism. The belief in the essential oneness of the universe is ultimately levelling down all spiritual and ethical distinctions. There is no essential difference between light and dark, good and evil, divine and demonic. Krishna himself is reported to have said, "I am the Prince of demons. I am the light and the darkness."

Some mystic experiences can be provoked psychologically by auto-suggestion but in some cases they are based on real encounters with the transcendent realm. It is that domain which, according to Biblical faith, is allocated to the created spiritual powers, the angels. After the primal rebellion of Lucifer there arose a division between angels of light in the ministry of God and angels of darkness in the service of Satan.[313] Spiritualism, i.e. the communication with disembodied spirits, cannot be explained as a mere illusion; rather, its aim is to get into real contact with the sphere of the demons.[314]

Likewise certain yoga practices like Mantra yoga or transcendental meditation induce occult experiences. This is not simply a momentary event. It may result in occult oppression or even demonic possession. It must be assumed that gurus are in fact demonized persons who exercise an occult influence on their clients. For that reason it is hard to get out of their mental grip. Being completely submitted to a guru means to become spiritually enslaved.

This is confirmed by some gurus who, by a miraculous conversion to Christ, became Christians.[315] It was only then that they fully realized what their former possession entailed. In certain cases they were not fully liberated at once. Instead, they sensed their being haunted by ghosts at night. Sometimes they felt the threat of being physically choked. They were rescued eventually by a determined renunciation of their former allegiance to Satan. They had to sever all ties with their former practices and be completely submitted to Christ as their per-

---

[313] Alois WIESINGER 1957, pp. 90-98. – Alan MORRISON [2]199,: pp. 25-41.

[314] Kurt KOCH 1972, pp. 120-130.

[315] Katrin LEDERMANN 1988, pp. 118-123.

sonal Saviour. Only then were they fully liberated. Such was the experience of *Rabindranath R. Maharaj*, a former Indian guru and son of a famous guru himself. He relates it in his spiritual autobiography, "Death of a Guru."[316]

This occult dimension explains the difficulty in evangelizing people influenced by Neo-Hindu thought and New Age mentality. Even TM is by no means simply a psychological technique, religiously neutral. Being a form of Mantra yoga, it is based on the continuous invocation of a Hindu deity, signified by the Mantra word.[317]

III. The Danger of a Hinduized Christianity

1. Modernist Theology Paving the Way for Neo-Hinduism

One important reason why Neo-Hinduistic thought could make inroads even into Western churches is found in the anthropocentricity of contemporary theology. It was *F.D.E. Schleiermacher* (1768-1834), the father of modern Theology, who early in the 18th century, located religion in the feeling capacity of the human mind. He shunned maintaining the supernatural essence of Biblical revelation because it was disavowed by rationalistic philosophy. Therefore he claimed a particular province of religiosity, situated in human feeling. He defined religion as the "feeling of absolute dependency on God." All Christian doctrines had to be based on the inner experience of the believer.[318] Thus the objectivity of God Himself and the authority of the Bible as His revealed Word were surrendered. Schleiermacher himself admitted that Christian emotional experiences had parallels in other religions. Consequently he pleaded for a natural theology based on the mystical experiences of all religions. Thus God became the object of spiritual subjectivism.

The existentialist theology of *Rudolph Bultmann* (1884-1976), based upon *Martin Heidegger*'s (1889-1976) philosophy also internalised God to become the cause of "man's changed understanding of himself." By denouncing the polarity between subject and object in favour of a personal act of decision, Biblical epistemology (the way of gaining

---

[316] Published 1977 by J. B. Lippincott Company Publishers, New York 1977.
[317] Up-date. New Religious Movements, vol. III, issue 3-4, Dec.1979, p. 47: "The Meaning of some TM Mantras."
[318] F. D. E. SCHLEIERMACHER 1799, p. 50.

true knowledge) is giving way to mysticism. Similarly, *Paul Tillich*[319] (1886-1965), another pioneer of modern theology, defined God as the "ground of being." We relate to him – or rather to it (!) – by an experience of close connection, in which all religions participate in their particular ways.[320] In this view Tillich found a basis of dialogue with Eastern religions.

Obviously modern theology in the West was not immune to a wholly subjective concept of divine reality as it is found in the Vedanta equation between *brahman* and *atman*. *Os Guinness* rightly comments that a theology which relinquishes the historicity of God's acts of salvation and the objectivity of the Word of God, will lead us towards Hinduism.

2. The Quest for an Ecumenical Spirituality

In Chapter VII on modern Syncretism, we referred to the quest for an "ecumenical spirituality." This is thought to be needed for an overcoming of the ecological problem of human beings exploiting nature for their selfish benefits and also for providing a common bond for a divided mankind. Therefore a spirituality is sought which emphasizes both the basic oneness between people of all cultures and also the oneness between man and nature. Such a spirituality is supposed to foster an ultimate respect for animal life and nature. It should counteract man's subjecting creation to his technological superiority. Here Neo-Hinduism steps into the gap. Gurus can point out that they do in fact presuppose such universal oneness for it is exactly its realization which is attained in the *"Krishna consciousness."*[321]

We have also pointed to the common ground for a pluralist theology of religions. This is sought in the alleged oneness of the mystical experience which is enjoyed analogously in all particular religions by their devout adherents. This in fact is also the basic thesis of the Neo-Hinduistic understanding of the plurality of religions. If the presupposi-

---

[319] Paul TILLICH 1964.

[320] Paul TILLICH 1956, vol I, pp. 16 ff.

[321] A.C. Bhaktivedanta Swami PRABHUPADA 1971: pp. 119-124. "Über die Internationale Gesellschaft für KRSNA-Bewußtsein:" *"It is the goal of ISKCON to flood the whole world with sankirtana, the chanting of the holy names of gods. ... This sankirtana-movement is a blessing for all mankind, because it spreads the highest blessing like moon light. It is the life of all transcendental knowledge, it causes the ocean of divine delight to grow more and more and makes us taste the nectar of eternity, which we constantly are longing for." p. 121.*

tion made here were true, Hindus, in following the theory of S. Rad-hakrishnan,[322] could very well claim that theirs is the mother of all hu-man religions and that it can provide a basis for uniting them in a relig-ion for the One World. No wonder that Hindu thought has become so influential in ecumenical theology. It is also fully accepted as a basic component in the development of a culturally, truly contextualized theology for the Indian church.[323]

In recent decades, the World Council of Churches has had some outstanding promoters of its dialogue programme which came from India. These include the Syrian Orthodox bishop *Paul Verghese*, Dr. *Stanley Samartha*[324] and *Wesley Ariarajah*.[325] They became more and more intrigued by India's Hindu religion as a major source of an ecu-menical spirituality.

IV. Affirming the Uniqueness of Christ against Hinduistic Universalism

Amongst Asia's great religions it is Hinduism which has made great efforts to come to terms with the basic tenets of Christianity. Its repre-sentatives are motivated by the desire to incorporate these into their own monistic system. At the same time it is Neo-Hinduism that tries to engage in missionary activities amongst Western Christians. By a sub-stantial offer of spiritual resources Gurus try to make it attractive, claiming that it is fully compatible with Christian convictions. Indeed they have been successful in winning many nominal Christians who had become uncertain about the real content of their own religion and who had craved for an inner enrichment. This makes it necessary to

---

[322] S. RADHAKRISHNAN 1939.

[323] In the report of a meeting of the Ecumenical Association of Third World Theologi-ans (EATWoT) in New Delhi in 1981 we find the following statement: *"People of other religions and creeds reveal some aspects of God's will and message for our time. Just as we Christians recognize the working of God in the events of Jewish history, so we must also learn to recognize the presence of God amongst the oppressed of other religions, who are fighting for their full humanity in the Third World today. Their sacred writings and traditions are also a source for us. If we consider this divine reve-lation, we are led to realize that the term 'people of God' must be extended in order not only to include the believers of other religions, but the whole of humanity – all those to whom the God of the Bible wants to bestow life and self-realization."* L. Wiedemann (ed.) 1983, p 131.

[324] S.J. SAMARTHA 1985, pp. 3-9.

[325] Wesley ARIARAJAH 1991. – Tosh ARAI / Wesley ARIARAJAH, (eds.) 1989.

make a clear evaluation of Hinduism with its ways of salvation in the perspective of Biblical revelation.

In order to pass a substantiated judgment it is important to juxtapose the corresponding key concepts of Hinduistic and Christian doctrine. We shall concentrate on five themes: Divinity, Anthropology, Creation, History and Salvation.

1. The Concept of God

In *Hinduism* God (i.e. Brahman) is, ultimately, not a personal but a neutral reality. This is identical with the universe in spite of its apparent diversity. In describing the Vedanta concept of God or divinity, Rudolf Otto – in reference to Shankara – has coined the term "theopanism"[326] (God is all). By that he wants to say that only the Godhead possesses reality. Brahman is not a dimension of creation; on the contrary, only God is there. The world emanates from that divine reality in order to become submerged in it as it eventually returns to it. The Hindu gods are part of that emanation. Thus their personalities do not have ontological reality.

In the *Biblical doctrine of God* He is a person who stands as a sovereign over against the world created by Him. He does not diffuse Himself into nature, as is thought in pantheism. Nor is the world absorbed by Him, as would be the case in theopanism. God remains independent as Creator and Preserver of the world; likewise He remains absolutely sovereign over against the history of mankind. He never could become identified with that history, as is done in process theology. Human beings are responsible to Him personally.

2. Anthropology

In *Hinduism* the human personality does not own ultimate reality. Man in his distinct essence and personality is only a sensual perception, blurred by *Maya*. Man's true self, Atman, is identical with Brahman; there is no I-Thou relationship between God and man. Consequently Hinduism does not acknowledge the sinfulness of man for that would mean an insult not only to man but also to God himself.

In *Biblical understanding,* man stands in an essential, close relationship with God. He does so on account of his being created in God's image. But this likeness is a created one; it does not mean identity. The

---

[326] Cf. Friederich HEILER [3]1980, pp. 250 f.

creational vis-à-vis between God and man is sharpened by man's sinful separation from God. On account of this, man is unable to uphold communion with God; his separation has to be overcome by an initiative from God's side. But even when this happens, the personal vis-à-vis is not removed by a melting into oneness. Rather, man remains subjected to God and his basic attitude is loving obedience and adoration.

3. Creation

For the *Hindu* the world does not have a reality in itself. This applies to nature, history and social community. Accordingly, it is not worthwhile for man to interfere actively in the world in order to shape, change and preserve it for the product of such activity does not possess abiding relevance. Only by the concept of *Karma* can worldly activity become envisaged. Even then the meaning of such action is not beneficial to the illusionary world as such; it is rather a help for man's self-liberation from karma. Thus it becomes difficult for Hindus to find a persuasive motivation for social engagement. Neo-Hinduism is only now trying that but it remains difficult to overcome the ancient Hindu tradition of escapism and to change Hindu mentality into a positive acceptance of secular duties.

In *Biblical perspective* the invisible and the visible universe were created by God out of nothing (Gen 1:1; Hebrews 11:3) by the Word of God. It is subject to him in essential difference from him (Is 64:7) and is in no way part of Him or identical to Him (1 Tim 6:14-16). God loves His creation (John 3:16). The created world is both real (Is. 48:13) and originally good. In its present condition after the Fall it bears the germ of decay and death in itself; but God sustains it by his fatherly benevolence in view of its future redemption and complete renewal (Hab. 2:14; Hebr. 1:3).

4. Time and History

Time, too, does not possess reality in *Hinduism*. Brahman is resting, unchangeable perfection.

Accordingly, history has no definite goal towards which it moves. World history is embedded in a cyclical movement of emerging and vanishing. The major historical cycles are connected with the revolution of the stars. Historical events, therefore, do not have an abiding significance; everything is cyclical, without goal or end.

In *Biblical faith*, on the other hand, time plays an important role.[327] Of course, our human concepts and measures of time become relative before the eternal God (Psalm 90:4). Yet earthly times contain meaningful events which happen at very specific, appointed moments (*kairos*). Moreover, history is moving towards a definite goal set by God himself. This is the meaning of eschatology, the doctrine of the endtimes. It is the historical task of man to seize the appointed times in order to find his salvation in them. Man lives only once and after that Judgment is awaiting him. Therefore it is necessary for the Christian to be prepared for death by being in a state of reconciliation with God.

5. Salvation

In *Hinduism,* the concept of *Moksha* means existentially to realize the essential oneness of the individual soul with the divine universal reality. This is the condition for aspiring to the reunification between *atman* with *brahman*. Moksha is anticipated here in life in the form of the mystical union, the experience of *sahmadi*. It is perfected when man is liberated from samsara, the compulsory reincarnation. The way towards it is the removal of the misty veil, *maya*. This happens when the seeker has arrived at the true understanding of his own essence, after having striven for self-realization through the various ways of yoga exercises. Man is able to attain his self-realization by his own power. Help from outside may give guidance but the way towards one's salvation must be accomplished by oneself.

In contrast to this, according to the *Bible,* salvation is the reinstallation of the man into his filial fellowship with God and the brotherly relation with his neighbours which were broken by sin. This reconciliation cannot be accomplished from the side of man. He is in need of the forgiveness of his sins by God against whom he trespassed. Yet forgiveness has been truly prepared for him by Christ's vicarious death on the cross. The new life, likewise, is imparted to him by grace alone through the regenerating power of the Holy Spirit.

Thus the way of salvation is the way of God coming down to man. Man's participation in his redemption is not an active performance of meritorious works; it is a passive reception of grace by faith, which enables him as a regenerated child of God to fulfil His commandments in obedience.[328]

---

[327] Oscar CULLMANN [3]1962, pp. 60-68.
[328] Bishop S. KULANDRAN 1964. – David F. WELLS 1978: pp. 23-35.

To summarize this: *In Hinduism, man's salvation is within the reach of his own exercise,* basically independent of particular moments and divine interventions.

In Christianity, salvation is inseparably connected with the unique person and accomplished work of Jesus Christ and it is confined to this one and only offer of God the Father. A repetition of God's historical act of salvation is excluded and so is its suggested completion by the offers of other religions.

Conclusion
Authentic Christian Spirituality Amidst a New Age Mentality

The appeal of Neo-Hinduism to the contemporary Western mind is based mainly on its offer of a "spirituality in depth." Ever since the appearance of Swami Vivekananda in Chicago in 1893, Indian gurus have criticized the people of Europe and America for their lack of spirituality. They say we have lost it due to the secularising effects of our post-enlightenment civilization. It is remarkable and alarming that some Christian leaders have not only confirmed this criticism but are inclined to accept the Indian spiritual offer without considering whether it is really compatible with our own Christian faith. Many seem to have forgotten that the Church, in her Biblical tradition, has access to a fountain of spiritual riches which is far more genuine and helpful than that stale water which is found in the cisterns of South Asian religions. Here the complaint of the Lord through His prophet Jeremiah (2:13) applies:

"My people have committed two sins:
They have forsaken me, the spring of living water,
and have dug their own cisterns,
broken cisterns that cannot hold water."

I want, therefore, to conclude this chapter on Neo-Hindu Missions in Christian countries with a concise theological statement. I shall, in 12 theses, try to point out the contrast between genuine Christian spirituality and the treacherous offer of a syncretistic, Hindu-inspired spirituality. It is also meant to be a help for diacritical discernment between the two.

1. Genuine Christian spirituality is a piety which originates from the Holy Spirit. It is the Spirit who proceeds from God the Fa-

ther; it is that Holy Spirit who at Pentecost was poured out on the Church by God's Son Jesus Christ on account of His completed work of atonement (Acts 2:33).

2. The Holy Spirit must never be confused with the subconscious dimension of the human mind. Even less must He be confused with spiritual forces of other religions or ideologies. Therefore we have to observe the intimate tie between the Spirit and the Word of God; this may not be undermined by appealing to an uncontrollable mystic experience of religious experts, past or present.

3. True Christian Spirituality directs our eyes to look constantly on Jesus Christ, our heavenly Lord and Saviour, and Him alone (Hebrews 12:2; Matthew 17:8).

4. Spirituality is a gift which must not be considered apart from its donor and the purpose for which He gives it to us. It is not permitted to be utilized for purely human, inner-worldly purposes, lest we are misled into magic.

5. The Church finds the centre and fountain of her life not in herself but in her heavenly Head (Eph 1:22; Col 1:18). Every day she has to be judged and directed by His living Word found in the Bible.

6. Genuine Christian Spirituality is given to us on account of our being pardoned sinners and children of God. We are included in the vital fellowship of the triune God and connected with that flow of love that unites the three divine persons: Father, Son and Holy Spirit from eternity into eternity (John 14:23; 15:26; 17:21). Christian Spirituality, thus, bears a *Trinitarian* character. It elevates us together with all invisible and visible creatures of God to praise Him as our Creator, Redeemer and Sanctifier.

7. The condition for a new breakthrough of vibrant spiritual life is a deepened awareness of our sinfulness. It comes from a shaken conscience, pierced by the judging law of God and consoled by the glad tidings of God's mercy on us for the sake of Jesus Christ. This is the experience of all historic and contemporary revival movements.

8. The Christian is always in danger of being swept away by the spirit of the present age. This applies particularly to our age of mass communication. It is easy to fall prey to the demonic wave

of contemporary antichristian currents. That makes us guilty of an unconscious participation in the general ethical and religious decay. Therefore, a genuine Christian Spirituality can only come forth as the fruit of a movement of repentance that purifies the Church of Jesus Christ.

9. The best thing we can do in order to experience a wave of spiritual renewal is to implore the Lord earnestly to pour out on His people the spirit of grace and supplication (Zech 12:10).

10. Christians must never forget that in the invisible, transcendent sphere, there are two forces directed against each other which we must not confuse. One is the Work of God and His Holy Spirit, administered by His holy angels. The other is the work of the devil and his demonic host (Rev. 12:7f.).

11. There wages an unmitigated war between the spirits, in which human beings, too, first of all Christians, are involved (Eph 6:10 ff.). From both sides spiritual influences proceed that try to penetrate us with the vital principle of their respective sources: God or Satan.

    The term "spirituality," therefore, is dangerously ambiguous. In Neo-Hinduism it is used on the basic assumptions of its monistic world-view. Therefore any dynamic enhancement of our human existence is welcomed as an enrichment.

    Consequently, we have to distinguish clearly between the personality of the Holy Spirit, the personality of the human spirit and the personality of the transcendent spiritual forces. We must never dissolve that distinction by using the term "spirituality" to denote an impersonal, cosmic or deep psychological vital force.

12. The supreme and only reliable standard for testing the spirits whether they are from God or not, is the infallible Word of God, the Bible. Its centre is Jesus Christ, crucified for our sins and raised to life for our justification (Romans 4:25).

Chapter 10
Neo-Buddhism –
The Fascination with the Dalai Lama

Introduction

One of the most dramatic experiences I had as a professor at Tue-bingen University was the ominous Dalai Lama controversy in Spring Term 1988. My theological Faculty holds the privilege of bestowing the prestigious *Leopold-Lucas prize*, as an annual award, upon persons who have distinguished themselves by outstanding academical contri-butions to promote the values of humanity and inter-cultural under-standing. In 1988, the faculty followed the recommendation to bestow the *Leopold-Lucas* prize upon the XIV. *Dalai Lama* for his peaceful policy in handling the Tibetan annexation by China (1950) and for his world-wide efforts to foster harmony between people of all races and religions.

A small minority felt that regardless of the noble character of the Dalai Lama it would be awkward for a protestant theological faculty to honour the head of a non-Christian religion who is worshipped by his followers like a god. Sadly, our appeals to reconsider the decision failed. Therefore we held a worship service of repentance and prayer during the very hour when the ceremony took place in the university's festival hall. When this was noted, my colleagues reacted in fury. I was rebuked for having acted disloyally and damaging the public reputation of our theological faculty. In spite of being ostracized, I remained defi-ant. I regarded the recorded reproach as a document of honour; I framed it and placed it on the wall of my study room. Like Peter and John, I rejoiced that we *"were counted worthy to suffer dishonour for the name"* (Acts 5:41).

This was the first time that I was confronted existentially with the challenge of the Buddhist religion to our once-Christian Europe. I also discovered the ignorance of German theologians about the essence of Buddhism, particularly in its Tantristic form, which had led them to such a naïve assessment. Today I wonder whether such ignorance might likewise prevail in other regions of the world-wide Church, in-cluding Korea, where these two religions live in such close proximity. In April 2003, an analogous event happened in Seoul at *Ewha Univer-*

sity: On the initiative of Mrs. Kyung-Hyun Chung, the Vietnamese Buddhist monk, *Thich Nat Than,* was invited to address the student body at their chapel service, to the dismay of the confessing evangelical members of the academic community.

I. Buddhism –
Self-remedy for Attaining Inner Peace

Like Islam and unlike Hinduism, Buddhism owes its origin to the work of one historic person, the prince *Gautama Siddharta,*[329] who lived in North India in the years from about 566 to 486 B.C. On account of his dramatic life story which climaxed in his famous *bodhi* (enlightenment), he came to be known by his religious title *Buddha,* the *Enlightened One.* He went around practising his experience based on the doctrine of *dharma,* initiated others into it and gathered his faithful followers in his *sangha* (monastic community). His teaching reflects his own realization of the insufficiency of all earthly pleasure and accomplishment. He taught that to strive for such vanities only increases the craving for more and leads into suffering *(dukkha).* Gautama's (or *Sakyamuni's*) spiritual insight gained at his "enlightenment" can be summarized in the *four noble truths*:[330]

I.   All life is essentially suffering.

II. The cause of suffering is thirst = *sitya* or craving for pleasure. Redemption, accordingly, is to rid oneself of such thirst by complete detachment and accepting the ultimate nothingness or emptiness - *sunyatta - behind* the deceptive world of appearances.

III. The removal of thirst leads to the elimination of suffering.

IV. The way towards such elimination is the *eightfold path*.[331] This consists of rules for self-discipline, five moral commands and instructions for meditation in ascending degrees.

Buddhism actually began as a distinct new school of thought in Hinduism.[332] It retained most of its central concepts, like *karma,*

---

[329] Helmuth von GLASENAPP 1963, pp. 69-80. – M. LADNER 1948. – H. BECK ⁴1958.

[330] *Vinayapitika, Mahavagga* 1,6. – Mahathera NYANAPONIKA 1981: pp. 2 ff.

[331] *Majhima-Nikaya* 44 A. Bertholet (ed.) 1929: pp 70 ff. – Gerhard ROSENKRANZ 1960.

[332] S. RADHAKRISHNAN 1955.

dharma, samsara, samadhi, bimoksha, sangham. The major difference is that Buddha eliminated the socio-religious caste system and, more than that, the concept of an ontological reality both of *brahman* and of *atman*, the individual soul. In its initial form, it is a religion without belief in a supreme eternal God which really means philosophical atheism. Buddhism teaches *anattan* (no-self). The human self is regarded as simply a temporary and transitory complex of several "factors of being there." They determine the present phase of existence. However, they are dissolved in death and will be re-structured in renewed forms of incarnation. This happens when one arrives at perfect enlightenment and complete detachment is achieved. Only then will the human being vanish into the *Nirvana*, the "nowhere" or "nothingness." That is an event which corresponds with the merging of the *atman* into the *brahman* in Hinduism. It is disputed amongst scholars whether the Nirvana really means nothingness,[333] which would classify Buddhism as metaphysical Nihilism. Perhaps the Nirvana is the incomprehensible and inexpressible?[334] In any case, we can characterize the essence of original Buddhism as the attempt of serious truth-seekers to find inner peace for their worried minds by making strong efforts of detachment and spiritual concentration. In other words, it is a *self-remedy to gain inner peace.*

Historically, Buddhism was divided up into three or four major schools or "confessions."[335]

The original teaching of Gautama Siddharta was preserved faithfully, as its monastic adherents claim, by the *first* school, that of **Theravada Buddhism**,[336] the tradition of the elders. Their rivals in the school of *Mangasikha* nicknamed it **Hinanyana**; the "little vessel" for it accommodates only individual souls striving for their own salvation. Theravada-Buddhism survived particularly in South East Asian countries.

The *second* school consequently called itself **Mahayana Buddhism**,[337] the "large vessel," for there is room for many on board. It promises to save many people by making the way to salvation easier

---

[333] ROSENKRANZ, op. cit. pp. 37 f.

[334] Suttanipata 1092-1095, in: A. Bertholet (ed.), op. cit. 11, p. 111. – G.R. WELBON 1968. – H. v. GLASENAPP 1996: pp. 147-152. – L.W. KING 1975: pp. 37-53.

[335] Hans W. SCHUMANN 1976. – Idem 1963.

[336] Moritz WINTERNITZ (ed.) 1929. – Dieter SCHLINGHOFF 1962.

[337] R. von MURALT 1956. – Dieter SCHLINGHOFF 1963.

for them. This is provided by the assistance of **Bodhisattvas**,[338] smaller semi-buddhas, who in their ascetic endeavour have already reached the experience of *samadhi*. They are driven by compassion for other creatures which are still suffering from their miserable karma in the never ending circle of samsara. Therefore they vowed not to enter into *Nirvana* until these other souls had reached enlightenment as well. A bodhisattva is a mighty, high ranking being who is regarded as a metaphysical saviour. Out of thankful attachment, their followers regard them and even worship them like gods. Some of the bodhisattvas have already died physically but invisibly they are present and available. Others are still alive and appear as human beings, *super-gurus*. That corresponds to the Hindu notion of *avataras*. One of them is the Dalai Lama.

A specific *third* type of Mahayana is **Zen-Buddhism**.[339] It originated in China (*chin*) but developed fully in several sects in *Japan*. Characteristic of Zen-B is a very austere practice of meditation, undergirded by a corresponding posture of immovable sitting (*Za-Zen*).[340] The practice of *Zen* can be learned only under the direction of a spiritual master who exercises a rigid discipline.[341] He suggests to his adept a *kuan*. That is an irrational riddle which assists the meditation to get rid of all attachment to empiric concepts. Thus he or she will finally experience the great universal oneness. Here all distinct appearances and notions, even the difference between life and death, are dissolved. The Japanese name for such enlightenment is *satori*. Zen is widely acclaimed as a means to overcome psychological tensions, to acquire perfect concentration and provide fitness for one's duties in secular life.

The fourth school of Buddhism is **Vadjrayana**, the "diamond vessel," often referred to as *Tantrayana*. It is derived from one of the major Hindu yoga-systems, *tantra yoga*, which is the way of ecstasy. This is reached by a variety of highly emotional experiences in dancing, drumming and singing, including sensual orgies of a sexual nature. It is widely developed in Tibet,[342] in continuation of the original *shamanist Bon-religion*. In section IV we shall go more into detail.

---

[338] H.v. GLASENAPP 1963: pp. 114-117. – H. DAYAL 1970.

[339] D.T. SUZUKI 1927. – Idem 1955. – Idem 1972. – A. W. WATTS 1961.– I. MIURA and R.F. SASAKI 1965. – Enomiya LASSALLE 1966 – H. DUMOULIN 1976.

[340] Peter BEYERHAUS 1972c, pp. 44-53

[341] Gerta ITTAL ²1968.

[342] Helmuth von GLASENAPP 1963: p. 94. – G. ROSENKRANZ 1960: pp. 94-97.

In **Korea** today, all types of Buddhism can be found, often combined with each other. The major traditional form is Mahayana.

Buddhism has about 300 million followers worldwide. It is the fourth largest religion. On account of its mission-activities and its appeal to the post-modernist Western mind, it is one of the greatest spiritual challenges to the Christian Church today.

II. Apparent Similarities and Essential Differences between Christianity and Buddhism[343]

A. Similarities[344]

There are some analogies in the biographies of Buddha and Jesus. Both, reportedly, were born under miraculous circumstances. Both had experienced a period of temptation and a calling to their ministry. Both performed miracles, one of them of the same nature - walking on the water.

In their spiritual diagnosis of the misery of present human life, Buddhism and Christianity agree in the "radical insufficiency of this shifting world"[345] on which consequently, humans should not fix their minds. Both religions encourage their adherents to search for and find true peace of an internal nature.

Ethics correspond widely when severed from their frame of reference. Buddha's five commandments reflect the six commandments of the second tablet of the Decalogue. Both Buddha and Jesus find the essence of the law in love. *Maitri* and *Karuna* (compassion and kindness) appear similar to *agape* (unselfish love for one's neighbour). They are, however, different in regard to their source and to their goal. These differences reflect the atheistic character of Buddhism on the one hand and the character of the image of God the Father in Jesus Christ on the other.

---

[343] L.W. KING 1963. – Hans KÜNG / H. BECHERT 1990. – Ursula von MANGOLDT 1959.

[344] Gustav MENSCHING 1978.

[345] Walter M. ABBOT (ed.) [10]1966, p. 662.

Biblical and Mahayana eschatology have parallels in the hope of a most enjoyable state which the obedient soul finds after death – Paradise in the Bible and the *Pure Land* in Buddhism.[346]

Some practices of ascetics and meditation are similar in Buddhist and Catholic/Orthodox monastic spirituality. In *Amida- (Amithaba-)* Buddhism, there is a concept of divine mercy and concern for salvation which is strikingly similar to the Biblical doctrine of grace without works. The suggestion has been made that both Amida Buddhism and Hindu *Bhakti yoga* show traits of Christian influences.[347] It would require a special study to discern both the similarities and the abiding differences. This, however, does not lie within the focus of this chapter. Quite a number of Christian theologians have already dealt with this, including *Karl Barth*.[348] It might suffice to say here that Amida faith is ultimately a projection of the attitude of the seeker himself, whilst in Christianity it is aroused by an objective reality coming from a personal, truly existing God. Secondly the *bodhisattva Amida* is a myth, whereas Jesus Christ is a historic person who eternally lives in a glorified state in heaven. However, the Christian missionary will gladly find particular points of contact in the "pure land" religion as well as in the other parallels pointed out.

B. Differences

All schools of Buddhism differ decisively from Christianity. Just like Hinduism they deny the reality of creation, of the existence of distinct eternal human souls and the meaning of time and history. Moreover, Buddhism in any form is emphatically **atheistic**.[349] Consequently, the soteriologies are entirely different. In Buddhism, the root cause of human misery is seen in self-deception concerning the vanity of empirical pleasures. In Christianity it is the separation of the sinner from a holy God. Consequently, salvation in Buddhism is ultimately nihilistic whereas in Christianity it is everlasting life in childlike fellowship with a loving Father through His Son in the Holy Spirit.

---

[346] Chr. LANGER-KANEKO 1986.

[347] H. HAAS 1912: pp. 1-13.

[348] Karl BARTH [1]1939 1960: vol. I/2, Ev., pp. 372-377. – G. HOSHINO 1956. – H. HAAS 1912: pp. 1-13. – Sh. BANDO 1973. – Fritz BURI, 1975: pp. 274-288. – G. MENSCHING 1936: pp. 339-350. – H. BUTSCHKUS 1940. – H. DUMOULIN [2]199,: pp. 99 f. – Nicholae ACHIMESCU 1993: pp. 195 – 299.

[349] Helmuth von GLASENAPP 1966: pp. 43-54.

C. The Resurgence of Buddhism[350]

A. In Asia

In most Asian countries renascent Buddhism was a corollary of the end of Western colonial imperialism. Buddhists of all schools now gained a reinforced sense of mission.[351] That, in fact, had always been essential to this religion since it was not ethnically tied to the social caste system.

What facilitates the rapid cross-cultural spread of Buddhism is the *strategy of adaptation* practised by all important Buddhist proselytizers in Eastern countries. They do not shun apparent syncretism. On the contrary, they even encourage the indigenous people to retain their national deities and spirits including the rituals of approach. Therefore regional Buddhism can show itself with very different features, giving the impression that these are separate religions. Behind this, however, there are the basic metaphysical concepts which provide a basis for world-wide Buddhist ecumenicity. I was amazed when a very erudite Korean Buddhist monk assured me that scholarly examination had proved the basic "orthodoxy" of the Dalai Lama!

Buddhist "missions" have to cope with one hereditary difficulty when they try to rival Christian missions. That is the other-worldliness of Buddha's philosophical system and his mysticism. *Neo-Buddhism* has taken up this challenge by copying the methods of Christian missions, sometimes even in such detail as adopting Christian hymns by substituting the name of Buddha for that of Jesus![352] There are Buddhist Sunday schools, orphanages, clinics, feeding projects, high schools, all with close similarities to the Christian models. The attempt to turn from 'inward looking' into 'external outreach' finds its programmatic articulation in the formation of 'engaged Buddhism'. Today it is organized world-wide in the *International Movement of Engaged Buddhists*[353] (IMEB).

Buddhists have developed their own sense of religious superiority. They emphasize the depth of their spiritual meditation and the peace-

---

[350] Ernst BENZ 1963.

[351] G. ROSENKRANZ 1960: pp. 54-57. – H.-W. GENSICHEN 1959. – Georg VICEDOM 195, pp. 128-132. – Maurice PERCHERON 1979, pp. 139-143.

[352] Werner SCHILLING 1979, pp. 128-143.

[353] Arnold KOTLER 1996.

fulness[354] of their doctrine. Therefore we meet vocal Buddhists in all Inter-Faith ventures, as e.g. the World Conference of Religions for Peace (WCRP) with its regional and national headquarters. In WCRP meetings, Buddhists of all brands pose as the really credible advocates of peace, in contrast to Christianity, in the name of which, they say, many wars have been fought or are still fought today, e.g. in Iraq and other countries. They do concede that there have been historical wars amongst the Buddhist people as well, and particularly in Tantristic Buddhism you frequently find paintings of an angry Buddha exercising his wrath against the evildoers.

B. In the West

Gautama Buddha predicted to his disciples that 2,500 years after his death his doctrine would be preached in the West. This prediction is being fulfilled today in full scale. All four major schools participate in it.[355]

Already during the 19th century, under the influence of Romanticism, philosophical **Theravada thought** influenced the philosophies of *Arthur Schopenhauer* (1788-1860) and *Friedrich Nietzsche* (1844-1900) in Germany and the compositions of Richard Wagner (1813-83). The *Theosophical Society* (founded in 1875 by Mrs. H.P. Blavatzky[356] and H. S. Olcot) introduced Buddhism systematically in Europe and America.

Towards the middle of the 20th century Japanese **Zen Masters** like *D. T. Suzuki* (1870-1966)[357] spread their system in the West which was met with great interest. Later, Roman Catholic monasteries endeavoured an inter-religious exchange with Zen Buddhist monasteries in Japan.

Today, under the influence of the New Age movement, the Western focus has shifted towards **Tantric Buddhism**.[358]

Tibet started to exercise a magnetic attraction on the phantasy of Western people,[359] many of whom thought that this was a country that

---

[354] V. TRIMONDI 1999, pp. 597-599.

[355] Stephen BATCHELOR 1994.

[356] Marion MEADE 1987. – H. J. SPIERENBURG 1991. – John SYMONDS 1959.

[357] D. T. SUZUKI 1927. – Idem 1955. – Idem 1968. – Idem: 1974. – Idem 1988.

[358] Shashi Bhusan DAGUPTA 1974. – Julius EVOLA: "What Tantrism means to modern Western Civilization," in: East and West I, No 1. – Alex WAYMAN 1973.

[359] Peter BISHOP 1993.

enjoys an original paradisiacal peace in harmony with the spirit world. It became popular to decorate one's home and even public buildings with colourful Tibetan paintings and Mandalas. Some people even went on a pilgrimage to Tibet. The negative reasons were found in the aftermaths of technological modernism and consumerism - unrest, stress, anxiety, loss of meaning, and search for internal and external peace.

One influential propagandist of Tantric Buddhism was the Dane *Ole Nydahl*. He managed to establish 220 *dharmadhatu*-centres in Western countries. In America, actresses *Tina Turner* and *Shirley MacLaine* professed themselves Buddhists.

However, no single person has done so much to introduce Tantristic Buddhism to the entire Western world as the present *Dalai Lama*.

D. Tibetan Tantristic-Buddhism

1. Historic Religious Background

Mahayana Buddhism reached Tibet via China and Nepal in the middle of the 7th century AD.[360] One hundred years later, the Tibetan king *Tisong Detsa* became interested in Vajrayana Buddhism. He invited the Indian mystic and magician *Padamansabhavam,* to come to Tibet. The latter is still venerated by Tibetans, even more than Buddha himself. There is a statue of him in *Dharamsala*, the exile capital of the Dalai Lama. Shortly after that, the famous guru *Rimpoche* founded the first monastery. They adapted their Tantric Buddhism to the indigenous *Bon religion*[361] in its "Black" or "pure type," which was a mixture of Animism and Shamanism. This was concerned with appeasing ancestor spirits and demons. In the 1920s, a German traveller, Alexandra David-Neél, underwent several ritual initiations and was even called a Lama woman. She observed: "Tibet is the cradle of sorcery and occult sciences."[362] For the Tibetans, interaction with demons and spirits is necessary to attain higher stages of consciousness and acquire superior magical power in contest with their rivals. The Dalai Lama, too, has shown such extra-ordinary capabilities, especially in clairvoyance.

---

[360] C. Austine WADDELL 1895.

[361] Helmut HOFFMANN 1956.

[362] Quoted in: T. and G. BALDIZZONE 1995, p. 51.

2. Lamaism

Until 1000 AD, Tantristic Buddhism, better known as *Lamaism*, has been the ruling religion of Tibet. It was characterized by the dominant role of the *Lamas*. Originally they were shamans (necromancers) who called on spirits or exorcized them. Then the Lamas became Buddhist priests. Today the term is identical with *guru but* in the capacity of the former, they are the mouthpieces and representatives of Buddha.

The two highest ruling Lamas were traditionally the *Dalai Lama* and the *Panchen Lama*. Dalai is a Mongol word, meaning "ocean" so he was the ocean-like Lama or embodiment of divine wisdom. He ruled as a political king in *Lhasa*. The Panchen Lama was the high priest. The Dalai Lama incarnates Avalokiteshvara, who was the highest God in the North Indian pantheon and the highest bodhisattva in Buddhism. That means, he is a redeemer who mediates between human beings and the universe of spirits. The Panchen Lama incarnated *Maitreya Buddha*, the bodhisattva of prosperity and also the coming ultimate Buddha. When the last Panchen Lama *Rimpoche* was murdered by the red Chinese after 1950, the present Dalai Lama, who is regarded as the 14th incarnation of Avalokiteshvara, combined both offices, the political and the spiritual, in a personal union.

Another important role is played by the state oracle, the *nechi kuten*. This is a most powerful *medium*. Animated by rhythmic music, dances and incense, he falls into a trance. The Tibetan god *Pehar* appears to him and makes him predict the outcome of major ventures and of the future in general. The present Dalai Lama retains this institution and relies fully on it. He never takes an important step before he has consulted the *nechi kuten*. That means that the exilic politics of the Tibetans is fully directed by spiritistic forces.

3. Mandala and Kalachacra

The central Tibetan Ritual since the 10th century has been the *Kalachacra*. In fact, the present Dalai Lama refers to his own religion as *Kalachacra*[363] and makes extensive use of it wherever he goes. *Kala* means time, *chacra* wheel (or knot). This time-wheel contains at its centre cosmic energy and through the ritual this energy is transformed

---

[363] DALAI LAMA XIV 1985.

and transmitted for the purpose of gaining enlightenment, both personally and corporately.[364]

The means to do this is the construction and meditation upon or
rather visualization of the **Mandala** (circle).[365] A Mandala is a mosaic,
laid in colours in sand. A good Mandala is highly artistic, laid by
monks who are experts. It may be called a "cosmogram," being a symbolic presentation of the universe. It is a spiritual palace, the abode of
the gods and spirit-powers that are invoked and visualized. The ornaments are arranged in concentric figuration. The inner ornaments represent the *microcosmos* (humanity); the outer figures stand for the *mac-
rocosmos* (universe). By visualizing the Mandala, the initiated spectator
experiences enlightenment. He realizes his oneness with the universe
and receives cosmic energy, passed to him by the spirits, for the universe is conceived as being filled with spirits. A proper visualization
can lift the spectator up to the 7th degree of *bodhisattvahood*, because
the energy of the entire cosmos is collected in the Mandala by the
Kalachacra ritual.

Today, the painting of mandalas is introduced in the fine arts education of Western schools. Already in the primary stage it is offered as a
new form of fanciful painting. In ordinary cases this may be religiously
neutral, but if a teacher has acquired guru faculties, that teacher can
abuse it by using the painting as a means of initiation into Eastern spirituality. S/he may be excited to do this when observing the proceedings
of the popular Dalai Lama. S/he lays *mandalas* not only privately but
also publicly wherever he performs. In a naïve interpretation he is simply adding to the exotic fascination with his appearance but there is
more behind it.

E. The Spiritistic Strategy of the Dalai Lama

1. His Biography

"His Holiness" the Dalai Lama, as he is addressed not only by his
Tibetan subjects but also at official functions in other countries, was
born in 1935 in a Tibetan village as a farmer's child.[366] His civil name
is *Tenzin Gyatso*. After the death of the then ruling Dalai Lama who

---

[364] Llarampa Ngawang DHARGYEY 1985. – Michael HENSS 1985. – Alex WAY-
MAN 1973.

[365] Martin BRAUEN 1992. – Carl Gustav JUNG 1981.

[366] DALAI LAMA XIV 1964.

was regarded as the 13[367] incarnation of the god *Avalokiteshvara*,[367] the lamas searched for a boy who by distinct similarities could be identified as his 14th incarnation and consequently become the new Dalai Lama. In 1937 he was eventually discovered in the person of little Tenzin. Tenzin was taken from his home and placed in a monastery to be educated and prepared for his future office by Lamaist monks. Soon the Tibetan people started to adore and worship him as *Kundu* (the loving Buddha) and their designated divine king. Tragically in 1950,[368] Tibet was annexed by Red China. The Tibetans tried to struggle with arms for their independence but in vain. Their new Dalai Lama strongly advised them to adopt a policy of non-violence. When the Chinese suppression increased and the Panchen Lama was killed, the Dalai Lama and his hierarchy escaped to Northern India in 1959. They established their exile capital in *Dharamsala* on the slopes of the Himalayas.

2. His Religious and Political World "Mission"

Very soon, the Dalai Lama embarked upon extensive travelling, pleading the cause of his oppressed people in all Western countries. He combined his diplomatic mission with a religious one. Wherever he appeared, mass meetings were convened which he addressed. In New York, Chicago and Indianapolis, between 5000-7000 people listened attentively to his message of tolerance and the basic oneness of all religions.[369]. They were attracted by the radiance of his spiritual personality which combined humility with kindness and humour.

His oral presentation was illustrated by the laying of Mandalas on every suitable occasion, even at the most unlikely sites, e.g. in the World Trade Centre! To this he gave an interpretation by coining as his watchword: **Kalachacra for world peace!**[370]

In his messages he adapted himself to the post-modernist mentality of the West, emphasising values of harmony, tolerance, creativity and spirituality.[371] He advocated brotherhood between cultures, nations and religions.

---

[367] "On the dissemination of the belief in the Dalai Lama as a manifestation of the Bodhisattva Avalokiteshvara," in: Acta Asiatica. Bulletin of the Institute of Eastern Culture, No. 64, Tokyo 1993.

[368] C. Melvyn GOLDSTEIN 1989.

[369] DALAI LAMA XIV 1996. – Idem 1997.

[370] DALAI LAMA XIV 1993.

[371] Marcia KEEGAN 1981.

Seen as a champion for peace on the foundation of religion, he was invited to meet Pope John Paul II on several occasions. On October 27th 1986 John Paul II convened the historic Prayer of World Religions for Peace in Assisi. He assigned to the Dalai Lama the honourable place of sitting next to him – to the left - in front of the Franciscan basilica. In 1988, the Dalai Lama was awarded the Leopold Lucas prize in Tübingen and the following year the Nobel Peace prize in Oslo.

Such recognition greatly enhanced the importance attached to his personality and mission. There was hardly a major religious meeting to which he was not invited, e.g. twice to the bi-annual German Protestant "Kirchentag" (Church Mass Assembly), to Munich in 1991 and to Berlin in 2003,[372] where tens of thousands of people hailed him as the bearer of hope.

It is hard to say what actually is the substance of such hope. It does not lie in the conceptual content of his message for that is very elementary or even common-place morality and wisdom. "Hope" in his case is rather a mental fascination both of individuals and of great multitudes which come in contact with him. With his kind smile, he seems to be the embodiment of his message of mercy, oneness and optimism. From his personality a mysterious spiritual energy seems to emanate. For many, this becomes all the more irresistible, the closer they get to him.

3. Evangelical Concerns about the Dalai Lama

a. First Changes in Public Opinion

The acceptance of the Dalai Lama within Western countries and churches specifically, seems to be general. To reject him would be considered an act of intolerance and lack of concern particularly in view of the tragic fate of his Tibetan people and the Dalai Lama's appeasing policy. His attraction appears to be the same, irrespective of nationality, denomination or standard of education of those with whom he comes into contact.

For quite some time, conservative evangelicals seemed to be the only exception. They were branded as fundamentalists. That was my personal experience in connection with the Lucas prize in 1988.

In 1999, however, some thinking people were induced to reconsider their admiration for the Dalai Lama. In that year a thoroughly docu-

---

[372] Wolfgang POLZER 2003, pp. 144 f.

mented volume of more than 700 pages appeared,[373] co-authored by a
German couple who had formerly been deeply initiated adherents of the
Dalai Lama, Victor and Victoria Trimondi.[374] They showed, by an
abundance of material, that there is another side of the Dalai Lama,
known only by those closest to him.

From then on, evangelicals were re-assured and supported in their
concern about the Dalai Lama and the fascination generated by him.

b. His Syncretistic Message

Theologically the message of the Dalai Lama is focussed on the
Eastern thought of the oneness of all particular religions. He sees it
firstly in their common origin, the mystical sense at the bottom of human consciousness. Secondly, it is seen in their common ethos of mutual love and compassion amongst all human beings (*maitri* and *karuna!*). Thirdly, they are assigned a common goal- the future paradisiacal state in a peaceful universal society. It does not matter what particular names and expressions are used to describe that goal. Consequently,
the Dalai Lama sees no point in mission and conversion. Everybody
should remain within the fellowship of his own religion. Their loyalty
to it will be, he says, even deeper on account of the enlightenment
which they receive from him. That, he believes, will help them to understand the real meaning of their traditional faith and will give a re-
laxed conscience to those nominal Christians who have decided to be
initiated by the Dalai Lama.

c. The Deceptiveness of the Dalai Lama's Approach

The claim of the Dalai Lama that his initiation into enlightenment is
religiously neutral **is** fraudulent. In reality it is based wholly on Tantristic concepts. Thus it focuses upon the realm of the spiritual forces in
Buddhist mythology.

Not all Tantristic myths are disclosed in the oral messages or even
books of the Dalai Lama. He is almost silent about the *Shambhala
myth*. Shambhala[375] is a small paradisiacal kingdom hidden in the
heights of the Himalayas. The Dalai Lama believes that it is a place
"which can be seen only by those who have been purified by their kar-

---

[373] V. and V. TRIMONDI 1999.

[374] Their civil names are Herbert and Mariana Röttgen.

[375] Chögyam TRUNGPA 1986. – Edwin BERNBAUM 1982. – Nicholas ROERICH
1988.

mic inclinations."[376] Shambhala will become visible in the end times, when Kalachacra-Tantra has become the official universal religion. A worldwide Buddhist kingdom of peace will then be established. The Dalai Lama is considered to be the forerunner of that eschatological king of Shambhala. Tibetans expect the establishment of that kingdom to be preceded by a final battle between the army of *Ruda Chakrin* (the coming universal redeemer) and the dharma of the barbarian hordes. Thus, in spite of its alleged tolerance, the Kalachacra of DALAI LAMA is ultimately intolerant of all monotheistic religions that do not submit to his dharma.

d. Immorality[377]

In principle, the Dalai Lama teaches ethics based on Buddha's five classical commandments. All moral prescriptions may be set aside, if that helps the person who is initiated to reach a higher stage of enlightenment. Alcohol, some gurus in the West claim, helps them to enlarge their consciousness. Even smuggling and theft can be tolerated under certain circumstances.

Especially disgusting are the *sexual practices* indulged in by many Lamas. According to Tantristic tradition, sexual copulation can be one way of divine communication with the spirits. Admittedly, this is tolerated also by the present Dalai Lama. He does not disclose what his own practices may be or have been. The meaning behind this practice is that the female sex-partner provides spiritual energy to the Lama, who uses her only for that purpose. Thus, after sexual intercourse, she is disregarded like an empty shell which reduces the woman to the status of a mere temporary instrument and disregards her human dignity.

e. Spiritualistic Strategy

We have already referred to the constant practice of the Dalai Lama of laying out Mandalas at any place where he finds an opportunity to celebrate his Kalachacra ritual in public. This is a beautiful ceremony but it has a double religious purpose. One is to initiate the audience attending the ritual into the basic experience of "enlightenment."

The other purpose is to serve the officiating Lama himself. At the end of the ceremony he destroys the Mandala at which point the spiritual energy enshrined in it by visualization and belief enters into his

---

[376] DALAI LAMA 1981. (Quoted in Michael HENSS 1992, p. 136.)
[377] Michael M. BROIDO 1988.

own person. At the same time, symbolically, he takes possession of the building, place or whole region in which the Kalachacra ritual has been performed. All the places where this has been done are connected by the spirit forces which have been invoked. That means a spiritualistic network is knitted which stretches from Dharamsala in North India to European cities like Graz in Austria, New York in America and Cape Town in South Africa. "Kalachacra on behalf of world peace" in fact lays the foundation for the world dominion of the highest Buddha, represented by the Dalai Lama who incarnates him. It should be noted that in Tibetan Tantristic Buddhism, religion and politics are closely connected.

f. Occult Nature

As we have seen, Tantristic Buddhism deals not merely with religious doctrines, mystical experiences, ethical and social utopias. It is in constant contact with spiritual forces. Here the distinction between good and evil matters less than their degree of power. The monistic world-view of Hinduism and Buddhism likewise does not contain an absolute opposition between dark and light forces. In Tantristic religion, every deity has a dual aspect of light and darkness. *Avalokiteshvara* is the highest god of creation but he is also the god of death, similar to *Shiva* in Hinduism. The Dalai Lama, when asked about this, freely admits that his Kalachacra religion has to do with spirits. In Zurich he said in an interview: "We rely on these spirits. They have more than 1000 years of history in Tibet without controversy about it."[378]

However, for the person who contacts such forces or even allows them to possess him/her, this must have serious effects. Psychologically analysed, they result in unrest, anxiety, depression and nightmares. The autobiographical accounts of former adepts of the Dalai Lama give striking accounts of that. Experienced evangelists and counsellors call this an "occult oppression," knowing that it is extremely difficult to deal with.

g. Antichristian Feature

We have spoken about the strange fascination which many people have for the person of the Dalai Lama. It is particularly disquieting that Christians - at least nominal Christians - do not make an exception. He has been hailed jubilantly at Christian mass-meetings as if he was a

---

[378] Zürich Newspaper 23.3. 1998.

saviour sent by God.[379] Even a German female bishop addressed him by the title "Your Holiness." Some even recognised him as a living image of Jesus Christ; others saw the goodness of our divine Father in Heaven streaming through him.

The Dalai Lama is by no means a professing Christian and implicitly refuses the authority of Jesus Christ by reducing him to the status of a *bodhisattva*. Therefore we cannot avoid the conclusion that the Dalai Lama, by making such extraordinary claims, is a forerunner of the Antichrist himself. The coming of this apocalyptic figure is predicted in the Old Testament by Daniel and in the New Testament by Paul and John. Jesus himself warns of him in his eschatological speech on the Mount of Olives (Matthew 24:24; 2 Thess 2:8-9; 1 John 2:18; Rev 13:13).

The true nature of the Antichrist in Biblical perspective is not that he openly opposes Jesus Christ or even persecutes the Church – at least initially. It is, rather, by his words, deeds and charming personality that he imitates Christ. In this way, he is able to deceive many Christians about his identity as we read in 2 Cor 11:4. In verse 14 Paul proceeds to say that *"Satan disguises himself as an angel of light."*

I am fully aware of the fact that it is terrible to pass such a judgment with regard to a living personality. On the human level, he is so akin to ourselves and his tragic fate calls for sympathetic understanding. I have, however, learned from the German reformer, Martin Luther, who described a theological opponent who tried to twist the clear wording of Scripture. Said Luther,"That I call him a devil I do not mind, for I am not referring to the man, but to the spirit that speaks through him." Likewise Jesus himself did not hesitate to command his favourite disciple, Simon, son of Jona, to *"Get behind me, Satan"* (Matth 16:23). It was the same person whom he just had blessed and highly honoured by calling him *Petros*, rock of the Church.

4. Evangelistic Response to Neo-Buddhism[380]

We have arrived at a most serious assessment of Tantristic Neo-Buddhism as represented by the Dalai Lama. Now, finally, we have to

---

[379] Manfred DREYTZA 2000, pp. 15-22.

[380] G. APPLETON 1958. – Werner GENSICHEN 1959. – Gerhard ROSENKRANZ 1941 – D.T. NILES 1967. – Lausanne Committee for World Evangelization: 1980. – Alex G. SMITH 1980.

clarify our approach to the adherents of such a contemporary movement which stands in clear contradiction to the Gospel of Jesus Christ.

1. Again, we have to point out the difference between the spiritual
   construction of the movement and our fellow human beings who
   have been captured by it. We have to denounce the system whilst
   being concerned sympathetically with its followers by meeting them
   in relation to their particular convictions.

2. With regard to Tantristic Lamaism, it is obvious that we should not
   try to demythologize the spirit-world in which its adherents live. On
   the contrary, we shall affirm it in the light of the Bible's demonic
   realism. The reality is that those spirits have been experienced and
   actively manipulated by the Lamas for thousand of years. The "Tibetan Book of the Dead" is used by Western Satanists as a source
   book of occult knowledge. We must not, on the other hand, be
   trapped by the danger of over-estimating and fearing the power of
   those dark forces. We are members of Jesus Christ who in his exor-
   cising ministry and by his victory on the Cross and his Resurrection
   has conquered them all (Matthew 28:18).

3. Negatively, we must point out the spiritual danger into which people
   are running if they allow themselves to be initiated into a Buddhist
   enlightening ceremony. The "light" which is gained thereby does
   not deserve its name. On the contrary, it is a spiritual blindfolding
   and exposure to the forces of darkness.

4. As Christians, we can take advantage of the term *"enlightenment"*
   by reminding ourselves what the Bible tells us about true enlightenment. This is conferred by the Word of God in the power of the
   Holy Spirit, *"the Spirit of Wisdom and of all revelation who enlightens the eyes of our hearts so that we may know what is the hope to
   which God has called us, what are the riches of his glorious inheri-
   tance of the saint, and what is the immeasurable greatness of the
   power in us who believe ... "* (Eph 1:17-19).

5. The Christian alternative to the Buddhist concept of salvation
   should be clearly explained. Salvation cannot be attained by self-
   dissolution through a mental discipline. It is a free gift of God based
   on the atoning sacrifice of His Son, Jesus Christ. By this, that terrible burden is taken away, a problem which Buddhism does not
   really tackle. It is the accusation of a guilty conscience which cannot
   escape the reality of the living God, our supreme Judge. That was

the experience of a young German woman[381] who deserted both her husband and her two children in order to find enlightenment by the guidance of the Dalai Lama. She was constantly haunted by her own conscience. She could not find real peace until finally she found forgiveness through the blood of Jesus Christ which made her abandon the false way of Tantristic initiation and return to her former Christian faith as well as to her family.

6. Buddhism puts as its highest ideal the attainment of absolute emptiness – *sunyata*. The Gospel offers the very opposite of this: Being accepted into the loving fellowship of the triune God, Father, Son and Holy Spirit.

7. The treacherous nature of all imaginary transcendent bodhisattvas like the Asian goddess *Kwan In*[382] as well as the self-acclamation of the Dalai Lama as a tangible bodhisattva, should be unmasked. To achieve this, we need to do more than demonstrate their futility in a negative way. Much more important and persuasive will it be to point to the divine and human person of Jesus Christ. On account of His self-sacrifice under Pontius Pilate, our sins are taken away when we repent and turn to Him. Moreover, he intercedes for us as our heavenly High Priest. At the same time he is near to us in the power of the *Holy Spirit*. He approaches us even tangibly by feeding us spiritually with His body and blood in the sacrament of Holy Communion.

8. Finally, we can give account of the hope which is in us (1 Peter 3:15). It is a hope not primarily in the pleasures of a heavenly paradise, although this is promised to us as well, but it is our ultimate hope which lies in the prospect of being united to God. We are going to see Him eternally and enjoy Him in His heavenly glory (Matthew 5:8).

---

[381] Martin KAMPHUIS 2000, pp. 117-119; 127 f.; 152f; 146 f.
[382] John Blofeld 1988.

Chapter 11

Upholding the Biblical Ethos
against "New Morality"

Introduction

In November 2003, the General Synod of the Protestant Church in Germany (EKD) had to elect a Chairman for its central Council (Ratsvorsitzender) for the next term of six years. The final ballot showed an overwhelming majority for the favourite candidate, Bishop Dr. *Wolfgang Huber* of Berlin. At first, he had declined to run for the election to this highest office of our church as his limited time and strength would compel him to resign from his participation in the State Commission on Ethics, a very important institution of the German Federal Government. Huber had felt that this newly established body had a crucial significance for the parliamentary legislation on issues vital to the future of our German people.

The fact that Chancellor *Gerhard Schroeder* had to create this unprecedented institution indicates that Germany, like other European countries nowadays, finds herself in a difficult situation, arising from the absence of self-evident moral standards. Formerly those were provided by the Biblical ethos which was enshrined in the cultural foundations of the formerly "Christian Occident." However, the validity of this tradition is denied by the majority of political parties which today are ruling in most Western countries. This fact is also endorsed by the failure to include at least a reference to this Christian heritage in the new constitution for the European Union. The secularist French opposed it, showing therefore that the West has forsaken its own spiritual roots from which ethical rules had been nourished for the past 1200 years!

I. The Undermining of Biblical Ethics by the Modern Quest for Human Emancipation

1. The Emancipatory Movement during the Enlightenment and French Revolution

The fundamental crisis of ethics in Europe did not suddenly emerge at this present time. It was not caused by an incidental shift of democratic balance. The cause was not even the worldwide neo-Marxist rebellion in the late 1960s, although that had a radical catalytic effect. The ideological sources reach back as far as the age of the rationalistic Enlightenment and the French Revolution which was, in its essence, anti-Christian. Then the authority of God was programmatically abolished in the name of the autonomy of human reason. Some thinkers trace it even earlier to the Renaissance, when man instead of God was placed into the centre of the Western world view. In general, the philosophical trend since the 15th century steadily moved towards mankind's **emancipation,** which found its most emphatic articulation in the modern ideologies.

The word *emancipation* stems from the Latin *"e manu capere,"* which means literally, to pull out of the hand. In the ancient Roman law it meant that a dependent person – a son or a slave – was rightfully taken out of the jurisdiction of his master or father and granted the right to make his own decisions. In the wake of Rationalism, man took his life into his own hands, refusing henceforth to be controlled by external instances such as the State, the Church or the Patriarchal family. These institutions drew their legitimacy from God whom their human heads represented. Consequently, emancipation means, ideologically, that man refuses to be under the governing hand of God in order that man himself can be the highest authority of appeal.

Such philosophical emancipation has far-reaching consequences not only in the field of scientific knowledge – *epistemology* – but also for the realm of *ethics.* The quest for *autonomia* (i.e. to legislate for oneself) is a spiritual rebellion against *heteronomia* (to be under the legislation of others and ultimately *theonomia*, i.e. to be under the Law of God.

Modern emancipation means to disregard any divinely sanctioned norms. It is a fundamental turning away from a millennial history with God, in the interest of human self-assertion, self-determination and self-realization. Man opts for developing all his inherent capacities and strives to attain the utmost satisfaction which life can offer. This quest builds upon the belief in the essential goodness of human nature, if left to itself. This idea had been guiding *Jean Jacques Rousseau's* (1712-78) principles of education, being trivialized by the programme of "anti-authoritarian education"[383] in their liberal and Marxist forms. Soon after their implementation, the dubious fruits became obvious: They resulted in a new generation widely marked by ruthless egotism and abuses of a "freedom" which exhibited outright disrespect both for moral and legal norms. Many had forgotten that true freedom cannot exist without reverence for God, unless it would head for ultimate self-destruction.

As we have seen in chapter III, the French Revolution ushered in the *age of ideologies.* Those appeared in various types: liberalism, individualistic idealism, scientism, Freudianism, evolutionism, Marxism, fascism, feminism. They all had one common denominator. In their programmatic striving to produce the "new man" (or "human being"), there were different appearances of a modern humanism without or even against God. Some of their protagonists were inspired by a fanatical hatred against God. It was significant that one of the most popular textbooks for the Student Rebellion in the late 1960s was *Joachim Kahl's bestseller*: "Humanism without God – The Misery of Christianity."[384] God was rejected because he appeared to be a harsh autocrat, a tyrant whose main concern was to suppress freedom and thereby deprive human beings of attaining happiness.

2. Three Historic Revolutions

The Swedish philosopher *Tage Lindbom,* converted to Christianity from Socialism, has promoted the thesis that the age of *Enlightenment* has geared three major revolutions, all inspired by social utopianism, in which the *new man* would come of age.[385] The *first* one was the *French Revolution* (1789-92). It was a political revolution, fighting against the inequality of social and governmental institutions. It strove for a social

---

[383] A.S. NEILL 1970. – G. AMENDT (ed.) 1968. – W. KLAFKI 1970. – W. MERTENS 1974. – **Critics:** W. BREZINKA 1974. – STEINBACHER ³1971. – Immanuel LÜCK 1979. – P. BEYERHAUS (ed.) 1979, pp. 110-149. – Verein zur Förderung der Psychologischen Menschenkenntnis (ed.) 1991.

[384] J. KAHL 1968.

[385] Tage LINDBOM 1979, pp. 106-118.

brotherhood (*fraternité*) without authoritarian ruling, which resulted in the bloody rule of the guillotine.[386]

The *second* one was the *Bolshevik revolution* (1917). It fought against the capitalist system of private property, the abolishment of which should lead to the *classless society* of Communism. This resulted in the "Gulag Archipelago,"[387] the continental network of labour camps.

At present – as Lindbom argues – we are experiencing the *third* one: the *biological revolution*. It seeks to produce the new man by liberating human beings from the slavery of sex distinction. That started with the social and juridical fields, but consequently led into the biological realm of sexuality. Radical feminists demand that women should be released both from the slavery of motherhood and from exclusive heterosexual satisfaction.[388] The obvious difference in the genital organs of females and males is regarded as a mistake in the biological construction which should be amended. This leads to advocating uninhibited sexual pleasure with the help of contraception of any kind, the legitimacy of abortion, extra-corporal conception and of Lesbian lifestyle.[389] The result of this is the physical and mental deformation of human nature and the undermining of the ordinances of matrimony and family.

Tage Lindbom ingeniously comments that the biological revolution is the most heinous one. It will have the most destructive consequences for the future of mankind. Whilst the two former revolutions fought against institutions founded by man i.e. social and economic organizations, the biological revolution rebels against the direct work of God Himself, for it was He who created the human, mental and physical nature. The biological revolution is therefore an open attack against God and His sovereignty.

Since Lindbom published his thesis in 1979, the biological revolution has progressed into new dimensions. Scientists embark on genetic engineering and technological manipulation of embryos artificially produced.[390] Trading with them is about to become legal. Through ex-

---

[386] Otto ZIERER 1980.

[387] Alexander SOLZHENITSYN 1974.

[388] Cf. Chapter VI.

[389] Wilhelm REICH [7]1971. – Helmut KENTLER 1970.

[390] Claudia KAMINSKY 2002, pp. 39-52. – Rudolf WILLEKE 2000, pp. 21-24.

perimenting with cloning, copies of animals and even human beings are produced. Thereby, autonomous man is interfering with the sacrosanct domain of God the Creator. Man is putting himself in His place.

What are the churches going to say in view of such apocalyptic development? I think my readers will now understand the difficulty *Bishop Huber* had in deciding which was the more important task assigned to him - becoming the ecclesiastical head of German Protestantism or giving ethical guidance to the German Government. The government finds itself entrapped in a scientific process which most other states, and even international bodies like the EU, have already decided upon.

3. The Breakdown of True Fatherhood

The German theologian *Georg Huntemann* (*1925), teaching in Belgium and Basel, analyses the contemporary ethical crisis as the result of the loss of fatherhood.[391] He finds that the present generation in the West is a generation of men and women who have never experienced the benefit of having a real father. Such a father is someone who, as an educator, is able to exercise genuine authority borne by loving concern. This, however presupposes his being conscious of his double responsibility, the responsibility towards his children and, above all to the transcendent authority from whom his own fatherhood is derived – God, our heavenly Father. Through his ideological emancipation in the wake of rationalistic Enlightenment, man lost God, not only as the source of revelation but also as a wise educator. His dealing with His children is characterized by a synthesis of authority and loving concern. According to Ephesians 2:24, it is from God that all human fatherhood has derived its name.

Admittedly, in the modern age men were forced to act as fathers, but, since they did so without divine legitimization, they appeared to be caricatures of true fathers. Becoming "bossy," they applied extreme authoritarianism. The opposite extreme was to become indulgent dads without demanding or receiving respect.

The drastic consequences of both extremes appeared in the 1960s: parts of the younger generation were involved in the antiauthoritarian rebellion, whereas other parts escaped into a hippy lifestyle. They practised loose sexuality and/or became enslaved in drug consumption.

---

[391] Georg HUNTEMANN 1981, pp. 38-64. – Idem 1995, pp.313-350.

Huntemann's theory about the loss of fatherhood should be complemented by what we said about the biological revolution and the ideology of *Feminism*. It is here we find the corresponding *loss of motherhood*. The latter results, as the Christian psychotherapist *Christa Meves* has shown in numerous publications, in neuroses and depression in many young women.[392]

All these disquieting contemporary phenomena are demonstrating how modernism, in its emancipation from God, has built on the wrong concept of man. The male and female victims of Freudian Marxism and romantic liberalism tragically proved that human nature cannot suffer manipulation.

II. The Cultural Crisis of
Post-Christian Western Society

1. The Absence of a Stable Basis for Culture and Politics

As we have pointed out already, our post-modern period of history is marked by an agonizing uncertainty about ethical norms and by an ongoing process of their erosion. Our governments, overburdened with problems, look for an ethical basis for their solution. After the abandonment of Christianity as the main source of spiritual information, they can no longer find it. Even the institution of "Ethical Councils" cannot be seen as a way-out, for they are pluralistically composed. Moreover, there are ideological, economic and scientific lobbies striving to influence our law-makers to meet their vested interests.

Meanwhile, the **Mass media** promote a loose lifestyle by over-emphasizing shallow amusement instead of promoting the importance of spiritual values and norms. Their degrading influence is complemented by the **Internet.** By surfing it, users are exposed to the dirtiest type of attraction and the spreading of it is out of control.

Under the pretense of creative freedom, **modern arts** have become polluted to the extent that not even pornographic features are shunned. Thus, by the combined efforts of movies, literature, fashion, and compulsory sex education, the natural instinct of **shame** has been systematically broken down. The promoters do not mind that even the Aus-

---

[392] Christa MEVES 1982. – Idem [42] 2000. – Idem [7]1980a. – Idem 1980b. – Idem 2002.

trian psychoanalyst *Sigmund Freud* (1856-1939) has warned that the loss of shame would lead to a state of idiocy.[393]

Party politics are severely haunted by the extent of **corruption**. Many decisions are made under the influence of bribery – no matter whether the parties are leftist or rightist oriented. Corruption had once been a phenomenon of non-Christian cultures like that of the Chinese and the Indians. Nowadays, the democratic West has followed this dangerous trait and even parties which carry the label "Christian" (e.g. the German "Christian **D**emocratic **U**nion) in their names are not immune to that trend.

With reference to the Christian doctrine of original sin, the Latin word *corruptio* traditionally has been used to describe the effects of the Fall on human nature. Economic corruption is just one form in which the sinful perversion is manifested. As we consider this, we can also see that the problem of corruption in society and private life cannot be solved by merely legislating against it and enforcing control. The real remedy is an ethical transformation of our sinful nature, which can come about only by a spiritual regeneration. Here the Christian testimony becomes extremely relevant even in the realm of politics and economics.

The most vexing problem of international politics is the question about the legitimacy of resorting to **violence** in order to suppress and prevent mortal danger. What about using arms in dealing with burglars? What about **capital punishment**[394] as a means of deterring potential murderers?

On a major scale the question presents itself as the **Peace problem**.[395] It is debated how far wars must and can be abolished as means to solve international conflicts. Here we are faced by two extreme opposites-unconditional pacifism on the one hand and the neo-conservative strategy of preemptive strikes on the other hand. The problem is aggravated by the invention and production of ABC-weapons of mass destruction.

Both sides are presenting their own ideological blue-prints. The "Peace Movement" holds on to its utopian belief in the essential goodness of human nature and the persuasive force of public pacifist opin-

---

[393] S. FREUD 1989. – Idem [4]2004.

[394] Emil Brunner 1932, pp. 464f. – N.H. Søe 1949, p. 348.

[395] Klaus MOTSCHMANN (ed.) 1982. – G. HUNTEMANN 1995, pp. 602-629.

ion. Neo-conservative US-politicians believe in America's calling to establish a New World Order built on the humanist principles of democracy. During the transitory stage, application of military power is seen to be justified as an acceptably unpleasant means to reach a nevertheless good and desirable purpose. The confrontation of the democratic world by terrorism has added new force to such reasoning.

In principle, Christian ethics do offer a solution by the traditional theory about a *"just* (or rather justified) *war."* Here we are confronted by the fact that neither side believes in the validity and applicability of Christian norms based upon biblical revelation and its traditional exposition. Even worse, they present their own controversial theories as upholding the Christian position, without being fully aware that their motives in fact contain some self-contradictory components.

2. Consequences of the Sexual Revolution

a. Breakdown of the Institutions of Matrimony and Family[396]

As we have seen in our chapters on Marxism and Neo-Marxism and also on Feminism, these mutually related ideologies do not uphold the institutions of monogamy and paternal families as essential for maintaining social order. On the contrary, they fight against them as products of capitalist or male-chauvinist self-interest, and both propose and practise "alternative lifestyles."

Apart from this particular trait, all modern ideologies are based on the two elementary principles which, in the wake of the Age of Enlightenment, were elevated to become supreme ideals -the principles of *lust* and of *power*. Giving abundant opportunities for enjoying uninhibited lust became a major feature in modern culture. Both cravings are idealized seductively in novels, theatres and films.

By many, **marriage** was contracted mainly as an opportunity for enjoying sensual pleasures with liberal concessions to occasional infidelity. Such exaggerated and unrealistic expectations, however, could not be fulfilled. Dissatisfaction and mutual suspicion undermined the stability of marriages with the result that the **divorce rate** rose drastically. Even in Korea it has reached 40%, whereby most marriages break up already during the first year. Here the cultural clash between Confucian patriarchalism and American feminist desire for self-realization shows devastating consequences for the social coherence of the Korean peo-

---

[396] Henning GÜNTHER 1979. – Günter ROHRMOSER 1979.

ple. Until now, churches have not dared to address themselves to the problem in a way consistent with Biblical ethics and with the Calvinist or Wesleyan concept of sanctity.

The most deplorable victims of such egotism are the *children*. Worldwide, a hundred million of them live in broken families or drop out from them. Mental disturbances and social abjection are unavoidable. Often the next step is to get involved in *infant prostitution*[397] and *juvenile delinquency*. The majority of younger and middle-aged criminals are themselves victims of broken families.

In the long run, such a rotten culture is doomed to self-destruction. The history of human cultures provides many illustrations of this. One Biblical example is the downfall of the Canaanite naturalist culture which, as archaeological excavations have revealed, was highly sexualized.

In modern times, some ideological imperialists, e.g. Bolshevists and Maoists, make use of moral undermining as a strategy to conquer powerful nations. Traditional Christianity provided a spiritual bulwark against such inroads. Therefore the Church became the particular target of anti-religious Marxist propaganda. One favoured means was making a mockery of alleged moral hypocrisy of priests and nuns.

b. Disrespect for Human Life

1. Abortion[398]

The philosophy of Enlightenment constituted a naturalist world-view. Consequently, human beings were considered as part of nature. Thus, only a *relative* superior dignity amongst other creatures was attributed to them. *Darwin*'s theory of biological evolution undergirded such a perspective. Socialists and liberals adopted the hypothesis that after insemination the embryo undergoes all stages of evolution from the one-cell amoeba through a fishlike being until it attains an inherent human dignity. It was, therefore, perfectly justifiable to kill it by abortion, if that served the interests of the pregnant woman. Thus, the pe-

---

[397] Phyllis KILBOURN and Marjorie McDERMID (eds.) 1998. In this book it is documented that one million children are forced into child prostitution every year and an estimated 10 million children worldwide are victims of the sex industry. The contributors also outline helpful strategies and specific actions to combat the crisis and present effective healing and prevention programmes.

[398] Martin H. SCHARLEMANN: Art. "Abortion," in: BDCE, pp. 1-3. – Die Heiligkeit des menschlichen Lebens,(the sanctity of human life). Special Issue of DIAKRISIS 23 (1/2 2002).

riod after the First World War saw the process of legalizing abortion initially under limited conditions. During the last three decades, however, the practice became more and more alleviated. Nowadays in Germany alone about 300,000 unborn children are sacrificed annually, a number which exceeds those Germans who died on the battlefield or Jews murdered in concentration camps. The term "babycaust," analogous to "holocaust," sounds outrageous, but it reflects the reality.

2. Euthanasia[399]

Another expression of the modern disregard for the untouchability of human life is the recommendation that "medical assistance to terminate a patient's life" should be granted under certain circumstances. These may be at his/her own request or, in case of reduced consciousness, at the request of relatives or even of the doctor himself. The *Netherlands*[400] has become the pioneer when its parliament in 2001 officially legalized euthanasia although it had already been practised and tolerated before that. Since similar motions are made in other European Union countries as well, it is likely that euthanasia will eventually become legal in all the member states. Here, again, it is fatal for it is highly unlikely that the EU constitution will refer to the authority of God.

c. Homosexuality[401]

Space does not allow us to deal with Homosexuality and Lesbianism to the extent to which they occupy the minds of the public through the world – including Korea! Both practices are consequences of maintaining the Enlightenment's principle of lust and of isolating the sexual instinct from its creational purpose to secure the reproduction of the human race. In this connection, it is important to make three observations:

1. The Propagation of Both

Homosexuality is no longer seen as a biological or mental abnormality. It is justified by its advocates as a "creational variant," with rights equal to those held by heterosexuality. Moreover, today's homosexual men and women are not satisfied with public tolerance of their unnatural lifestyle. They even try to propagate it and confront society with its proud exhibition of "love parades" and similar obscenities. This shows

---

[399] Glanville L. WILLIAMS 1957. – Donald S. Robertson: Art. "Euthanasia," in: BDCE, pp. 222 f.

[400] Emerson VERMAAT 2001.

[401] Richard F. LOVELACE 1984. – Roberto de MATTEI (ed.) 1996.

that in modern culture neither Biblical nor natural law is recognized any more, even if this violates a taboo universally held in former times.

2. Their Sanctioning by Legal Reforms

There is an international lobby for promoting "gay rights" which is using almost mafia-like methods. Posing as a discriminated or even persecuted minority, they try to introduce legislation in the name of "tolerance"[402] which outlaws any criticism of homosexual and lesbian practice. The new Swedish anti-discrimination law places these on the same level as racist instigation, so that it can be draconically punished. Attempts are even made to introduce this into EU legislation. That would make it a crime, even in church, to maintain the validity of the Biblical view on homosexual practices.

3. Ecclesiastical Conformity Following

The Gay and Lesbian movements make specific efforts to penetrate the churches. They urge church councils, synods and parishes to discuss the significance of homosexuality as an enrichment of ecclesiastical life. Consequently, demands are made to recognize homosexual partnerships as equally legitimate as marriages between husband and wife. Wedding ceremonies should be granted to them and even the right to adopt children. The next step, others having been taken already with partial success, has been the demand for the ordination of homosexuals to the pastoral ministry. In some denominations that has become possible. The climax of the efforts made by the movements was reached when, in November 2003, the American clergyman *Gene Robinson* was consecrated to become the first Anglican bishop and the head of the diocese of Hampshire. He had openly confessed to being a practising homosexual. Moreover, he was known to be divorced from his wife, with whom he had two children.

This consecration took place in spite of worldwide protests – even from the Vatican – and at the risk of the Anglican communion splitting apart.[403] In fact, two African Archbishops have, as their response, already discontinued sacramental communion with the Episcopalian Church in the USA. That decision was taken more in the hope that it might bring about a breakthrough on sexual ethics in the Church at large.

---

[402] Josh McDOWELL and Bob HOSTETLER 1999.

[403] "Anglicans try to avert schism," in: KNA, 23. May 2004.

d. Gène Techniques

The latest accomplishment of the biological revolution is the scientific embarking on genetic engineering and embryo manipulation. This is done under the moral pretext that a way might be opened to find therapies for incurable and hereditary illnesses and abnormalities. The ultimate goal reaches much further. Scientists try to select strong specimens out of a greater number of artificially begotten embryonic cells. By interfering with their genetic composition, ideal human beings might be created with only good genes. It is hoped these human beings would be healthy, strong, and talented. So, the "new man" is to emerge out of the test tube, that new man, at whom all ideologies have been aiming. Such a production would not have been created by God. It would be an artifact made by human beings.

What is going on reminds us of the Biblical story of the tower of Babylon: When the Lord saw what they had done, he said: *"If ... they have begun to do this, then nothing they plan will be impossible to them ..."* (Gen 11:6). The Biblical author tells us how God brought to nothing that hybrid plan. This shows that God will respond to the contemporary human hubris with a catastrophe analogous to the Babylonian one. Should not the Church perform her prophetical ministry before that divine punishment becomes necessary?

III. Situation Ethics versus Normative Bible Ethics

1. A Modern Theological School: "Situation Ethics"

a. Terminology

The word *"situation ethics"* was coined by the American theologian *Joseph Fletcher* who in 1966 published his revolutionary book "Situation Ethics – New Morality."[404] Another pioneer of this school of thought was the Anglican bishop of Woolwich (London), *John A. T. Robinson,* author of the notorious bestseller: "Honest to God."[405] He dealt sympathetically with that concept in his chapter on ethics. Later on, he expanded it in his book "Christian Morals Today," (1964). Fletcher and Robinson contrasted their dealings with ethics against the traditional one which deduced the unfolding of ethical behaviour from given norms. Those norms were found in the Bible and in the tradition

---

[404] The title for the German translation was "Morals without norms?" (1967).
[405] John ROBINSON 1964.

of the Church's teaching on her established moral principles. That school of thought would be called *"norm ethics."* Alternative terms were "ordinance ethics" or "commandment ethics."

b. Critics

1. Philosophical Background

The concept of situation ethics was severely criticized especially by conservative systematic theologians like the evangelical Anglican *James I. Packer,*[406] the dispensational theologian *Erwin Lutzer*[407] and German evangelicals like *Klaus Bockmühl*[408] and *Karl-Heinz Bormuth.*[409]

The Austrian theologian *Helmut Weber*[410] criticized it from a Catholic perspective. He sees the roots of situation ethics in mediaeval nominalistic voluntarism, in the modern idealistic and existentialist philosophies' individualism and in scientific-technological thinking. In 19th century *Idealism* it was held that the individual follows his own conscience, not being bound by others. *Existentialism* is opposed to any binding system of orthodoxy and correct doctrines. It claims that man must act in obedient response to a given situation in order to realize his freedom.

2. Theological Background

Bockmühl and Bormuth showed that Fletcher and Robinson were not so original after all. They borrowed from former greater theologians such as Rudolph Bultmann, Karl Barth, Emil Brunner and Paul Tillich.

In his book on Jesus,[411] **Bultmann** paved the way. Man has to respond to the actual demands of God. Those are not found in the formal authority of Scripture. They grow from the "decision" in a given situation before God into which man is placed. There are no standards taken from the past nor from common convention. The wording of the Bible is not binding, neither that of the Old Testament nor of the New Testa-

---

[406] "Situations and Principles," in: Bruce Kaye/ Gordon Wenham (Eds.) 1978.

[407] Measuring Morality: A Comparison of Ethical Systems. Probe Ministries Texas, 1989, in: Kaye/Wenham loc. cit. 29-44.

[408] K. Bockmühl 1975.

[409] K.-H. Bormuth 1972.

[410] Helmut Weber 1991, pp. 123-136.

[411] 7th edition Berlin, 1926, pp. 82 f.

ment. Historical-critical research shows, he claimed, that biblical texts are culturally conditioned. Thus man has to respond in obedience to the existential challenge today.

Against idealistic liberalism, **Dialectical Theology** wanted to re-emphasize the authority of the "Word of God" but since it accepted the claims of the historical-critical method, it did not want to be charged with "literalism." For the representatives of this theology, the Biblical texts as such, are not the Word of God. They may become such if God should, at any time, choose to speak through them.

Consequently, **Barth** refuses to speak of the commandments as God's universally valid legislation. He rather agrees with Bultmann that the commandments *can* communicate God's will to the individual in a concrete situation.
Modern "atheistic theologians" speak even more radically. *Dorothee Soelle* (†2003), for example, emancipated herself totally from Biblical authority. For her, Christian ethics do not have a fixed basis. They only put the demand upon man "to be open for the future."

K.-H. Bormuth critically sums up: Since the Bible does not provide us with eternally valid divine commandments, "the result of that theology in the ethical realm is that the world follows its own laws and is entitled to do so."[412]

c. Basic Assumptions of Situation Ethics

1. Main Propositions

i. The starting point of these ethics is not God nor any revealed commandments. Man is invested with an inner compass that directs him to do what is good and right. That compass is his *conscience, informed by love*. All given laws and commandments, therefore, are suspended in favour of creative love. Since we live in a world of constant change, it is argued, we must be motivated by love in order to discover for ourselves what is good in a certain situation.

ii. It is claimed that **The OT Law and the NT commandments** are culturally conditioned. They were given with reference to historical situations. Ours, however, are different as they require new forms of right action.

iii. Appeal to Christ Himself. It is said that Jesus did not introduce nor refer to absolute norms. Rather, He pointed out that loving one's

---

[412] Bormuth op. cit., p. 11.

neighbour is the source of ethical behaviour. Even the instructions of his Sermon on the Mount are only examples. They illustrate how love acts in certain situations.

An analogous appeal is also made to *Paul's doctrine of law and grace*. Christians are no longer under the law but under the rule of grace. Love is the fulfillment and the end of the law.

c. Consequences of Situation Ethics

On the basis of such arguments, nothing is right or wrong in itself. It all depends on the requirement of a certain situation. Man has to be watchful and sensitive and then decide according to the concrete need.

Consequently, no law or commandment is absolutely binding. The only sin is lack of love.

That means in practice that extramarital sex is wrong in most cases but sometimes it may be good, if it is an expression of true love. Under certain circumstances, it might be a duty to break a rule or even all rules. Fletcher goes so far to state that, in an extraordinary situation, lying and bribery, violent actions and even killing may be the only good and just thing to be done.

The **juridical consequences** of modern situation ethics became apparent in Germany in the career of the famous politician *Gustav Heinemann* (1899-1976). As a Christian layman, he regarded himself as a disciple of the Dialectical Theology which he had studied extensively. In 1970, he became Minister of Justice. In this function, he immediately began to liberalize German laws with regard to blasphemy, pornography, homosexuality, adultery and abortion. When criticized by conservative Christians, he appealed to the authority of his ethical teachers.

2. Critical Evaluation of Situation Ethics

a. Elements of Truth

The Bible and dogmatic tradition do not provide us with definite prescriptions for right behaviour in all possible situations. Attempts to form such a system end up in endless casuistic arguments. God's Commandments, even in the Decalogue, are, to a certain degree, historically and culturally marked. The 10th Commandment, for example, speaks of servant, ox and ass - not of motorbikes or computers. Given

for an ancient rural culture, surely flexibility in adapting them to new situations is needed.

There exists however the *danger of legalism*. Legalism consists in a one-sided application of certain Biblical rules without consideration of those others which are complementary to them. Of such a nature was Pharisaism which Jesus criticized so severely (Matth 23:16-36). He used the example of a donkey fallen into a well on the Sabbath Day, clarifying thereby that the Sabbath was made for man and not man for the Sabbath. That means that the OT law must be interpreted according to its divine intention, i.e. that love is the fulfillment of the law (Rom. 13: 8-10). Here we need the *Holy Spirit* in order to discern how the law should be used and which one should be applied in a given moment (I Tim 1:8).

b. Fallacy

The errors of situation ethics outweigh its relative merit by far. This can be shown as follows:

1. Underrating the Abiding Content of Biblical Commandments

The supreme commandment of love for God and for one's fellow-man, the commandment which contains all others (Matth 22:36-40), is not an abstract principle nor a 'categorical imperative': 'Do practise love!' It needs substantial filling as indeed is provided concretely in the Bible. Adultery, for example, is wrong without exception. The same applies to showing love by not stealing (Ex 20:15; Matth 19:18; Eph 4:28), lying, acting treacherously nor resisting defamation. It pertains to homosexual practices as well, because these are strongly condemned in both Testaments (Lev 18:22; Rom 1:22f.)

It is true that we need to be flexible in obeying God's commandments according to various situations but this does not change the principle and basic content (Matth 28:20a). It just pertains to their concrete application.

2. Overlooking the Source and True Meaning of Love

Love can be practised only when it is constantly fuelled with divine love. That, however, presupposes that we live in the state of grace and do not violate it by being disobedient to God.

The entire *concept of "love"* in situation ethics is highly questionable. It is not the compassionate love of Jesus who, in his vicarious sacrifice on the cross, respected God's holiness. Situational love can become tantamount to sentimentality and indulgence.

3) Wrong Concept of Man

Man is not constantly inspired by the love residing in him. His nature is corrupted by evil (Gen 8:21; Matth 15:19; Rom 7:14-25). He is inclined to be immoral and to follow his instincts of covetousness and aggression. Human beings often bend the law to make it benefit themselves. Moreover, the manifold situations in which we should act cannot be assessed by each individual in all their implications and consequences.

Jesus and His Apostles did, indeed, give very concrete instructions for ethical behaviour and endorsed the Law of the Old Testament (Matth 5:15; Luke 16:17; Rom 3:31).

Furthermore, man, in situation ethics, is seen *too individualistically*. He lives in community and his actions have consequences through imitation by others. Breaking a law "out of love," e.g. living in a loose partnership without marriage has the effect of being followed by others. Even done out of presumed love, it will serve as incitement to general licentiousness. Finally, that could lead to the justification of any wrongdoing under the pretence of love.

4. Creational Purpose of Law Misunderstood.

God gave His Law not in order to dominate human beings but to enable them to live a healthy life and to facilitate their social existence. His *revealed* laws were intended to secure and stabilize human relations and institutions in the socio-political life of the people of Israel. However, unless they were revoked (Acts 10:15) and they have not been so, they still fulfill the same purpose for other nations.

Natural law is instituted in the ordinances of creation and preservation (Rom 2:14f.): Matrimony, family, state. All these institutions can function only in accordance with their innate rules. If, however, they are neglected or willfully eliminated, those institutions will tumble. That applies both to individual members and also to the communities as such.

Confronted with the attacks on these institutions by emancipatory ideologies, responsible citizens, and not only Christians, are regaining the important ancient insight that no culture can prevail without an ethical basis. Moreover, no ethical basis will prove to be stable without divine undergirding.

5. Divine Personal Character of Commandments Overlooked

The Biblical laws and commandments are not abstract principles. Such devaluation belongs to situation ethics. On the contrary, they are instructions given by the living God, whose essence is both holiness (Rev 4:8) and love (1 John 4:8.16). He watches over their fulfillment and at the same time guarantees the good outcome by obeying them. They are backed by his power and his provision, as it is fundamentally stated in the preamble to the First Commandment, and that refers to the entire Decalogue: *"I am Yahweh your God who brought you out of the land of Egypt, out of the house of bondage"* (Ex 20:2). He is Lord also over contemporary situations. The commandment does not arise out of a situation; it rather determines and changes the situation. If we doubt God's lordship even over turbulent situations, we make Him a puppet, inferior to the demands of the historic situation. Some liberation theologians tend to identify God with the situation.

The basis of obedience to God's commandments is *confidence in Him*. This was realized by *Martin Luther*. In the explanation of the Decalogue in his Small Catechism he introduced each commandment by the formula: *"We shall fear God and love Him."* Thus God's authority must not be confused with tyranny. He commands out of fatherly concern!

3. The Churches' Failure in Their Ministry of Shepherding and Teaching

The deepest tragedy in our cultural crisis in the West is that our established churches and their leaders were, to a high degree, informed by distorted concepts of ethics. The historical-critical exegesis had made them uncertain about the abiding authority and reliability of Biblical ethics. Therefore they shunned any identification with "fundamentalism." In addition, they were misdirected by some chief authorities in Systematic Theology, as previously indicated.

That led to the consequence that our churches yielded to the political demands to liberalize our national laws and to the softening of moral rules in general.

Much worse is that in many cases churches did not simply surrender but actually gave the lead in wrong directions. A famous German fighter for ethical resistance and renewal, the medical doctor *Siegfried Ernst*,[413] found that in many cases major amendments of law had been prepared by consultations in Church Academies. That was the case in reference to pornography, abortion, homosexuality and blasphemy. In the political realm some theologians justified revolutions in the Third World and also violence in combating racism.[414]

Another forum for propagating the new morals was the German "Kirchentage." Radical theologians like *Dorothee Soelle* were constantly invited as main lecturers. Consequently, the spokespersons of our established churches often did not act as counsellors and prophets, but as seducers.

IV. Contemporary Christian Movements for Ethical Renewal

We have described the present ethical crisis in the West and indeed across the whole world. This will probably have drawn a gloomy picture of what the future holds in stock. Is there no hope that both the churches and our peoples as a whole may return to the path of God? I do not dare to give an optimistic prognosis with regard to a changing situation in general but it would be fatal if we overlooked the many concerned Christian individuals and groups who try to stem the tide. We even see dynamic movements prophetically attempting to remind our nations and national churches of the necessity to reinforce their ethical standards and teaching. Let me mention some exemplary ones:

1. International Movements for Ethical Renewal

a. Moral Re-armament (MRA)

This movement was founded by *Frank N.D. Buchmann* (1878-1961)[415] in 1938 and was very influential during several decades. Its centre is the Swiss settlement *Caux*, where many international conferences have taken place. Caux attracted responsible persons from all cultures and levels of society. Their approach was based upon the "Four Absolute Demands" – absolute purity, honesty, truthfulness and unselfishness.

---

[413] Siegfried ERNST 1974. – Peter BEYERHAUS 2001, pp. 227-232.

[414] Bernard SMITH [2]1979. – P. BEYERHAUS / W. KÜNNETH (eds.) 1987.

[415] Carl F.H. HENRY 1973, p. 433.

b. World-Wide Temperance Movement

This movement fights against the evils of alcoholism and addiction to other obnoxious drugs which ruin the personal character and the stability of families and whole societies. Some of its branches have a clear Christian orientation. Here Korea has given an impressive lead.[416]

c. Pro-Life Movement

This movement came into being in reaction to the alarming number of abortions in many Western countries. The afore-mentioned friend of mine, Dr. med. *Siegfried Ernst*, founded the "World Federation of Doctors Who Respect Human Life" in 1973. The members fight against both abortion and euthanasia by providing information on the criminality and dreadful consequences of this legalized murder. Signatures are collected and demonstrations held outside courts and abortion clinics.

d. Moral Majority

This is a predominantly Christian movement of conservative orientation, led by *Jerry Falwell*. It fights for reinforcing God's commands in American politics and keeps a close connection with the Pro-Life movement. It interferes in the process of legislation. It also demands that morning prayers should be re-instated in public schools.

e. Initiative "True love waits"

This came into being in 1994, starting in South Africa and spreading to Central Europe and America. Young people, often being more conscientious than their parents, sign a vow to preserve chastity before marriage in order to undergird the purity of wedded life as a gift of God. In a short time, 90,000 young people gave their signature. Such an obligation is also a strong antidote against the terrible spread of AIDS especially in African countries.

2. Efforts of the Confessing Fellowships

During the course of these lectures, the work of the Confessing Fellowships in Germany and worldwide has been referred to several times. They came into being in the late 1960s as a conservative Christian protest against the devastating effects of radical Biblical criticism and against the intrusion of Neo-Marxism into the churches. Very soon we realized that ideological and religious currents were endangering the

---

[416] Kwi-Ook YEU 1988.

faith and ethical behaviour of Christians on a much wider scale. These currents were closely observed and analyzed by the theological commission (Theologischer Konvent) of the *Conference of Confessing Fellowships*. It did its work in consultation with like-minded theologians and responsible Christians in other countries. For that purpose the *International Christian Network* was founded in 1978 in London.

We are motivated by a sense of a prophetical mission as we feel obliged to act vicariously as watchmen, shepherds and teachers wherever we see our official churches neglecting this central duty. Thus our pronouncements have always the tone of deep concern and warning.[417] We do not want to fall into legalism as we are driven by a compassionate concern for the misguided people. Therefore our diagnosis is always followed by an exposition of a positive alternative. We point to the Bible as the revealed Word of God. This alone gives us reliable guidance and opens up truly reliable sources for spiritual renewal.

The means to communicate our messages are public appeals, books, and pamphlets containing Biblical orientation with regard to specific challenges. We try to get into conversation with the authorities in Church and State and we sponsor mass rallies like *"Gemeindetag unter dem Wort"* (Church Days under the Word).

With regard to the breakdown of ethical standards, we have issued several manifestos, the last one in 2001. It is called: *"The Ten Commandments – God's Signpost for our Times."*

It has found a very positive reception among many concerned Christians both in Germany and in other countries and continents as well. It may be appropriate to conclude this chapter by quoting from the Preamble and the Conclusion of that Document:

"Our post-modern era is characterized by a profound spiritual uncertainty and dissolution of ethical norms. The departure of our Western peoples from the Christian faith has led to fatal inroads into our ethics … Into this crisis of our society speaks the living God, the Creator, Provider and Saviour of mankind. All who trust in Him find a source of orientation in Him for their lives … through the Ten Commandments."

The Ten Commandments are binding because behind them stands the unchangeable God as the highest commanding authority. Whoever disregards them and follows his own ideas will destroy himself and

---

[417] R. Bäumer / P. Beyerhaus / F. Grünzweig 1980, pp. 297-342.

have to account for this in the Last Judgment (Ex 20:5; 2 Cor 5:10). For the LORD who has destined us for life will not hold guiltless the one who invalidates His Holy Law ... Even today it is true what was once spoken to the first recipients of the Ten Commandments:

"Behold, I set before you this day a blessing and a curse: the bless-ing if you obey the commandments of the LORD your God, which I command you this day; and the curse, if you do not obey the com-mandments of the LORD your God, but turn aside from the way I com-mand you ... " (Deut 11:26-28).

Chapter 12

The Church of Jesus Christ in the Tension between True and False Unity

Our present age is characterized by endeavours for unification in all realms. The fascinating watchword is *"globalisation."* High expectations are set on a unity in which all separating barriers are broken down. Nations should melt into a single community of states, a community in constant development towards higher standards of life and cultural exchange.

At the same time, however, there are other people who are scared by a monopolist system into which nation for nation is incorporated. That would deprive us of our national autonomy and organic peculiarity. Thus, globalisation is very far from being a self-evident ideal for all people; for social, economic and political unity is an ambivalent phenomenon.

What attitude should members of the Church hold towards the prospects of unity? In the religious field we meet it in the form of the *Ecumenical Movement*.[418] Even that is not welcomed unanimously.[419] On the contrary, it has, paradoxically enough, resulted in a new internal separation between the conciliar and the evangelical movements.[420] There is a tension between progressive and conservative Christians and churches.

The question, however, is not whether a community of believers should stand in favour of or against ecclesial unity. The theological problem is this: ***What kind of unity*** should disciples of Christ wholeheartedly keep and strive for and what promise is given to us that this unity is going to be realized? I intend to answer these questions in four steps:

---

[418] Harold E. Fey (ed.) 1970. – George H. TAVARD 1960.
[419] David Hedegard 1954. – Edgar C. BUNDY 1975.
[420] Donald McGAVRAN ²1977.

I. True Unity which Christ Grants

We take our point of departure from the high-priestly prayer of Jesus in John 17. He addressed it to the Father on the night before his crucifixion, when he bade farewell to his disciples. Thereby he bequeathed to them his spiritual testament, his last will. The subject of unity which is dealt with in verses 11 to 23 is in its core expressed in verse 21:

"I pray that all of them may be one, Father, just as you are in me and I am in you. May they also be in us so that the world may believe that you have sent me."

Jesus prays here for his Church and her future, whilst a serious concern depresses his heart. He anticipates that the coherence of the Christians will be severely contested by the "prince of this world" (John 14:30). The Devil's evil aim is to tear asunder that which God has joined together. The Church is going to be haunted by separations, beginning with the basic one, the separation between her members and her Lord. That would be a tragedy; for it would mean that the Church's spiritual blood circulation which proceeds from the heart and flows into all organs of the body (cf. Eph 4:16) would be hindered from supporting her members by the power of his grace. The members, whenever the Evil One succeeds, could no longer serve each other in the mind of Jesus Christ. Moreover, by their isolated existence Christians would deny their own message of God's reconciling love for the world (John 3:16; 2 Cor 5:19). Against such a danger Jesus poses his prayer. During her inner discords the Church will be borne up by its power. For our ascended High Priest is sitting at the right hand of God the Father and continues to intercede for us (Heb 8:1).

1. The Divine Foundation of the Church

Primarily, the "unity of the Church" is neither an ecumenical problem nor a programme. No, her essential unity is already given to her as a basic quality and an indestructible spiritual reality. It consists in the mystery that the Church is Christ's body (Eph 1:22; 5:23; 1 Cor. 12:12f.), inseparably grown together with her heavenly head. Likewise she is – to use another Biblical symbol – the bride of Christ (Rev 21; 2. 9: Eph 5:25 f.), bought by his blood and betrothed to him. Once she will even visibly be united with him, in all eternity. That is the *Christological dimension* of unity.

Equally important is its **trinitarian dimension**. The Church has come into being as an emanation of that internal love that exists between the three divine persons - Father, Son and Holy Spirit. The communion which unites the members of the Church is an earthly reflection of the internal communion of the triune God (John 17:11,21; 2 Cor 13:13). That pertains first of all to the mutual internal relations between the three divine persons. Thereafter it is also directed outwards in their cooperation for enacting the plan of salvation.

The Church likewise is a *koinonia* (communion) in a double sense: She owns, first of all, an internal communion between her members.

This is rooted in that *koinonia* which she has with the Father through the Son in the Holy Spirit (1 John 1:3). Furthermore, Christians have an active fellowship which is directed outwards in the form of their *martyria* (witness) and *diakonia* (service). In performing theses assignments, she participates in God's own mission, the *"missio Dei."*[421]

Consequently, the Church's unity is not built on clever ideas, pious feelings and strategic plans. It consists more so in her integral participation in the oneness of the three divine persons. That communion is mediated through the Son, the eternal word of truth, and through the Holy Spirit, whose temple she forms.

2. Essence and Shape of the Church

It is important to distinguish between the *spiritual essence* and the *empirical shape* of the Church. This Augustinian and Calvinistic distinction is treated dogmatically under the terms *"visible"* and *"invisible church."*[422] In the NT understanding, *ekklesia* is both a spiritual and a corporal concrete reality. Regarding her spiritual nature, she is invisible; but in her outward articulation she is visible as her fellowship is formed by living human beings, who consist of soul and body. As an institution taking part in time and history, she is invested with tasks and means such as ministries, services, ordinances, sacraments and Scriptures. These are tangible, so that it can be tested whether they are concordant with their divine institution.

This unity which Jesus entrusts to his disciples is in the same way invisible and visible at the same time. It is *invisible* regarding her spiri-

---

[421] Georg VICEDOM 1960.

[422] G. D. HENDERSON 1952, pp. 95 f. – Leonard HODGSON, 1946., pp. 133 f.

tual nature, *visible* regarding her empirical shape. Since that shape, however, belongs to the created world which is affected by the Fall, the visible side of the Church – her members, ordinances, ministries – can become distorted. That pertains particularly to ecclesial *unity*. With regard to its external appearance, it will always be threatened by the sinful tendency towards separation or even by perversion.

Thus we can state that, *from God's side,* the Church's unity is a *gift* that cannot be lost. Seen from her *human side,* unity is a *task* that can be accomplished only by God's special assistance. This task can be called her *ecumenical commission.* It consists in rendering visible, to a certain extent, the inner, spiritual unity of the Church (Eph 4:15f. I Peter 4:10). This articulated oneness shall be realized by the activity of the universal *Church.* It takes place in *leitourgia* (worship), *martyria* (mission) and *diakonia* (service in love).

3. Four Essential Marks of the Church

Quite early, the Church Fathers had declared which fundamental marks indicate the identity of the Church. These should help us to seek for her *true unity* and to discern it from *false unity*. The latter one consists only in the outer form but it is filled with content quite contrary to the Biblical elements of the Church of Christ. We describe the nature of the Church by four fundamental characteristics: We believe in the *one, holy, catholic* and *apostolic* Church. Let us treat them one by one:

1. The Church is *one* because she is not a human association, of which there are many. Much more, she is God's own people, with whom, by his New Covenant, He stands in an exclusive relationship. Just as God is only one, even his Church which is made up of all born-again people, is only one. Christ has bound himself to her. She is the elect instrument of God the Father to fulfil his plan of salvation, for he wants to bring together in Christ as a single head, all that is in heaven and on earth (Eph 1:9f.). She is enabled and commissioned by her ministry of reconciliation (2 Cor 5:18) to constitute fellowship in a divided mankind, because she reflects God's oneness.

2. The Church is *holy*, because she is sanctified by Christ's sacrifice (Eph 5:25 f.), and is a temple of the Holy Spirit. She is holy in the sense that she is separated from the world and belongs exclusively to God. He, Himself is the absolutely holy One and uses her as His instrument.

The Church's holiness is recognized *firstly* by her using the *means of grace* which Christ has bestowed on her for her sacred commission. These means are the Word of God and the holy sacraments.

Secondly: Her holiness is recognized by the fact that she enjoys the communion of saints. I am referring both to those in heaven – the angels and the "spirits of righteous men being perfected" (Hebr 12:22 f.) – and also to the saints on earth, our fellow Christians (1 Cor 1:2).

Thirdly: The holiness of the Church is recognized by the *fruit of the Spirit*. These are the good works that attract people to the Church and through her to God (Gal 5:22-25; Mt 5:16).

3. The Church is **catholic**, a term which in ecumenical usage nowadays, is no longer limited to the Roman Catholic Church[423] as it was formerly amongst Protestants. In fact, "Catholic" means "all-embracing," in contrast to sectarian isolation.

In her capacity of being *catholic*, the Church possesses all means of grace and spiritual gifts which God has given to her through her institution by Christ and through the Holy Spirit. She bears witness to the whole truth about God's essence and work, as He has revealed Himself to His people.

In the *dimension of time* she embraces all Christians who have ever been incorporated into the body of Christ. In the *dimension of space* she embraces all congregations on earth. She comprehends all cultures which have been Christianized and have enriched her worship service. In her mission she directs her efforts to the entire human race as the object of evangelization.

4. The Church is *apostolic* and that in a double sense. She is apostolic because she is built on the foundation of the Apostles and Prophets, in which Jesus Christ forms the corner-stone (Eph 2:20). She is apostolic also because she too, just like the Apostles, is sent by Jesus into the world to proclaim the Gospel. It is her apostolicity by which the identity of the Church as Christ's true Church in recognized, perhaps even more clearly than by the former three essential marks. She stands in a relationship with Jesus of Nazareth, which is demonstrated (Acts 1:21 f.) when she faithfully preserves the *doctrine* which Jesus has entrusted to his Apostles (Mt 28: 20a: ..." *teach them to keep everything I have commanded you.*") It can also be

---

[423] Peter BEYERHAUS 2000, pp.566-590. – Karl BARTH ¹1939: Vol. IV, 1, p. 782 writes: "The Church is either catholic or she is not a Church at all."

shown by her possessing an authorized *ministry*. In this she shares in the threefold ministry of Christ himself as Prophet, Priest and King, ministries which he, in the sense of participation, has delegated to his Apostles (John 20:21-23; Mt 10:40). From them it has been continued from one generation to the next (2 Tim 1:6).

These four essential marks penetrate each other and constitute an inseparable totality. Jointly they guarantee the faithfulness and integrity of the Church. The legitimacy of all ecumenical endeavours for reunion must be tested by questioning how far they aim at the Church's Oneness, Holiness, Catholicity and Apostolicity.

II. False, Anti-Christian Unity

Having described the true unity of the Church, let us now look at the *false unity*, lest we confuse the two.[424]

The survival of our world is threatened by great crises and conflicts. Because of that, "unity" has become the highest ideal for most people. Even many Christians are inclined to identify "unity" with God's will. Consequently, separation is regarded as one of the greatest sins. This is a dangerous conclusion as they seem to have forgotten that there may be and, indeed, will be an external, comprehensive unity which does not emerge from God. It comes, on the contrary, from his satanic antipode, the *"prince of this world"* (John 14:30; 16:11).

In the 17th chapter of John's Revelation, we read about a future dreadful figure which has the character of a beast. That man ascends to the highest political position and attains power over all mankind. The ten[425] major rulers at this time will voluntarily confer their power on him, in order, as his vassals, to govern jointly with him over a universal political system. That system is marked by absolute uniformity because, as we read in v. 13, "they have *one purpose*" (Greek *mia gnome*). We may think of an ideology of political, maybe also economic oneness.

However, before John speaks of that, he has already depicted another horrible vision. It is a glamorous woman who rides on the beast and is thus closely related to the Antichrist (Rev 17:1-6). She is called the *"great Babylon,"* who prostitutes herself with the kings of the

---

[424] Arthur JOHNSTON 1988, pp. 22-42.

[425] The number 10 here is probably used in a symbolical sense, meaning "fullness."

earth. Her golden cup is "full of abominable things and the filth of her adulteries" (v. 4). Moreover she is "drunk with the blood of the saints" who suffered martyrdom under her.

Who is the whore Babylon? Various theories have been proposed which usually were entailed by their historical circumstances. To me, the most persuasive interpretation seems to be that this harlot is the symbolic personification of a syncretistic world- religion and a united world church. This one does not adore the true God. It worships instead many kinds of idols in order to satisfy the unquenchable spiritual thirst of people and their carnal desires. It is going to be, in this sense, a religious system that gains immense influence,[426] since it offers itself to the political rulers of the world as a spiritual and moral support for their dictatorship.

Old Testament prophets, particularly Hosea (2:7; 5:3; Is.1:21; 23:16), speak of Israel or Jerusalem by using such a symbolic figure in certain contexts. By her continuous infidelity against her God Yahweh, Israel has perverted her position as God's wedded wife into that of an adulterous vagrant. Israel worshipped the idols of her neighbouring peoples and the spirits of nature and she constantly offended against the ethical commandments of the Decalogue.

Analogous to this example, it appears to be plausible to discern in the great Babylon a comprehensive religion, which incorporates in itself the elements of traditional religions, including Christianity.[427] Thereby it satisfies the personal craving of people but also satisfies the need of the political world-system for a spiritually uniting bond to undergird international order and peace. The watchword then is sounded: "One world – one religion!"[428]

---

[426] "Babylon is the means (as a counterfeit of God's plan) through which, from the earliest human history, Satan's evil philosophy ... worms its way into the religious developments of the world. The ultimate purpose of this has been the creation of an anti-Jehovah-world-system – known in Scripture as 'Mystery Babylon' – which would set itself up against the redemptive plan of God, but which surely will be destroyed when the Lord returns at the end of this present evil age (Rev. 17:1 – 18:2)," says Alan MORRISON 1999, p. 39. – A similar view is held by Martin KIDDLE 1946, pp. 337-344: "The Fall of Babylon the Great." Likewise M. R. De . HAAN [32]1982, pp. 214-231 and Brooks ALEXANDER 1988, pp. 43 – 55.

[427] Fritz GRÜNZWEIG 1982, pp. 113-171: "Der Fall der religiösen Weltkulturmacht" (Downfall of the religious world cultural power).

[428] P. BEYERHAUS/Lutz E. von PADBERG 1988b.

The sinister trait of such a religion is its combination of spiritual fascination and totalitarianism. It offers space for any religious phenomenon, whether it is ritual, mysticism, ecstasy techniques or even telepathy and miracles. On the other hand it also engages itself in sublime philosophical speculations in order to substantiate the essential unity of all religions. The modern New Age Movement gives a certain foretaste of that.[429] The conditions for participation are "openness" and "tolerance." No theological reservations are made anymore for everybody is entitled to make his own spiritual experience and to witness about it. One category of pious people, however, is excluded: It is those who still believe in an authoritative revelation and confess their faith in the Lord Jesus Christ as the one Lord and only way to salvation (John 14:6; Acts 4:12). They are the ones described in Rev 12:17 and 17:14. By their religious and theological exclusiveness, they place themselves outside the community. They are regarded as those who disturb peace and block multicultural harmony. Therefore the Babylonian whore looks on them with contempt and hatred and exposes them to moral and even physical persecution.

The delicacy of this observation is obvious. Those who have observed the Ecumenical Movement during the last 40 years have experienced it as a double-faced phenomenon. *On the one hand* we can witness about many gladdening events with regard to the mutual discovery of the churches' wealth: joint worship services with liturgical elements from the various confessional traditions; inter-Church Aid, world diaconate and hope- inspiring progress on the way towards doctrinal consensus.[430]

But *on the other hand*, within the same movement, extremely dubious types of secular theologies have been developed and sponsored. Some of them were (and still are) nothing else but political ideologies articulating themselves with a Christian vocabulary.[431] At the WCC's Uppsala Assembly in 1968, the ecumenical goal was widened from unifying churches to building up a world community.[432] In that fellowship the churches were given the role of acting as humble partners of political liberation movements and non-Christian religions.[433] The spiri-

---

[429] Cf. Chapters VII and IX.

[430] H.-M. Moderow / Matthias Sens 1979. – Heinz SCHÜTTE [4]1986. – Ernst LANGE 1972 – P. BEYERHAUS / U. BETZ (eds.), 1976.

[431] Rolf SAUERZAPF 1975. – Bert Beverly BEACH 1974.

[432] Ekkehard BIEHLER 1974.

[433] P. BEYERHAUS 1992, pp. 79-92.

tual treasures of these were supposed to be discovered and introduced to the inter-religious dialogue.

At the same time, we observe with concern and grief how our European and American mainline churches open themselves up to the spirit of the age. Worship services are modernized with elements of pop-culture to become more attractive. Sexual licentiousness was approved, and churches even introduced ceremonies to bless homosexual partnerships and divorces. Venerable cathedrals have been opened for pornographic expositions.[434] Thus, we could not escape from realizing how pointedly different Babylon has become to occidental Christianity. Churches are about to be pulled into the pluralistic cross-currents which are bound to confluence in that anti-Christian world system, the symbols of which are the *beast* and the *harlot*.

That underlines the necessity for Bible-believing Christians to have the ability to discern all tendencies towards an inner-worldly type of ecumenism. Such an aid has been offered by the First European Confessional Congress, which on the Day of Ascension in 1974 promulgated its "Berlin Declaration of Ecumenism."[435] Four years later, the International Christian Network was established in Westminster Chapel, London. There we realized again the need to call upon Christians in all countries to devote themselves to that unity for which Jesus prayed according to John 17:22-23.[436]

III. New Hope for the Churches' Re-uniting

If I interpret the signs of the times rightly, I see the Holy Spirit in our generation performing a new work in the Church's bi-millennial history: On the basis of Christ's atoning sacrifice he seeks *"to bring together the scattered children of God and make them one"* (John

---

[434] This happened during the summer of 1998 in Sweden, when, with the consent of the Archbishop of the (Lutheran) Swedish Church, a pornographic homosexual photo exhibition was put up in the cathedral of Uppsala and later on in other major dioceses as well. "Umstrittener schwedischer Erzbischof," in: DIAKRISIS 19 (4/1998), pp. 285-287.

[435] W. KÜNNETH/P. BEYERHAUS (eds.) 1975: Part I: "Das Bekenntnis von Berlin." – P. BEYERHAUS: Art. "Berlin Declaration," in: S.B. Ferguson et al. (ed.) 1988: p. 90 – Idem: 2004,: pp. 71-76 – The English text of the Berlin Declaration is found in the website of ICN: www.institute-diakrisis.de.

[436] P. BEYERHAUS: "Der Auftrag der Kirche Jesu Christi und der Ökumenische Rat der Kirchen," in: J. Heubach/K.-D. Stephan (eds.) 1999: pp. 76-98. – Idem 2004: pp. 71-76.

11:52; cf. 10:16). His purpose is to bring about genuine oneness by challenging the traditional self-sufficiency of the separated confessional and denominational communities, and this in conformity with the apostolic injunction of Eph. 4:13,15f.

We cannot see yet how this unification is going to be achieved in practice. Neither do we know how long we still have to walk until we have reached a *genuine unity* of the churches. What do I mean by this expression? It is the earthly shape of the one holy, catholic and apostolic Church, which is the home of all true followers of Jesus Christ. In an eschatological perspective, we can be sure that at the Second Coming of Christ as prophesied in John 10:16, and highlighted in Ez 34:23 and Jer 32:39, that promise will be fulfilled: *"... and there will be one flock and one shepherd."* Already, however, we can discern *signs* – light and dark ones – that are pointing to the fact that the age between Christ's ascension and His return in power and glory is rapidly moving towards its consummation.

As positive signs I can evaluate three historic processes which are very encouraging.

The *first sign* is that in our generation we witness a *missionary revival*, especially in the younger churches in Africa, Asia and Latin America.[437] It has led to the fact that world evangelization is progressing rapidly. There is hardly any country or people which have not been reached with the Christian message. Jesus predicts in Matthew 24:14: *"And this gospel of the kingdom will be preached in the whole world as a testimony to all nations, and then the end will come."*

The *second sign* is in fulfilment of Old Testament prophecies that God's ancient elected people *Israel has returned to the country* of her forefathers. This is the external side; but that is not everything. Even the other inner side is starting to be realised. There is a growing number of *"Messianic Jews"*[438] who openly confess their faith in *Yeshua ha Mashiach* (Hebrew for Jesus Christ). They are expecting his return in glory to establish his messianic kingdom of peace from Zion.

The *third sign* is encouraging as well. It is the burning *desire for ecclesial unification* of those Christians who are separated by the hard walls of denominations and confessions. This has reached a degree of intensity unknown to previous generations, although I do not see it in

---

[437] Panya BABA (Coordinator) 1990, pp. 390-392. – Larry D. PATE (ed.) 1989.
[438] Baruch MAOZ 1986. – Kelvin CROMBIE 1991.

Korea as yet! Church leaders, theologians and indeed laymen are strongly motivated to become involved in inter-denominational deliberations and activities.[439] Newly established spiritual fraternities and communities render an important contribution by their intercession. Most of them include working for unity in their rules and formulae of worship.

I am, however, quite conscious of the fact that the hindrances are still very tough. In most churches you will find individuals and groups who are worried about the unification development. They warn to be cautious. This is quite understandable in view of what we have said in Part II about false, antichristian unity with ideological and syncretistic features. That could, indeed, interfere with true Biblical catholicity.

What then is the course that should be steered by responsible Christians? How can we live in conformity with the prayer of Jesus for true oneness amongst his disciples and at the same time, preserve that genuine spiritual heritage which is entrusted to us in our various confessional traditions?

We have recognized the will of Jesus that his Church should be one in God the Father and the Son. We also have seen that the Holy Spirit will lead us towards a realization of her catholicity. Therefore we must neither be disinterested nor even hostile to the quest for Christian unity throughout the world.

We have also become conscious of the acute threat exercised by the forthcoming anti-Christian world system. Therefore we should not fight for unity at any expense. What is the golden middle way by which we can avoid temptations from both sides?

In answering this question I want to propose the following points of orientation:

IV. Eight Signposts on the Way towards True Christian Unity

In Ephesians 4:1-3 Paul admonishes the church to live worthy of its calling:

"Be completely humble and gentle; be patient, bearing with one another in love. Make every effort to keep the unity of the Spirit through the bond of peace."

---

[439] Harding MEYER (ed.) 1983.

In accordance with that, I want to give the following ecumenical advice:

1. Let us prayerfully submit to the *leading of Christ*, which he gives us through his holy Word and the presence of the Spirit. It is the heavenly shepherd himself who is able to gather his scattered flock and wants to defend it against the Evil One. Therefore enduring prayer in our small chamber and in the community is our most important task, which can be fulfilled by all Christians, following Jesus' prayer in John 17.

2. We have to observe carefully the *essential elements* which according to Eph 4:4-6 are the indispensable presuppositions of true catholicity and apostolicity. *"one body and one Spirit – as you were called to one hope when you were called – one Lord, one faith, one baptism; one God and Father of all ...."* When we faithfully comply with this apostolic injunction, we shall not be led astray by either secular ecumenism or by religious pluralism.

3. Practise the gift and task to *discern the spirits*. We have clearly to determine whether a modern movement for unity is really founded in Christ and is aiming to meet Him when He comes again. We must consider if this "unity" bears a Babylonian character. Does it sever us from communion with the living Christ and introduce heterogeneous elements of secular nature, strange to biblical faith? In the latter case we must be courageous and refuse to cooperate – even if that leads to our becoming despised and isolated.

4. All genuine Christian endeavour for unity is a process which cannot merely be organised by external means from the administrative top. It is rather a work of the Spirit that proceeds from the hearts of the faithful who, according to Rom 8:14, are men and women "driven" by the Spirit.

This is the truth of what some Christians call *"spiritual ecumenism."*[440] What is meant by that expression? Like any genuine revival

---

[440] G. H. TAVARD, op. cit., Chapter XIII: "Spiritual Ecumenism" quotes **Paul Couturier** 1881-1953, who was called "the apostle of Christian unity" and initiated the annual week of prayer for the unity of the Church: "The time has not yet come for the work of theologians and superiors, but it is time for psychological purification by means of prayer, kindness, mutual esteem of individuals and of all their human and Christian values, all the fruits of charity." As an "apostle of Christian oneness" on the regional level we can also think of the American pioneer missionary to Korea *Horace Grant Underwood*. He was an ardent promoter of unity between Christians of different de-

movement, ecumenical revival starts with repentance and conversion. It is a soul-searching renewal of our relationship with our brothers and sisters in other denominations and traditions.

It is true that in the history of Christianity such separations occurred which, for the sake of truth, were unavoidable. Moreover, the salvation of souls was at stake. On the other hand, however, purely human and as such also sinful factors did frequently interfere as well, e.g. ambition, lust for power, and socio-political tensions. Consequently, the spiritual atmosphere was poisoned by mutual polemics as, in fact, the Spirit of God, the forger of unity, draws back when he is quenched. Traumatic wounds were left in the hearts of fellow Christians who were despised as "dissenters."

Mutual persecutions even produced martyrs on both sides, mainly amongst the Protestants.[441] "Cleansing of memory" and mutual admission of guilt should be the first step before theologians engage in the discussion of doctrinal differences. The driving motive for reunification is that *love which* corresponds with the love of the Good Shepherd for his flock, for he has redeemed it on Calvary by his precious blood, when we still were estranged to God and to each other (Rom 5:10). When we seek to be unified with the members of other churches, we should not do this in order to build a larger ecclesial organization. No, we do it because they, too, bear the features of Jesus on their faces and together with us they belong to one family. Therefore we are concerned about them and about their spiritual convictions and experiences. We are not envious of each other but, on the contrary, we rejoice over the successes of the others and we support each other spiritually and materially.

5. In the present situation we should start by aiming at an *internal gathering* in our own ecclesial communion in which we contact those concerned representatives and groups which strive for Biblical orthodoxy against the inroads of heretical modernism and syncretism. Then we can move on concentrically, for similar movements can be discovered in many denominations, especially in the West.

---

nominational backgrounds. In the biography *Underwood of Korea* his widow Lillias UNDERWOOD writes on p. 238: "One of the chief desires of Dr. Underwood's heart was organic union on the mission field: for this he longed, prayed, worked and hoped as long as he lived, and he lived to see it a probability of the not distant future."

[441] Josef TON 1997, Chapters 14 and 15.

6. On the other hand, magnificent ecumenical schemes might even be dangerous, for they are promoted by the official representatives of such mainline churches which themselves are split up spiritually, i.e. because of modernistic inroads. Sometimes those churches' "liberal" leaders even exercise pressure on conservative Christians who are faithful to the Bible.

Therefore it is desirable that in times when the true faith is falsified and suppressed even within certain church bodies, faithful Christians across traditional divisions seek each other for a joint defence of the Gospel.

What we should aim at today is an ecumenical (in the sense of worldwide) movement of confessing Christians that utilizes the truly evangelical and truly catholic heritage.

A widely-known movement that assembles evangelical Christians across the traditional denominational borderlines within Protestantism is the *World Evangelical Alliance* (WEA, established 1846 in London). A younger venture is the *International Christian Network* (ICN, established 1978 in London). In defending the faith, the latter endeavours to knit together confessing groups in various countries in Europe and other continents.

7. When Jesus in John 17 prayed for oneness amongst his disciples, he was particularly moved by the divine desire *"that the world may believe that you have sent me"* (v. 21). As a matter of fact, the huge task of evangelizing the world in our generation can only be tackled successfully if it is done jointly by all Christian Churches and communities. Such evangelistic cooperation might also foster true unity. This was the insight that brought together the Lausanne Movement for World-Evangelization in 1974.[442] In Germany it is *joint evangelisation*, in which Christians from mainline churches and free churches and even Catholic congregations have found each other. They have realized that the opposition of the world is too strong for such a Christianity which by its own inner divisiveness has lost credibility.

8. The *community of martyrs* holds a great ecumenical potential that connects all traditions of Christian faith.[443] In certain situations, our joint witness can lead to a joint suffering for Christ's sake. It is then

---

[442] Arthur JOHNSTON 1978, Chapters VI-VIII.

[443] Josef Ton, op. cit. pp- 140 f. – P. BEYERHAUS 1992: pp. 163-180.

that we get most closely together. Such was the experience of evangelical pastors and Roman Catholic priests in a German concentration camp, when they started to pray and study the Bible together. In the Soviet Gulag Archipelago orthodox and evangelical prisoners held joint worship services.

At present, confessing Protestants in Germany have a peculiar experience: Our spiritual manifestos against abortion, euthanasia, sexual licentiousness and syncretism are ridiculed in liberal circles. They are simply ignored by the majority of Protestant church leaderships. On the other hand, our manifestos meet with the friendly consent of Catholic bishops – at least some of them.

Those negative experiences of confessing Christians today may be a mild anticipation of that persecution to which all faithful Christians will be exposed in coming times (Matth 24:9; Rev 6:9-11; 17:6; see also Rev 3:10.) In the eschatological hour of trial, all Christians will be faced with the option - Christ or Antichrist? The faithful number of those who do not shrink back will surely come out of various ecclesial traditions. All of them however will belong to the one holy, catholic and apostolic Church, the indivisible Bride of Christ. After their martyrdom, they will be gathered around the throne of the Lamb (Rev 7:9-17). United with the heavenly congregation, they will sing the everlasting praise of the triune God.

Bibliography

Abbreviations

BDCE: Baker's Dictionary of Christian Ethics

EDWM: Evangelical Dictionary of World Missions

EVA: Evangelische Verlagsanstalt Berlin

KNA: Katholische Nachrichten-Agentur

MEW: Karl Marx and Friedrich Engels – Works

NDT: New Dictionary of Theology

WCC: World Council of Churches

ZThK: Zeitschrift für Theologie und Kirche

A

AAGAARD, Johannes (ed.) 1979: "TM's Secret Texts," in: UPDATE: A Quarterly Journal on New Religious Movements, vol. III, (issue 3-4, Dec. 1979), Århus.

AAGAARD, Johannes, 1993: "A Christian Encounter with New Religious Movements," in: Update & Dialogue, No. 3, Oct. 1993, Århus, Denmark.

ABBOT, Walter M. (ed.), 1966: The Documents of Vatican II. Geoffrey Chapman Publ.

Abd al-Rahman al-Jaziri 1991: Die Strafen für den Abfall vom Islam nach den vier Schulen des islamischen Rechts. (The Punishment for Apostasy from Islam according to the four Schools of Islamic Law. Translated from the Arabic Original (Kairo 1987 by Ishak Ersen, Licht des Lebens):Villach, Austria 1991

ACHIMESCU, Nicholae, 1993: Die Vollendung des Menschen im Buddhismus: Bewertung aus orthodoxer Sicht, unpubl. Diss. Tübingen.

AFSCHAR, Moussa, 2002: Die letzte Schlacht des Islam um Jerusalem: Juden und Jerusalem aus der Sicht des Islam. M. Blaich-Verlag.

ALEXANDER, Brooks, 1988: "Die kommende Weltreligion," in: P. Beyerhaus / Lutz E. Von Padberg: Eine Welt – eine Religion?

AMENDT, G. (ed.), 1968: Kinderkreuzzug oder Beginnt die Revolution in den Schulen? Reinbeck.

ANDERS, K., 1963: Mord auf Befehl, Tübingen.

ANDRAE, Tor, 1932/1977: Mohammed. Sein Leben und sein Glaube. Georg Olms-Verlag: Hildesheim.

Anonymous 1967: Documentation: The Odessa Trial. Judicial Hearings of Gospel-Christians-Baptists in Odessa, 2nd-7th Feb. 1967.

ANWAY, P., 1982: "Das Wesen der geschlechtlichen Unterschiede," in: E. Moltmann-Wendel (ed.): Frauenbefreiung .

APPASAMY, A. J., 1970: The Theology of Hindu Bhakti. CLS: Madras.

APPLETON, G., 1958: The Christian Approach to the Buddhist, I.M.C. Edinburgh House: London.

AQUINAS, Thomas, 1975: Summa contra Gentiles, tr. A. C. Pegis et al., On the Truth of the Catholic Faith, 5 vols. (Garden City, NY, 1955-57), reprinted Notre Dame, IN.

ARAI, Tosh and ARIARAJAH, Wesley (eds.), 1989: Spirituality in Interfaith Dialogue, WCC Publications: Geneva.

ARIARAJAH, Wesley, 1991: Hindus and Christians: A Century of Protestant Ecumenical Thought, Eerdmans: Grand Rapids.

ASIAN SOCIAL WELFARE FOUNDATION (ed.), 1986: "Modern Society and Women."

ASSOCIATION OF KOREAN CHRISTIAN FAMILIES (ed.), 1983: The Task for Korean Feminist Theology, Seoul.

ATKINSON, John, 1982: Martin Luther and the Birth of Protestantism, Basingstoke.

AUGUSTINUS, Aurelius: Confessiones Book I.

B

BABA, Panya, 1990: "Track 140 – Two-Thirds World Missions," in: Proclaim Christ Until He Comes. Lausanne II in Manila. International Congress on World Evangelization, 1989, World Wide Publications: Minneapolis.

BAHR, Marius, 1980: Das Abendland am Scheideweg, Schulte & Gerth: Asslar. Baker's Dictionary of Christian Ethics 1973, ed. Carl F.H. Henry, Baker Book House: Grand Rapids, MI (abbr.: BDCE)

BALDIZZONE, T. and G.: Tibet 1995: Eine Reise auf den Spuren von Alexandra David-Nél, Belser-Verlag: Stuttgart.

BAILEY, Alice B., 1944: Discipleship in the New Age, 2 vols. Lucis Press, 1955, (republished London 1981).

BAILEY, Alice, 1945: The Reappearance of the Christ, London (first publ. Lucis Press 1922).

BANDO, Sh., 1973: "Jesus Christus und Amida. Zu Karl Barths Verständnis des Buddhismus vom Reinen Land," in: S. Yagi/U. Lutz (eds.): Gott in Japan, Kaiser Verlag: München.

BARNHOUSE, R. T., 1976: "An Examination of the Ordination of Women to the Priesthood in Terms of the Symbolism in the Eucharist," in: Anglican Theological Review 56 (1976).

BARTH, Karl, 1939 1960: Kirchliche Dogmatik vol. I/2, Ev. Verlag: Zollikon Zürich.

BATCHELOR, Stephen, 1994: The Awakening of the West. Encounter of Buddhism and Western Culture, Berkeley.

BAUCKHAM, R., 1987: Moltmann: Messianic Theology in the Making, London.

BÄUMER, R. / BEYERHAUS, P. / GRÜNZWEIG, F. (eds.), 1980: Weg und Zeugnis. Bekennende Gemeinschaften im gegenwärtigen Geisteskampf 1965-1980, Missionsverlag: Bielefeld.

BEACH, Bert Beverly, 1974: Ecumenism – Boon or Bane? Herald Publ. Assn.: Washington, D.C.

BECK H., 1958: Buddha und seine Lehre, Stuttgart. Bekenntnisschriften der evangelisch-lutherischen Kirche, Vandenhoeck & Ruprecht: Göttingen, vol II.1955.

BELKE, Thomas, 1999: Juche – A Christian Study of North Korea's State Religion, Living Sacrifice Book Company: Bartlesville, OK.

BELL, Daniel, 1960: The End of Ideology.

BENT, Ans J. van der, 1980: Christians and Communists. An ecumenical perspective. WCC: Geneva.

BENZ, Ernst, 1963: Buddhas Wiederkehr und die Zukunft Asiens, Nymphenburger Verl.: München.

BERGMANN, G., 1963: Alarm um die Bibel, Schriftenmission:Gladbeck (1974).

BERNBAUM, Edwin, 1982: Der Weg nach Shambala. Auf der Suche nach dem sagenhaftenKönigreich im Himalaja, Hamburg.

BERTHOLET, A. (ed.), 1929: Religionsgeschichtliches Lehrbuch, Tübingen.

BEYERHAUS, Peter, 1971: Missions – Which Way? Zondervan: Grand Rapids,

BEYERHAUS, Peter, 1972a: Shaken Foundations. New Foundations for Mission, Zondervan: Grand Rapids.

BEYERHAUS, Peter, [2]1972b: Missions which Way? Humanization or Redemption. Zondervan: Grand Rapids.

BEYERHAUS, Peter, 1972c: In Ostasien erlebt. Ev. Missionsverlag: Stuttgart.

BEYERHAUS, Peter, 1973: Bangkok '73 – the Beginning or End of World Mission? Zondervan:Grand Rapids.

BEYERHAUS, Peter / BETZ, Ulrich 1976: Ökumene im Spiegel von Nairobi 1975, Bad Liebenzell.

BEYERHAUS, Peter (ed.), 1979: Ideologien – Herausforderung an den Glauben, Bad Liebenzell.

BEYERHAUS, Peter / HEUBACH, Joachim (eds.), 1979: Zwischen Anarchie und Tyrannei. Vorträge und Ergebnisse des 3. Europäischen Bekenntniskonvents, Bad Liebenzell.

BEYERHAUS, Peter / KÜNNETH, Walter (eds.), 1987: Gewalt in Jesu Namen? Verlag St. Johannis-Druckerei: Lahr.

BEYERHAUS, Peter, 1988a: Theology as Instrument of Liberation. The role of the new "People's Theology" in Ecumenical Discussion. Pro Fide Defendenda, Cape Town.

BEYERHAUS, Peter / PADBERG, Lutz E. von (eds.), 1988b: Eine Welt – Eine Religion? Die synkretistische Bedrohung unseres Glaubens im Zeichen von New Age, Schulte & Gerth: Asslar.

BEYERHAUS, Peter, 1988: Art. "Berlin Declaration," in: New Dictionary of Theology, ed. by. S.B. Ferguson et al., InterVarsity Press: Leicester, p. 90.

BEYERHAUS, Peter, 1992: God's Kingdom and the Utopian Error, Crossway Publ.: Wheaton.

BEYERHAUS, Peter, 1996a: "Das Zeugnis vom Heil in unserer multikulturellen Gesellschaft," in: DIAKRISIS 17 (4/1996).

BEYERHAUS, Peter, 1996b: Er sandte sein Wort. Theologie der christlichen Mission, R. Brockhaus:Wuppertal.

BEYERHAUS, Peter, 1996c: "The Authority of the Gospel and Interreligious Dialogue," in: Trinity Journal 17 (Fall 1996).

BEYERHAUS, Peter, 1999: "Der Auftrag der Kirche Jesu Christi und der Ökumenische Rat der Kirchen," in: J. Heubach/K.-D. Stephan (eds.): Berufsethik – Glaube – Seelsorge. FS für Rolf Sauerzapf, Ev. Verlagsanstalt: Berlin.

BEYERHAUS, Peter, 2000: "Evangelisches Fragen nach der Katholizität der Kirche," in: Die Weite des Mysteriums. FS für Horst Bürkle, ed. by K. Krämer and A. Paus, Herder: Freiburg etc.

BEYERHAUS, Peter, 2001 : "Siegfried Ernst – Wächterstimme des christlichen Gewissens," in: DIAKRISIS 22 (4/2001).

BEYERHAUS, Peter, 2004: "Von Berlin 1974 nach Freudenstadt 2004," in: DIAKRISIS 25 (2/2004).

BEYREUTHER, Erich, 1958: August Hermann Francke und die Anfänge der ökumenischen Bewegung, EVA:Berlin.

BIEHLER, Ekkehard, 1974: Der Umbruch der Ökumene zwischen Neu-Delhi und Uppsala. Unpubl. Diss. Kirchliche Hochschule: Berlin.

BISHOP, Peter, 1993: Dreams of Power. Tibetan Buddhism in the Western Imagination, London.

BLIGNIÈRES, Louis-Marie de, 2003: "Überlegungen zu Assisi," Una Voce-Korrespondenz, 33 (no. 1, Jan.-Febr. 2003).

BLOCH, Ernst, 1954-59: Das Prinzip Hoffnung, 3 vols. Leipzig.

BLOCH, Ernst, 1962a: Werke, Gesamtausgabe, 4 vols., Suhrkamp: Frankfurt/M.

BLOCH, Ernst, 1962b: Thomas Müntzer als Theologe der Revolution. Suhrkamp: Frankfurt/M.

BLOCH, Ernst, 1969: Atheismus im Christentum – zur Religion des Exodus und des Reiches. Suhrkamp Verlag: Frankfurt/M.

BLOCH, Ernst, 1970: Man on His Own, Herder & Herder: New York.

BLOFELD, John, 1988: Bodhisattva of Compassion. The mystical tradition of Kuan Yin, Boston.

BLUMENBERG, Werner, 1967: Karl Marx in Selbstzeugnissen und Bilddokumenten. Rowohlts Bildmonographien vol. 76: Hamburg.

BOCKMÜHL, Klaus, 1975: Gott im Exil? Zur Kritik der 'Neuen Moral'. Aussaat: Wuppertal.

BOCKMÜHL, Klaus, 1986: Das Evangelium und die Ideologien, Wuppertal.

BORMUTH, K.-H., 1972: Alte Gebote und neue Moral, Hänssler: Stuttgart.

BORSCH, F., 1970: The Christian and Gnostic Son of Man, London.

BOWES, Pratima, 1977: The Hindu Religious Tradition. A Philosophical Approach. London/Henley/Boston.

BRAUEN, Martin, 1992: Das Mandala. Der heilige Kreis im tantrischen Buddhismus, Bachem: Köln.

BRECHT, Martin, 1993-2003: Geschichte des Pietismus. 4 volumes, Vandenhoeck & Ruprecht: Göttingen.

BREZINKA, W., 1974: Erziehung und Kulturrevolution. Die Kulturpolitik der Neuen Linken, München.

BROIDO, Michael M., 1988: Killing, Lying, Stealing and Adultery. A Problem of Interpretation in the Tantras, in: Donald P. Lopez: Buddhist Hermeneutics. Studies in East Asian Buddhism no. 6, Honolulu 1988.

BROMILEY, G. W., 1980: Introduction to the Theology of Karl Barth, Edinburgh.

BRUNNER, Emil, 1932: Das Gebot und die Ordnungen. Entwurf einer protestantisch-theologischen Ethik, Ev. Verlag: Zürich.

BULTMANN, Rudolf: Art. "Aleethei," Theol. Wörterbuch zum Neuen Testament vol.I.

BULTMANN, Rudolf, ³1954: "Neues Testament und Mythologie," in: Kerygma und Mythos, vol I.

BUNDY, Edgar C., 1975: Collectivism in the Churches. A Documented Account of the Political Activities of the Federal, National and World Councils of Churches, The Church League of America: Wheaton.

BURGSMUELLER, A./R. WETH (Eds.), 1984: Die Barmer Theologische Erklärung Einführung und Dokumentation, Neukirchen.

BURI, Fritz, 1975: Der Begriff der Gnade bei Paulus, Shinran und Luther, in: Theologische Zeitschrift 31.

BUSCH, Eberhard, 1976: Karl Barth, London.

BUTSCHKUS, H., 1940: Luthers Religion und ihre Entsprechung im Amida-Buddhismus, Diss. in Bonn, publ. Emsdetten.

C

CAIRNS, E. E., 1986: An Endless Line of Splendour. Revivals and their Leaders from the Great Awakening to the Present, Tyndale House Publishers: Carol Stream, IL.

CALVEZ, Jean-Yves, 1964: Karl Marx – Darstellung und Kritik seines Denkens, Olten u. Freiburg.

CANCIC, Hans, et. al. (ed.), 2001: Art.: "Götternamen," in: Handbuch religionswissenschaftlicher Grundbegriffe, Kohlhammer: Stuttgart, Vol. IV.

CAPRA, Fritjof, 1983: The Turning Point. Science, Society and the Rising Culture, Bantram Books: New York.

CASSIERER, E., 1951: The Philosophy of the Enlightenment, Princeton, USA

CHENCHIAH, P. / CHAKKARAI, V. / SUNDARISANAM, A. N., 1941: Ashrams Past and Present, CLS: Madras.

CHILDS, B.S., 1970: Biblical Theology in Crisis, Philadelphia.

CHO, Paul Yonggi, 1979: The Fourth Dimension, Bridge Publishing: South Plainfield, NJ,

CHOO, Kwang-Cho, 1997: My Father, Rev. Ki-Cheul Choo, the Martyr. (Korean and English), UBF Press: Seoul.

CHRISTIAN, A, 1962: Handbook on Communism. New York: National Council of the Churches of Christ in the U.S.A. Committee on World Literacy and Christian Literature: New York.

CHUNG, Kyung-Hyun, 1991: "Komm Heiliger Geist, – erneuere die ganze Schöpfung." In: Im Zeichen des Heiligen Geistes. Bericht aus Canberra 91, Verlag Otto Lembeck: Frankfurt 1991.

CHUNG, Kyung-Hyun, 1992: "The Contribution and the Future of Asian Women's Theology," in: Hanna Stenström (Ed.): Kan vi tro på Gud Fader? Uppsala.

COMMITTEE OF THEOLOGICAL STUDY / KNCC, (ed), 1982: Minjung and Korean Theology, Seoul.

COX, Harvey, 1977: Turning East – the Promise and Peril of the New Orientalism, Simon and Schuster: New York.

CROMBIE, Kelvin, 1991: For the Love of Zion. Christian Witness and the Restoration of Israel, Hodder & Stoughton: London.

CULLMANN, Oscar, 1962: Christus und die Zeit: Die urchristliche Zeit- und Geschichtsauffassung, EVZ-Verlag:Zürich

CULLMANN, Oskar, 1970: Petrus: Jünger, Apostel, Märtyrer, EVZ: Zürich.

CUMBEY, Constance, 1983: The Hidden Dangers of the Rainbow, Huntington House: Louisiana.

D

DAGUPTA, Shashi Bhusan, 1974: An Introduction to Tantric Buddhism, London.

DALAI LAMA XIV, 1964: My Land and my People, London.

DALAI LAMA XIV, 1981 "On the Kalachacra Initiation," Address in 1981, printed in Tibetan Review 17, 1981.

DALAI LAMA XIV, 1985: The Kalachacra Tantra. Rite of Initiation for the Stage of Generation, London.

DALAI LAMA XIV, 1993: Frieden für die Welt, Frieden für Tibet, Hamburg.

DALAI LAMA XIV, 1996: Beyond Dogma, Dialogues and Discourses, Berkeley.

DALAI LAMA XIV, 1997: Das Herz aller Religionen ist eins. Die Lehre Jesu aus buddhistischer Sicht, Hamburg.

DALY, Mary, 1968a: The Church and the Second Sex, Boston.

DALY, Mary, 1968b: Beyond God the Father, Boston, German edition 1982.

DALY, Mary, 1978: Gyn/Ecology. The Metaethics of Radical Feminism, Boston, (German edition München 1981).

DAYAL, H., 1970: The Bodhisattva Doctrine in Buddhist Sanskrit Literature, Basanidas: Delhi.

DEAN, Thomas, 1979: Post-Theistic Thinking: The Marxist-Christian Dialogue in Radical Perspective. Fortress University Press: Philadelphia.

DENNIS, L. T., 1986: Francis Schaeffer. Portraits of the Man and His Work, Westchester IL.

Deutsche Bischofskonferenz (ed.) 1984: Instruktion der Kongregation für die Glaubenslehre über einige Aspekte der "Theologie der Befreiung," 6. August 1984, Verlautbarungen des Apostolischen Stuhls No. 57.

DHARGYEY, Llarampa Ngawang, 1985: A Commentary on the Kalachakra Tantra, New Delhi.

DILLON, George F., 1965: Grand Orient Freemasonry Unmasked, London.

DÖRMANN, Johannes, 1988: Assisi: "Anfang einer neuen Zeit," in: Respondeo. Theologische Schriftenreihe No. 8: Abenberg.

DÖRMANN, Johannes: Der theologische Weg Johannes Pauls II. zum Weltgebetstag der Religionen in Assisi, 5 vols., Sitta Verlag: Senden 1990-1998.

DONNER, T. G., 1988: Art "Apologists," in: NDT.

DOSTOJEWSKI, Fjodor M., 1922: Die Dämonen. R & Co. Piper: München. (Russian: "Besy")

DOUGLAS, J. D. (ed.), 1989: Proclaim Christ Until He Comes. Lausanne II on Manila, IcoWE: Minneapolis.

DOWLING, Lévy, 1964: The Aquarian Gospel of Jesus Christ: The Philosophic and Practical Basis of the Religion of the Aquarian Age of the World, L. N. Fowler.

DREYTZA, Manfred, 2000: "Die Faszination des Dalai Lama," in: DIAKRISIS 21 (1/2000).

DULLES, Avery: A History of Apologetics, Philadelphia 1971.

DUMOULIN, H., 1976: Der Erleuchtungsweg des Zen im Buddhismus, Fischer TB: Köln.

DUMOULIN, H., 1991: Begegnung mit dem Buddhismus, Herder: Freiburg.

E

EBELING, Gerhard, 1950: "Die Bedeutung der historisch-kritischen Methode für die protestantische Theologie und Kirche," ZThK, Vol 47.

EISSLER, Hans / NÄNNY, Walter, 2001: Wegbereiter für Israel. Aus der Geschichte der Anfänge 1850 bis 1950. Ernst Franz Verlag: Metzingen.

ENGELS, Friedrich, 1975: Der Ursprung der Familie, des Privateigentums und des Staats, in: MEW, Dietz-Verlag Berlin, vol. 21.

ENROTH, Ronald & Others (eds.), 1983: A Guide to Cults & New Religions. Intervarsity Christian Fellowship of the U.S.A. Downers Grove. Ill.

ERNST, Siegfried, 1974: Das größte Wunder ist der Mensch. Antwort auf die sexuelle Konter-Evolution, Martin Verlag: Buxheim.

Evangelical Dictionary of World Missions 2000, ed. by A. Scott Moreau et al., Baker Book House: Grand Rapids, Mi.

Evangelisches Verlagswerk 1969: Theologiestudenten 1969. Dokumente einer revolutionären Generation. EVW: Stuttgart, 1969.

EVANS, Donald, 1965: Communist Faith and Christian Faith. SCM Press: London.

EVOLA, Julius: "What Tantrism means to modern Western Civilization," in: East and West I, No 1.

F

FARQUHAR, J. N., 1912: A Primer on Hinduism, Oxford.

FERGUSON, Marilyn, 1980: The Aquarian Conspiracy: Personal and Social Transformation, J.P. Tarcher, U.S.A.

FERNANDEZ, Ajith, 1995: The Supremacy of Christ, Crossway Books: Wheaton.

FEY, Harold E. (ed.), 1970: The Ecumenical Advance. A History of the Ecumenical Movement, vol. 2, 1948-1986, S.P.C.K.: London.

FINNEY, C. G., 1960: Lectures on Revival of Religion, (ed.) by W. G. McLaughlin, Cambridge MA.

FLETCHER, Joseph, 1966: Situation Ethics – The New Morality, John Knox Press: Westminster.

FREUD, S., 1989: Sexualleben, Reprint Fischerbücherei.

FREUD, S., 2004: Jenseits des Lustprinzips, Fischerbücherei (Gesammelte Werke vol. 13).

FREY, Hellmuth, 1972: Die Krise der Theologie. Historische Kritik und pneumatische Auslegung im Licht der Krise, Brockhaus: Wuppertal.

FREYTAG, Walter, 1961: Reden und Aufsätze vols. I+II, Christian Kaiser Verl.: Munich.

G

GABRIELI, Francesco, 1973: Die Kreuzzüge aus arabischer Sicht, Zürich/München.

GARAUDY, R., 1968: Kann man heute noch Kommunist sein? (Can one still be a Communist today?), Suhrkamp: Frankfurt/M. .

GARDET, Louis, 1968: Islam. Bachem: Köln.

GAY, P., 1970: The Enlightenment: An Interpretation, 2 Vols. London.

GEISLER, N.L. (ed.), 1979: Inerrancy: Zondervan: Grand Rapids.

GENSICHEN, H.-W., 1959: Buddhistische Mission und christliches Zeugnis, MBK Verl.: Bad Salzuflen.

GERBER, U., 1987: Die feministische Eroberung der Theologie, Munich.

GIESECKE, H., 1973: Bildungsreform und Emanzipation, München.

GLASENAPP, Helmuth von, 1956: Die Religionen Indiens. Deutscher Bücherbund: Stuttgart.

GLASENAPP, Helmut von, 1963: Die fünf Weltreligionen, Dt. Bücherbund: Stuttgart.

GLASENAPP, Helmut von, 1966: Der Buddhismus, eine atheistische Religion, Szczesny: München.

GNILKA, Christian, 1984: Chreesis. Die Methode der Kirchenväter im Umgang mit der antiken Kultur I. Schwaben-Verlag: Basel/Stuttgart.

GÖTTNER-ABENDROTH, Heide, 1984: Die Göttin und ihr Heros. Die matriarchalischen Religionen in Mythos, Märchen und Dichtung, Munich.

GODEL, E., 1989: "Die Heilige Geistin," in: Radius - Zeitschrift der Evang. Akademikerschaft, Oct. 1989.

GOLDSTEIN, C. Melvyn, 1989: A History of Modern Tibet 1913-1951. The Demise of the Lamaist State, Berkeley.

GONDA, Jan, 1963/1978: Die Religionen Indiens, Stuttgart.

GOODSPEED, E. J., 1914: Die ältesten Apologeten, Göttingen.

GORITSCHEWA, Tatjana, 1997: Von Gott zu reden ist gefährlich. Vandenhoeck & Ruprecht: Göttingen 1984.

GRANT, R. M., 1969: Gnosticism and Early Christianity, New York.

GROOTHUIS, Douglas: Art. "New Age," in EDWM.

GRÜNZWEIG, Fritz, 1982: Johannes-Offenbarung, Vol. II, Hänssler: Neuhausen-Stuttgart.

GÜNTHER, H., 1956: Der Buddha und seine Lehre, Zürich.

GÜNTHER, Henning, 1979: Alarm um die Familie, Bad Liebenzell.

GUINNESS, Os, 1989: "The Impact of Modernization," in: DOUGLAS 1989.

GUNDRY, S.N., 1910: The Life and Work of D.L. Moody, London.

GUTIÉRREZ, Gustavo, 1972: Theologia de la Liberaciòn, Ediciones Sigueme, Salamanca; (English tr.: A Theology of Liberation: History, Politics and Salvation). Orbis Books: Maryknoll 1973.

H

HAAN, M. R. de, 1982: Revelation. 35 Simple Studies in the Main Themes in Revelation, Zondervan: Grand Rapids.

HAAS, H., 1912: "Christliche Klänge im japanischen Buddhismus," in: Zeitschrift für Missionskunde und Religionswissenschaft 20 (1912).

HADDON, David, 1983: "Transcendental Meditation," in R. ENROTH (ed.) 1988.

HALKES, C. J. M., 1982: Gott hat nicht nur starke Söhne. Grundzüge einer Feministischen Theologie, GTB Siebenstern:Gütersloh.

HANNAH, J.D. (ed.), 1984: Inerrancy and the Church, Chicago.

HARRINGTON, W.J., 1973: The Path of Biblical Theology, Dublin.

HAUSCHILDT, Ingeborg, 1983: Gott eine Frau? Weg und Irrweg der feministischen Theologie, R. Brockhaus: Wuppertal.

HAUSCHILDT, Ingeborg, 1989: Die feministische Versuchung und die Antwort der christlichen Frau. R. Brockhaus: Wuppertal/Zürich.

HAWTING, G.R, 1982: "The Origins of the Muslim Sanctuary at Mecca," in G.H.A. Juynboll (ed.): Studies on the First Century of Islamic Society. Southern Illinois University Press: Carbondal.

HECKER, Hellmuth, 1971: Das buddhistische Nirvana. Mit einer Stellenlese aus den Pali-Texten, Hamburg.

HEDEGARD, David, 1954: Ecumenism and the Bible, Lund: Sweden.

HEILER, Friederich et. al., 1980: Die Religionen der Menschheit in Vergangenheit und Gegenwart, ed. by Kurt Goldammer, Stuttgart.

HENDERSON, G. D., 1952: "The Reformed (Presbyterian) Churches," in: The Nature of the Church. Papers presented to the Theological Commission of the World Conference on Faith and Order, ed. by. R. Newton FLEW, SCM Press: London.

HENRICK, James A., 2003: The Making of the New Spirituality, InterVarsity Press: Leicester.

HENSS, Michael, 1985: Kalachakra. Ein tibetisches Einweihungsritual, Zürich.

HEMPELMANN, Reinhard et.al. (eds.), 2001: Panorama der neuen Religiosität, Gütersloher Verlagshaus.

HESS, Moses, 1841: Letter to Berthold Auerbach, September 2, 1841.

HEYWARD, Carter, 1986: Und sie rührte sein Kleid an, Kreuz-Verlag: Stuttgart.

HICK, John (ed.), 1977: The Myth of God Incarnate. SCM Press: London/Westminster.

HICK, John (ed.), 1987: The Myth of Christian Uniqueness: Towards a Pluralistic Theology of Religions, Orbis Books: Maryknoll.

HINNELS, John R. (ed.), 1984: The Penguin Dictionary of Religions, Penguin.

HOCK, Klaus, 1986: Der Islam im Spiegel der westlichen Theologie. Böhlau Verlag: Köln.

HODGSON, Leonard, 1946: The Doctrine of the Church as Held and Taught in the Church of England, Oxford: Blackwell.

HOEFER, Herbert E., 1991: Churchless Christianity, Gurukul: Madras.

HOFFMANN, Helmut, 1956: Religionen Tibets. Bon und Lamaismus in ihrer geschichtlichen Entwicklung, Freiburg.

HOLMSTRAND, I., 1980: Karl Heim: Philosophy, Science and the Transcendence of God, Stockholm.

HORKHEIMER, Max, 1968: Kritische Theorie, 2 vols., Frankfurt/M.

HORNIG, G., 1961: Die Anfänge der historisch-kritischen Theologie. Johann Salomo Semlers Schriftverständnis und seine Stellung zu Luther, EVA:Berlin.

HORNUNG, Klaus, 1978: Der faszinierende Irrtum: Karl Marx und die Folgen, Herderbücherei: Freiburg.

HOSHINO, G., 1956: "Das Verhältnis des buddhistischen Denkens zu Karl Barth," in: Antwort. Festschrift zum 70. Geburtstag von K. Barth, EVZ:Zürich.

HOVE, Odd Sverre, 1991: "Der Weltkirchenrat am Scheideweg," in: DIAKRISIS 12 (2/1991).

HUMMEL, Reinhart, 1980: Indische Mission und neue Frömmigkeit im Westen, Kohlhammer: Stuttgart-Berlin.

HUMMEL, Reinhart, 1984: Gurus in Ost und West, Quell Verlag: Stuttgart.

HUNDLEY, Raymond C., 1987: Radical Liberation Theology: An Evangelical Response, Bristol Books: Wilmore.

HUNDSBERGER, George: Art. "Accommodation," in: EDWM.

HUNT, Dave /MacMAHON, T. A., 1985: The Seduction of Christianity, Harvest House Publishers: Eugene, Oregon, USA.

HUNTEMANN, Georg, 1981: Die Zerstörung der Person: Umsturz der Werte – Gotteshaß der Vaterlosen – Feminismus, Bad Liebenzell.

HUNTEMANN, Georg, 1995: Biblisches Ethos im Zeitalter der Moral-revolution, Hänssler: Neuhausen-Stuttgart.

I

Institute of Eastern Culture 1993: "On the dissemination of the Belief in the Dalai Lama as a Manifestation of the Bodhisattva Avalo-kiteshvara," in: Acta Asiatica. Bulletin, No. 64, Tokyo

International Christian Network 1996: 25 Jahre alternatives Theologiestudium. Special issue of DIAKRISIS vol. 17 (1/1996).

International Christian Network 2000: No Other Name! (Acts 4:12). Theological Declaration Concerning the Assessment of the Religions in the Light of the Gospel, (separate print); the German original in: DIAKRISIS Vol. 21 (1/2000).

ISHAQ, Ibn, 1976: Das Leben des Propheten. Translated by G. Rotter, Tübingen.

ITTAL, Gerta, 1968: Der Meister, die Mönche und ich: Im Zen-buddhistischen Kloster. O.W. Barth Verlag: Weilheim.

J

JACOBS, Manfred, 1989: Assisi und die Neue Religion, Pro Fide Catholica: Durach.

JAQUARD, Roland, 2001: Die Akte Osama Bin Laden, München.

JEBASINGH, Emil, 2003: "A New Experimental Approach of Holistic Mission in the Indian Context," unpubl. Lecture read at the A.M.A. Congress in Moscow in September 2003.

JOHANNES PAUL II, 1994: Die Schwelle der Hoffnung überschreiten, Hoffmann & Campe: Hamburg.

JOHNSON, R.A., 1974: The Origins of Demythologizing, Brill: Leiden.

JOHNSTON, Arthur, 1978: The Battle for World Evangelism, Tyndale House Publishers: Carol Stream, IL.

JOHNSTON, Arthur, 1988: "Wahre und falsche Einheit der Christen," in: P. Beyerhaus / L. E. v. Padberg 1987.

JOMIER, R.P., 1962: Bibel und Koran, Klosterneuburger Verlag.

JONAS, Hans, 1963: The Gnostic Religion, Boston.

JONES, E. Stanley, 1925: The Christ of the Indian Road, SCM: London.

JUNG, Carl Gustav: Mandala: Bilder aus dem Unbewußten, Olten 1981.

JUYNBOLL, G.H.A. (ed.), 1982: Studies on the First Century of Islamic Society. Southern Illinois University Press: Carbondal.

K

KÄSEMANN, E., 1964: "Einheit und Vielfalt in der neutestamentlichen Lehre von der Kirche," in: Ökumenische Rundschau 13 (I/1964).

KAHL, J., 1968: Das Elend des Christentums – oder Plädoyer für eine Humanität ohne Gott. Rowohlt Taschenbuch Verlag: Hamburg.

KAHL, Susanne et al., 1981: Feministische Theologie - Praxis. Ein Werkstattbuch, Evangelische Akademie: Bad Boll.

KAMINSKY, Claudia, 2002: "Medizinischer Fortschritt am Menschen vorbei," in: DIAKRISIS 23 (1-2/2002).

KAMPHUIS, Martin, 2000: Ich war Buddhist, Pattloch Verlag: München.

KARST, Heinz, 1979: "Die ideologische Gemeinsamkeit von Marxismus und Faschismus," in: Peter Beyerhaus (ed.) 1979.

KAYE, Bruce / WENHAM, Gordon (Eds.), 1978: Law, Morality and the Bible, IVF-Press Leicester.

KEEGAN, Marcia, 1981: The Teachings of His Holiness, the Dalai Lama, New York.

KELLERHALS, Emanuel, 1961: ... und Mohammed ist sein Prophet. Basileia Verlag: Basel.

KENTLER, Helmut, 1970: Sexualerziehung, Reinbek.

KIDDLE, Martin, 1946: The Revelation of St. John, Hodder & Stoughton: London.

KILBOURN, Phyllis / McDERMID Marjorie (eds.), 1998: Sexually Exploited Children. Working to Protect and Heal, World Vision Resources.

KIM, Yong-Bock (ed.), 1980: Minjung Theology. People as the subject of history. Christian Conference of Asia: Singapore.

KING, L.W., 1963: Buddhism and Christianity. Some Bridges of Understanding. Allen/Unwin: London.

KING, L.W., 1975: The Impersonal Personalism and Subjectivism of Buddhist Nihilism, in: Japanese Religions, VIII, 4.

KIPLING, R., 1927: The Ballad of East and West, Hodder & Stoughton: London.

KITTEL, Gerhard: Art. *"eidos"* in: Theologisches Wörterbuch zum Neuen Testament, vol. II.

KLAFKI, W., 1970: Erziehungswissenschaft als kritische Theorie, Suhrkamp: Frankfurt.

KLOSTERMAIER, K., 1963: Hinduismus, Bachem: Köln.

KOCH, Kurt, 1972: Between Christ and Satan, Evangelization Publ.: Berghausen, Germany.

KOTLER, Arnold, 1996: Engaged Buddhist. Reader: Berkeley.

KRATTIGER, U., 1987: Die perlmutterne Mönchin. Reise in die weibliche Spiritualität, Kreuz Verlag: Zürich

KRENTZ, E., 1976: The Historical-Critical Method, London.

KRÜGER Erich, 1962: Der Buddhismus im Lichte der Christusoffenbarung, Verlag Stursberg: Neukirchen.

KRÜGER, Hanfried (ed.), 1976: Jesus Christus befreit und eint. Vorträge von der Fünften Vollversammlung des Ökumenischen Rates der Kirchen in Nairobi, Verlag O. Lembeck: Frankfurt.

KÜNG, Hans / ESS, Josef van et. al., 1984: Christentum und Weltreligionen: Islam – Hinduismus – Buddhismus. Piper: München, "Muhammad – ein Prophet?".

KÜNG, Hans / BECHERT, H., 1990: Christentum und Weltreligionen, vol. III Buddhismus, München.

KÜNNETH, Walter / BEYERHAUS, Peter (eds.), 1975: Reich Gottes oder Weltgemeinschaft? Die Berliner Ökumene-Erklärung zur utopischen Vision des Weltkirchenrates, Bad Liebenzell.

KÜNNETH, Walter, 1979: "Ideologie und Evangelium in systematisch-theologischer Deutung," in: Peter Beyerhaus (ed.): Ideologien - Herausforderungen an den Glauben, Bad Liebenzell.

KÜNZLI, Arnold, 1966: Karl Marx – Eine Psychographie, Wien/Frankfurt/Zürich.

KUHL, Dieter, 2002: "Hat Gott einen Plan auch mit den Muslimen?" In: DIAKRISIS 23 (No. 5/6 2002).

KULANDRAN, Bishop S., 1964: Grace: A Comparative Study of the Doctrine in Christianity and in Hinduism. Lutterworth Press: London.

KUSCHEL, Karl, 2001: Streit um Abraham. Was Juden, Christen und Muslime trennt und was sie eint. Patmos Verlag:Düsseldorf.

KUX, Ernst, 1967: Karl Marx – Die revolutionäre Konfession, Zürich/Stuttgart.

L

LADNER, M., 1948: Gotamo Buddha, Zürich.

LAMBERT, Lance, 1998: "Islamischer Fundamentalismus in endgeschichtlichem Licht," in: DIAKRISIS vol. 19 (2/1998).

LANGE, Ernst, 1972: Die ökumenische Utopie oder Was bewegt die ökumenische Bewegung? Kreuz Verlag: Stuttgart.

LANGER-KANEKO, Chr., 1986: Das Reine Land. Zur Begegnung von Amida-Buddhismus und Christentum, Brill:Leiden.

LASSALLE, Enomiya, 1966: Zen-Buddhismus, Bachem: Köln.

LASZLO, E., 1974: Goals for Global Society. A Positive Approach to the Predicament of Mankind, A Report to the Club of Rome, mimeographed document November.

LAUSANNE COMMITTEE FOR WORLD EVANGELIZATION 1980: The Thailand Report on Buddhists: Report of the Consultation on World Evangelization. Mini Consultation on Reaching Buddhists, held at Pattaya, Thailand from 16-27 June 1980, Wheaton.

LEDERMANN, Katrin, 1988: "Zeugnis eines ehemaligen New-Age-Gurus," in: P BEYERHAUS/Lutz E. von Padberg (eds.) 1988.

LEE, Dong-Joo, 1991: Koreanischer Synkretismus und die Vereinigungskirche. Edition VLM, St. Johannis-Druckerei: Lahr.

LEHMANN, Arno (ed.), 1957: Alte Briefe aus Indien, EVA: Berlin.

LENZ, Reimar, 1969: Der neue Glaube. Bemerkungen zur Gesellschaftstheologie der jungen Linken und zur geistigen Situation. Jugenddienst-Verlag: Wuppertal.

LINDBOM, Tage 1979: "Wohlfahrtsstaat mit Totalitätsansprüchen," in: P. Beyerhaus / J. Heubach (eds.), Zwischen Anarchie und Tyrannei. Bad Liebenzell.

LINDSELL, Harold (ed.), 1966: The Church's World-Wide Mission.

LÖW, Konrad (ed.), 1985: Marxismus Quellenlexikon, Kölner Universitätsverlag.

LÖW, Konrad, 2001: Marx und Marxismus. Eine deutsche Schizophrenie, Thesen, Texte, Quellen. Verlag Langen Müller: München.

LOPEZ, Donald P., 1988: Buddhist Hermeneutics. Studies in East-Asian Buddhism no. 6, Honolulu.

LOVELACE, Richard F., 1984: Homosexuality: What Should Christians do about it? Fleming H. Revell: New Jersey.

LÜCK, Immanuel, 1979: Alarm um die Schule – die neomarxistische Unterwanderung, Hänssler: Stuttgart-Neuhausen.

LÜLING, Günter, 1977: Der christliche Kult in der vorislamischen Kaaba als Problem der Islamwissenschaft und der christlichen Theologie. Erlangen.

LÜTHIE, Kurt, 1978: Gottes neue Eva: Wandlungen des Weiblichen, Kreuz Verlag:Stuttgart.

LUTHER, Martin, 1955: Works, Weimar Edition, 55 vols. St Louis and Philadelphia.

M

MACHOVEC, M., 1972: Jesus für Atheisten (Jesus for Atheists), Kreuz Verlag:Stuttgart.

MACHOVEC, M., 2000: Die Frage nach Gott – die Frage nach dem Menschen (The Quest for God – a quest for man), Tyrolia Verlag: Innsbruck.

MACQUARRIE, J., 1955: An Existentialist Theology, London.

MAHARAJ, Rabindranath R., 1977: Death of a Guru. J. P. Lippincott Publ.: New York.

MAIER, Gerhard, 1987: "Die Kirche im Matthäusevangelium. Hermeneutische Analyse der gegenwärtigen Debatte über das Petrus-Wort in Matt. 16:17-19," in: C. P. Thiede (ed.): Das Petrusbild in der neueren Forschung. R. Brockhaus: Wuppertal.

MANGOLDT, Ursula von, 1959: Christentum und Buddhismus: Verwandtes und Unterscheidendes. Barth Verl.: München-Planegg.

MANNHEIM, Karl, 1962: Ideologie und Utopie, Suhrkamp:Frankfurt.

MAOZ, Baruch, 1986: The Gospel Scene in Israel, CWI: Kent.

MARCUSE, Herbert, 1966: Das Problem der Gewalt in der Opposition (The Problem of Violence in the Opposition), Suhrkamp: Frankfurt/M.

MARCUSE, Herbert, 1974: "Marxismus und Feminismus," in: Jahrbuch Politik No. 6, Berlin.

MARGULL, H.-J. / SAMARTHA, St. J. (eds.), 1972: Dialog mit anderen Religionen. Material aus der ökumenischen Bewegung, O.Lembeck: Frankfurt/M.

MARSDEN, G. M.: Art. "Fundamentalism," in: NDT.

MARSDEN, G. M., 1980: Fundamentalism and American Culture. The Shaping of Twentieth-Century Evangelicalism 1870-1925, New York.

MARX, Karl: The Union of the Faithful with Christ. MEW, Suppl vol. 1.

MARX, Karl, 1882: Letter of Karl Marx to Friedrich Engels (May 20, 1882), in: MEW, XXXV.

MARX, Karl, 1971: Thesen über Feuerbach, in: Die Frühschriften, (ed. B. Kautsky), Kroner Verlag: Stuttgart.

MATRISCIANA, Caryl, 1985: Gods of the New Age, Harvest House Publ., U.S.A.

MATTEI, Roberto de (ed.), 1996: Kirche und Homosexualität, Christiana:Stein am Rhein.

McDOWELL, Josh / HOSTETLER, Bob, 1999: The New Tolerance, Tyndale House: Wheaton.

McGAVRAN, Donald, 1977: The Conciliar-Evangelical Debate: The Crucial Documents 1964-1976, William Carey Library: Pasadena.

MEADE, Marion, 1987: Madam Blavatsky. The Woman behind the Myth, New York.

MEADOWS, D., et al (ed.), 1972: The Limits to Growth, Universe Books: New York.

MELTON, J., 1990: New Age Encyclopaedia, Gale Research.

MELZER, Friso, 1976: Christliche Ashrams in Südindien, Ev.-Luth. Mission:Erlangen.

MENSCHING, Gustav, 1936: "Luther und Amida Buddha," in: ZMR 51.(1936).

MENSCHING, Gustav, 1955: Buddhistische Geisteswelt: Vom historischen Buddhismus zum Lamaismus, Baden-Baden.

MENSCHING, Gustav, 1978: Buddha und Christus – Ein Vergleich. DVA: Stuttgart.

MERSAROVIC, M / FESTEL, E. (ed.), 1974: Mankind at its Turning Point, Dutton: New York.

MERTENS, W., 1974: Erziehung zur Konfliktfähigkeit, München.

MERTENSACKER, Adelgunde, 1992: Geführt von Dämonen (Led by demons). Mohammed im Urteil seiner Zeitgenossen. Christliche Mitte: Lippstadt.

MERTENSACKER, Adelgunde, 1998: Muslime erobern Deutschland (Muslims Conquer Germany). Eine Dokumentation, Christliche Mitte: Lippstadt.

MERTENSACKER, Adelgunde, 2001: Moscheen in Deutschland: Stützpunkte islamischer Eroberung [Mosques in Germany: Strongholds of Islamic Conquest]. Christliche Mitte: Lippstadt.

MEVES, Christa, 1980a: Unser Leben muß anders werden, Herder: Freiburg.

MEVES, Christa, 1980b: Der Weg zum sinnerfüllten Leben, Herder: Freiburg.

MEVES, Christa, 1982: Die ruinierte Generation, Herder: Freiburg.

MEVES, Christa, 2000: Manipulierte Maßlosigkeit, Herder: Freiburg.

MEVES, Christa, 2002: Aufbruch zu einer christlichen Kulturrevolution, Christiana: Stein MEYER, Harding (ed.), 1983: Dokumente wachsender Übereinstimmung. Bonifatius / Lembeck Verl.: Paderborn / Frankfurt.

MIGUEZ-BONINO, Josè, 1976: Christians and Marxists: The Mutual Challenge to Revolution. Hodder and Stoughton, London.

MILDENBERGER, Michael / SCHÖLL, Albrecht, 1977: Zauberformel TM. Die Bewegung der Transzendentalen Meditation, Aussaat Verlag: Wuppertal.

MILLHEIM, John, 1991: "Ecumenism in Canberra," in: TAM Newsletter of the Associated Missions; No. 85 April-August 1991.

MIURA, I. and SASAKI, R.F., 1965: The Zen Koan, Kyoto.

MODEROW, Hans-Martin / SENS, Matthias, 1979: Orientierung Ökumene.EVA: Berlin.

MOJZES, Paul (ed.), 1978: Varieties of Christian-Marxist Dialogue. A special number of the Journal of Ecumenical Studies, Vol. 15, No. 1.

MOLLENHAUER, K., 1968: Erziehung und Emanzipation, München.

MOLTMANN, Jürgen, 1968: Messianismus und Marxismus," in: Über Ernst Bloch. Mit Beiträgen von M. Walser et. al., Suhrkamp: Frankfurt/M.

MOLTMANN, Jürgen, 1969: Religion, Revolution and the Future, Harper & Row New York

MOLTMANN, Jürgen, 1972: Theology of Hope, Harper & Row: New York

MOLTMANN, Jürgen, 1975: The Experiment Hope, London.

MOLTMANN-WENDEL, Elisabeth, 1980: Ein eigener Mensch werden. Frauen um Jesus, (GTB 1006), Gütersloh.

MOLTMANN-WENDEL, Elisabeth (ed.), 1982: Frauenbefreiung, Munich.

MOLTMANN-WENDEL, Elisabeth, 1985: Das Land, wo Milch und Honig fließt. Perspektiven feministischer Theologie. Verlagshaus Gerd Mohn: Gütersloh.

MORA, Fernandez de la, 1955: Der Untergang der Ideologien (Spanish), Madrid.

MOREAU A. Scott, 2000: Art. "Syncretism," in: EDWM.

MORRISON, Alan, 1999: The Serpent and the Cross, K & M Books: Trelawnyd, Wales

MOTSCHMANN, Klaus (ed.), 1982: Flucht aus der Freiheit? Zur Frage des Friedens in einer friedlosen Welt, Verl. Dietrich Pfaehler: Bad Neustadt.

MÜLLER-RÖMHELD, Walter (ed.), 1983: Bericht aus Vancouver, O.Lembeck: Frankfurt/M.

MÜLLER-RÖMHELD, Walter (ed.), 1991: Bericht aus Canberra 1991. Offizieller Bericht der Siebten Vollversammlung des Ökumenischen Rates der Kirchen, Verlag O. Lembeck: Frankfurt.

MULACK, C., 1983: Die Weiblichkeit Gottes, Kreuz Verlag: Stuttgart/Berlin.

MURALT, R. von, 1956: Meditations-Sutras des Mahayana-Buddhismus, 2 vols., Zürich.

MURRAY, I. H., 1987: Jonathan Edwards. A New Biography, Edinburgh.

N

NEILL, A.S., 1970: Theorie und Praxis der antiautoritären Erziehung, Rowohlt TB:Hamburg.

NEILL, Stephen, 1974: Bhakti: Hindu and Christian. CLS: Madras.

NEWBIGIN, L., 1985: Unfinished Agenda. An Autobiography, Eerdmans: Grand Rapids.

NEWBIGIN, L., 1986: Foolishness to the Greeks. The Gospel and Western Culture, Eerdmans: Grand Rapids.

NEWBIGIN, L., 1991: Truth to Tell: The Gospel as Public Truth, Grand Rapids/Geneva.

New Dictionary of Christian Theology 1988: Editors Sinclair B. Ferguson et al., Inter-Varsity Press: Leicester, England – Downers Grove Illinois, USA

NICHOLLS, Bruce J. (ed.), 1995: The Unique Christ in Our Pluralistic World. Publ. On behalf of the World Evangelical Fellowship. Paternoster Press/Baker Book House.

NICOLE, Roger R, 1973: Article "Authority," in: BDCE.

NILES, D.T., 1967: Buddhism and the Claims of Christ, John Knox Press: Richmond, Va.

NONNENGASS, Urda, 1970: Der androgyne Mensch, Gladenbach.

NUNN, H. P. V., 1932: What is Modernism? London.

NYANAPONIKA, Mahathera, 1981: Buddhismus – Weg zur Leidfreiheit. Ein Grundriß der Buddha-Lehre. Buddhist Publication Society: Kandy, Sri Lanka.

O

OH, Sung Choon, et. al., 1992: Ministry and the Ordination of Women. Presbyterian Theological Seminary Press: Seoul.

OLOFSSON, F., 1995: Vart är Svenska Kyrkan på väg? Verbum Förlag: Stockholm.

OLVEDI, Uli, 1985: "Evas Apfel der Erkenntnis – Weibliche Geistigkeit," in: Esotera No. 11 (Nov. 1985)

ORGAN, T.W., 1974: Hinduism: Its historical development. New York.

OTTO, Rudolph, 1930: India's Religion of Grace and Christianity Compared and Contrasted. Macmillan: New York.

P

PACKER, James I.: Art. "Infallibility and Inerrancy of the Bible," in: NDT.

PADBERG, Lutz E. von, 1985: Feminismus – eine ideologische und theologische Herausforderung, Schriftenmission der Evangelischen Gesellschaft: Wuppertal.

PADBERG, Lutz von, 1987: New Age und Feminismus, Schulte & Gerth: Aßlar.

PAIK, R.G., 1929: The History of the Protestant Missions to Korea. Pyongyang.

PALMER, Bernard, 1980: Understanding the Islamic Explosion. Horizon House Publ.: Camp Hill, PA.

PARET, Rudi, 1980: Mohammed und der Koran. Kohlhammer: Stuttgart/Berlin.

PARSHALL, Phil, 1983: Bridges to Islam. A Christian Perspective on Folk Islam. Baker Book House: Grand Rapids.

PATE Larry D. (ed.), 1989: From Every People: A Handbook of Two-Thirds World Missions, MARC: Monrovia.

PATON, David M. (ed.), 1976: Breaking Down Barriers. Nairobi 1975. Official Report of the Fifth Assembly of the WCC, Nairobi, 23 Nov. – 10 Dec., 1975, SPCK: London / Eerdmans: Grand Rapids.

PENN, Lee: "The United Religions Initiative," in: New Oxford Review, December 1998 and May 1999 issues.

PERCHERON, Maurice, 1979: Buddha in Selbstzeugnissen und Bildnissen. "Der Buddhismus und der Westen."

PINNOCK, C.H, 1988: Art "Apologetics" in: NDT.

PIUS IX, 1846: Qui Pluribus – On Faith And Religion – 9 November 1846, Vatican, Rome.

POLZER, Wolfgang, 2003: "Der Dalai Lama – 'Superstar' des Evangelischen Kirchentages in: DIAKRISIS 24 (3/2003).

POSDEEFF, Helena, 1976: "Die Rolle des Moskauer Patriarchats in Nairobi," in: P. Beyerhaus/U. Betz (eds.) 1976.

POSTON, Larry, 2000: Article "Ramon Lull" in: EDWM.

PRABHUPADA, A. C. Bhaktivedanta Swami, 1971: Sri Isopanissad, Bhaktivedanta Book Trust: Los Angeles – London – Bombay – Hamburg.

PROKSCH, Otto, 1950: Theologie des Alten Testaments, Bertelsmann:Gütersloh.

R

RAD, G. von, 1969: Theologie des Alten Testaments Vol. II., EVA:Berlin.

RADDATZ, Hans-Peter, 2002: Von Allah zum Terror? Der Djihad und die Deformierung des Westens. Herbig: München.

RADFORD RUETHER, Rosemary, 1975: New Woman – New Earth. Sexist Ideologies and Human Liberation, New York; (German edition: Frauen für eine neue Gesellschaft, Munich 1979).

RADFORD RUETHER, Rosemary, 1982: "Frauenbefreiung und Wiederversöhnung mit der Erde," in: E. MOLTMANN-WENDEL (ed.): 1982.

RADHAKRISHNAN, S., 1939: Eastern Religions and Western Thought, George, Allen & Unwin: LONDON.

RADHAKRISHNAN, S., 1955: Indische Philosophie, vol. I: Von den Veden bis zum Buddhismus, Holle: Darmstadt.

RAEDER, Siegfried, 1997: Biblische Traditionen im Koran, in: Jahrbuch für Biblische Theologie, vol 12 (1997).

RAEDER, Siegfried, 2001: Der Islam und das Christentum, Neukirchener Verlag.

RÄISÄNEN, Heikki, 1971: Das Koranische Jesusbild. Finnische Gesellschaft für Ökumenik: Helsinki.

RAISER, Konrad / SENS, Matthias, (eds.), 1991: "Botschaft der multireligiösen Konsultation an die Teilnehmer an der Vollversammlung des ÖRK in Canberra 1991, in: Canberra 1991. Beiheft 63 zur Ök. Rundschau, O. Lembeck: Frankfurt/M.

REICH, Wilhelm, 1971: Die sexuelle Revolution, Suhrkamp: Frankfurt.

REISSINGER, Walter, 1980: "Der Theologische Konvent Bekennender Gemeinschaften," in: R. Bäumer/P. Beyerhaus/F. Grünzweig (eds.)1980.

RICHARDSON, C. C., (ed.), 1953: The Early Christian Fathers, Philadelphia.

ROBERTSON, Donald 1973: Art. "Euthanasia," in BDCE.

ROBINSON, John, 1798: Proofs of the Conspiracy Against all the Religions and Governments of Europe Carried on in the Secret Meetings of Freemasons, Illuminati and Reading Societies: London.

ROBINSON, John, 1964: Honest to God, SCM Press: London.

ROERICH, Nicholas, 1988: Shambala. Das geheime Weltzentrum im Herzen Asiens, Herder:Freiburg.

ROHRMOSER, Günther, 1976: Das Elend der kritischen Theorie, Rombach:Freiburg.

ROHRMOSER, Günter, 1979: Angriff auf die Familie – Kulturrevolution auf leisen Sohlen, Hessischer Elternverein: Wiesbaden.

ROSENKRANZ, Gerhard, 1941: Buddha und Christus im Ringen um die Seele Chinas, Bertelsmann:Gütersloh.

ROSENKRANZ, Gerhard, 1960: Der Weg des Buddha, Ev. Missionsverlag: Stuttgart.

ROY, Ram Mohan, 1820: The Precepts of Jesus - The Guide to Peace and Happiness, extracted from the Books of the New Testament, ascribed to the four Evangelists. Baptist Mission Press: Calcutta.

RUDOLPH, Wilhelm, 1922: Die Abhängigkeit des Qorans von Judentum und Christentum, Stuttgart.

S

SAMARTHA, Stanley J., 1970: Hindus vor dem universalen Christus, Evang. Verlagswerk: Stuttgart (English original: The Hindu Response to the Unbound Christ).

SAMARTHA, Stanley J., 1985: "Christian Concern for Dialogue in India," in: Current Dialogue 9 (Dec. 1985).

SARTRE, Jean-Paul, 1948: Existentialism and Humanism, London.

SAUERZAPF, Rolf, 1975: Die Säkularisierung der Genfer Ökumene. Diss. University of Pretoria: South Africa.

SCHAEFFER, Edith, 1969: L'Abri, London.

SCHAEFFER, Francis, 1985: Complete Works, 5 vols., Westchester IL.

SCHARLEMANN, Martin H.: Art. "Abortion," in: BDCE.

SCHEFFBUCH, Rolf, 1976: "Ein Christus in vielen Christussen" (One Christ in many Christs), in: P. Beyerhaus/U. Betz (eds.).

SCHENK, Herrad, 1981: Die feministische Herausforderung. 150 Jahre Frauenbewegung in Deutschland, Munich.

SCHILPP, Paul A. (ed.), 1952: The Philosophy of Sarvepalli Radhakrishnan, Tudor Publ. House: New York.

SCHILLING, Werner, 1979: "Reaktionen des Buddhismus auf unsere gewandelte Theologie," in: U. Asendorf/F.-W. Künneth (eds.): Christuszeugnis im Nebel des Zeitgeistes, Hänssler: Stuttgart.

SCHIRRMACHER, Christine, 1994: Der Islam. Geschichte, Lehre, Unterschiede zum Christentum, vol. I, Hänssler: Stuttgart,

SCHIRRMACHER, Thomas (ed.), 1999: Kein anderer Name. Die Einzigartigkeit Jesu Christi und das Gespräch mit nichtchristlichen Religionen. VTR: Nürnberg.

SCHLEIERMACHER, F. D., 1799: Über die Religion, Berlin.

SCHLINGHOFF, Dieter, 1962: Die Religion des Buddhismus, vol. I "Der Heilsweg des Mönchtums." De Gruyter: Berlin.

SCHLINGHOFF, Dieter, 1963: Die Religion des Buddhismus, vol II "Der Heilsweg für die Welt." Sammlung Göschen No. 770, Berlin.

SCHMIDT-LEUKEL, P., 1993: "Das pluralistische Modell in der Theologie der Religionen. Ein Literaturbericht," in: Theologische Rundschau 89 (1993/3).

SCHÜTTE, Heinz, 1986: Ziel: Kirchengemeinschaft. Zur ökumenischen Orientierung, Bonifatius Verlag: Paderborn.

SCHUMANN, Hans W., 1963: Buddhismus, Philosophie zur Erlösung: Die großen Denksysteme des Hinayana und Mahayana, Francke Verlag: Bern/München.

SCHUMANN, Hans W., 1976: Buddhismus: Stifter, Schulen und Systeme, Walter Verlag: Olten.

SCHWARZER BRIEF – Informationen aus Kirche und Politik, 34 (no.31/2000), reprinted in DIAKRISIS 24 (No.3/2003).

SEMLYEN, Michael de, 1993: All Roads Lead to Rome, Dorchester House Publications, Chapter 19 "Biblical Prophecy and the Antichrist."

SHEIKH, Bilquis, 1977/2002: I Dared to Call Him Father. The miraculous story of a Muslim woman's encounter with God. Baker Book House, Grand Rapids.

SIMON, Gottfried, 1920: Der Islam und die christliche Verkündigung, Gütersloh.

SMITH, Bernard, 1979: The Fraudulent Gospel: Politics and the World Council of Churches, Foreign Affairs Publ. Co.: Richmond, Surrey.

SMITH, G. A., 1899: Henry Drummond, 2 vols. London.

SMITH, Alex G., 1980: The Gospel Facing Buddhist Cultures. Asian Perspectives No. 27, ATA: Taichung 1980.

SMITH, W., 1948: An Annotated Bibliography of D. L. Moody.

SÖDERBLOM, Nathan, 1931: Kompendium der Religionsgeschichte, Berlin.

SØE, N.H., 1949 : Christliche Ethik, Chr. Kaiser Verlag: München.

SÖLLE, Dorothee, 1985: Lieben und Arbeiten. Eine Theologie der Schöpfung, Stuttgart.

SOHN, Dong-Hee, 2001: My Cup Overflows, Christian Literature Crusade: Seoul.

SOLOWJEW, Wladmir, 1968: Short Narrative of the Antichrist, (German edition by Ludolf Müller, Wevel Verlag: Munich 1968).

SOLZHENITSYN, Alexander1974: Der Archipel Gulag, Scherz Verl.:Bern, 3 vols.

SORGE, E., 1987: Religion und Frau. Weibliche Spiritualität im Christentum, Stuttgart.

SPANGLER, David, 1978: Reflections on the Christ, Findhorn, UK.

SPIERENBURG, H.J., 1991: The Buddhism of H. P. Blavatsky, San Diego.

STEINBACHER, 1971: The Child Seducers, Educators Publ.: Anaheim, CA.

STENSTRÖM, Hanna (ed.), 1992: Kan vi tro på God Fader? Uppsala, Sweden.

STEPHENSON, A. M. G., 1984: The Rise and Decline of English Modernism, London.

STEUBING, Hans, et. al. (ed.), 1977: Bekenntnisse der Kirche. Bekenntnistexte aus zwanzig Jahrhunderten, Theologischer Verlag Rolf Brockhaus: Wuppertal.

STIEGLECKER, Hermann, 1983: Die Glaubenslehren des Islam. F. Schöningh: Paderborn.

STOEFFLER, F. E., 1965: The Rise of Evangelical Pietism, Brill: Leiden.

SUZUKI, D.T., 1927: Essays in Zen-Buddhism, vol I, Luzac and Co: London.

SUZUKI, D.T., 1955: Studies in Zen, Rider: London.

SUZUKI, D.T., 1968: The Essence of Buddhism, Hozokan: Kyoto.

SUZUKI, D.T., 1972: Die große Befreiung – Einführung in den Zen-Buddhismus. Weilheim.

SUZUKI, D.T., 1974: Amida: Der Buddha der Liebe, tr. fr. English U. Olvedi, Barth Verlag: Bern.

SUZUKI, D.T., 1988: Der westliche und der östliche Weg. Essays über christliche und buddhistische Mystik, Frankfurt/Berlin.

SWING, William E., 1998: The Coming United Religions. United Religions Initiative & CoNexus Press.

SYMONDS, John, 1959: Madame Blavatsky. Medium and Magician, London.

T

TAM NEWSLETTER of the Associated Missions, 1991: No. 85 April-August.

TAVARD, George H., 1960: Two Centuries of Ecumenism, Burns & Oates: London.

THIEDE, Carsten Peter (ed.), 1987: Das Petrusbild in der neueren Forschung. Wuppertal.

THIEDE, Carsten Peter, 2000: Geheimakte Petrus. Auf den Spuren des Apostels, Kreuz-Verlag: Stuttgart.

THOMAS, M. M., 1970: The Acknowledged Christ of the Indian Renaissance, CLS: Madras

TIL, C. van, 1955: The Defence of The Faith, Philadelphia.

TILLICH, Paul, 1956: Systematische Theologie, Kreuz Verl.:Stuttgart, vol I.

TILLICH, Paul, 1964: Das Christentum und die Begegnung der Weltreligionen, Ev. Verlagswerk: Stuttgart (American edition: Christianity and the Encounter of the World Religions, Columbia University Press: New York 1962).

TITTMANN, H., 1816: Suprarationalismus, Rationalismus und Atheismus, Leipzig.

TON, Josef, 1997: Suffering, Martyrdom, and Rewards in Heaven, University Press of America.

TRIMINGHAM, J. Spencer, 1962: Islam in East Africa, I.M.C. Research Pamphlet No. 9, Edinburgh House Press.

TRIMONDI, Victor und Victoria, 1999: Der Schatten des Dalai Lama. Sexualität, Magie und Politik im tibetanischen Buddhismus, (The Shadow of the Dalai Lama – Sexuality, Magic and Politics in Tibetan Buddhism – To my knowledge only the German translation is available at the moment) – Patloch Verlag: Düsseldorf.

TROEGER, Eberhard, 1996: Kreuz und Halbmond: Was Christen vom Islam wissen sollten. R. Brockhaus: Wuppertal.

TROELTSCH, Ernst, 1913: "Über historische und dogmatische Methode in der Theologie," in "Gesammelte Schriften II," J.D.B. Mohr (Paul Siebeck, 1913): Tübingen.

TRUNGPA, Chögyam, 1986: Shambala. The Sacred Path of the Warrior, New York.

U

UNDERWOOD, Lillias H. 1983: Underwood of Korea., reprinted by Yonsei University Press: Seoul.

V

Verein zur Förderung der Psychologischen Menschenkenntnis (ed.) 1991: Standort Schule. Schul"reform" – die heimliche Abschaffung der Schule. 4 vols., Verlag Menschenkenntnis: Zürich.

VERMAAT, J.A.E., 1975: Signalen van die Eindtijd? Ch. VIII "Occult-Religious Background of the Third Reich," Utrecht.

VERMAAT, J.A.E., 1976: "Für und gegen einen erweiterten Ökumenismus," in: P.Beyerhaus/U. Betz (eds.) 1976.

VERMAAT, J.A.E., 2001: Euthanasia: Herhaalt de Geschiedenis zich? De Banier:Utrecht.

VICEDOM, Georg, 1959: Die Mission der Weltreligionen, Kaiser: München.

VICEDOM, Georg, 1960: Missio Dei, Chr. Kaiser: München.

VIVEKANANDA, Swami, 1946/47: Complete Works, vols I-VII, Advaita Ashram: Almora, India.

VORLÄNDER, K., 1929: Karl Marx – Sein Leben und sein Werk, Leipzig.

VREE, Dale, 1976: On Synthesizing Marxism and Christianity, Wiley: New York.

W

WADDELL, Austine L., 1895: The Buddhism of Tibet or Lamaism, London.

WALKER, Benjamin, 1968: Hindu World. An Encyclopaedic Survey of Hinduism. 2 vols., London.

WALSER, M. et. al. (ed.), 1968: Über Ernst Bloch. Suhrkamp: Frankfurt/M.

WARNOCK, M., 1970: Existentialism, London.

WATTS, A. W., 1961: Zen-Buddhismus. Tradition und lebendige Gegenwart, Rowohlt: Hamburg.

WAYMAN, Alex, 1973: The Buddhist Tantras. Light on Indo-Tibetan Esotericism, New York.

WEBER, Helmut, 1991: Allgemeine Morallehre, Styria: Graz.

WEINGÄRTNER, L., 1969: Umbanda – Synkretistische Kulte in Brasilien, Erlangen.

WEISHAUPT, A., 1787: Das verbesserte System der Illuminaten. vol. I, (Reprint Delmenhorst).

WEIZSÄCKER, Carl Friedrich von, 1988: Bewußtseinswandel, München/Wien.

WELBON, G.R., 1968: The Buddhist Nirvana and its Western Interpreters, Chicago/London.

WELLS, David F., 1978: The Search for Salvation, InterVarsity Press: Downers Grove

WETTER, Paul, 1998: Der Missionsgedanke bei Martin Luther, Culture and Science Publication: Bonn.

WIEDEMANN, L. (ed.), 1983: Herausgefordert durch die Armen: Dokumente der Ökumenischen Vereinigung von Dritte-Welt-Theologen 1976-1983, Herder: Freiburg.

WIESINGER, Alois, 1957: Occult Phenomena in the Light of the Bible, Burns & Oates: London.

WILLEKE, Rudolf, 2000: Hintergründe der 68er Kulturrevolution: Frankfurter Schule und Kritische Theorie, Absteinach.

WILLEKE, Rudolf, 2002: "Bio-Technik, Bioethik, Biopolitik," in: DIAKRISIS 23 (1-2/2002).

WILLIAMS, Glanville L., 1957: The Sanctity of Life and the Criminal Law, Knopf: New York.

WILLIS, Avery, 1997: Indonesian Revival: Why two million came to Christ. William Carey Library: Pasadena.

WINDELBAND, Wilhelm, 1950: Lehrbuch der Geschichte der Philosophie: "Das System des Idealismus," Tübingen.

WINTERNITZ, Moritz (ed.), 1929: Religionsgeschichtliches Lesebuch: Der Ältere Buddhismus, nach Texten des Tipitaka, Verlag Mohr: Tübingen.

WOELLER, H., 1983: "Weibliche Aspekte der neutestamentlichen Botschaft," in: Berichte und Analysen aus der Arbeit der Evangelium. Akademie Nordelbien No. 3/1983.

WOLFF, R. et al. (Eds), 1967: Kritik der reinen Toleranz, Frankfurt/M.

World Council of Churches 1967: Drafts for Sections Prepared for the Fourth Assembly of the World Council of Churches, Geneva.

WURMBRAND, Richard, 1985: Marx and Satan, Crossway Books: Westchester.

Y

YAMAMOTO, J. Isamu, 1983: "Hare Krishna (ISKON)," in: Ronald ENROTH et al. (eds): A Guide to Cults and New Religions, Inter-Varsity Press: Downers Grove.

YEU, Kwi-Ook, 1988: Beautiful Memories, (Parts Two and Four), CLS: Seoul.

Z

ZACHARIAH, Aleyamma, 1990: Modern Religious & Secular Movements in India, Theological Book Trust: Bangalore.

ZIERER, Otto, 1980: Robespierre oder die reine Ideologie, Herbig: München/Berlin.

ZWEMER, Samuel, 1907: Islam, a Challenge to Faith. New York.

ZWEMER, Samuel M., 1912: The Moslem Christ. An Essay on the Life, Character and Teachings of Jesus Christ according to the Koran and Orthodox Tradition. Oliphant, Anderson & Ferrier: Edinburgh /London.

Arbeitskreis für evangelikale Missiologie (AfeM)

Der 1985 in Korntal gegründete **Arbeitskreis für evangelikale Missiologie** will im deutschsprachigen Raum biblisch fundierte Missionslehre und Missionswissenschaft fördern. Er tut dies vor allem durch eine jährlich stattfindende missiologische Tagung, durch die Zeitschrift **Evangelikale Missiologie** und durch die Förderung missiologischer Veröffentlichungen. Auskünfte zur Mitgliedschaft usw. erteilt das Sekretariat: AfeM-Geschäftsstelle, Kristina Weirich, Postfach 1360, D-51702 Bergneustadt, email: afem.em@t-online.de.

Evangelikale Missiologie (em)

Die Zeitschrift **Evangelikale Missiologie** erscheint seit 1985 vierteljährlich mit je 40 Seiten und kostet 17,-- € pro Jahr (Missionare im Ausland und Studenten die Hälfte). Die Schriftleitung hat Dr. Klaus W. Müller. Eine Probenummer kann beim AfeM-Büro (s.o.) bezogen werden.

edition afem

mission classics

Bd. 1: William Carey. Eine Untersuchung über die Verpflichtung der Christen, Mittel einzusetzen für die Bekehrung der Heiden. Hrsg. von Klaus Fiedler und Thomas Schirrmacher. 2. verbesserte Auflage 1998. 108 S. Pb. 12,00 € - ISBN 3-926105-84-4 (VKW)

Bd. 2: John L. Nevius. Die Gründung und Entwicklung missionarischer Gemeinden. Hrsg. von Wolf Christian Jaeschke. 2. korrigierte Auflage 2001. 124 S. Pb. 13,00 € - ISBN 3-932829-24-7 (VKW)

Bd. 3: James Hudson Taylor. Rückblick. Hrsg. von Simone Jaumann-Wang. 1999. 134 S. Pb. 14,00 € - ISBN 3-932829-10-7 (VKW)

Bd. 4: Martin Baier. Glaube, Liebe und Hoffnung auf Borneo. Religionswissenschaftliche und kulturanthropologische Erkenntnisse bei den Kotawaringin-Dayak aus den Tagebüchern von Johann Georg Baier, 1928-1932 Pioniermissionar in Südwest-Borneo. 2001. 167 S. Pb. 14,00 € - ISBN 3-932829-20-4 (VKW)

Bd. 5: Georg F. Vicedom. Missio Dei – Actio Dei. Neu hrsg. von Klaus W. Müller. Mit Beiträgen von Bernd Brandl und Herwig Wagner. 2002. 252 S. Pb. 19,80 € - ISBN 3-933372-52-6 (VTR)

mission academics

Bd. 1: William Lyle Wagner. North American Protestant Missionaries in Western Europe: A Critical Appraisal. Englisch mit deutscher Zusammenfassung. 1993. 248 S. Pb. 10,00 € - ISBN 3-926105-12-7 (VKW)

Bd. 2: Klaus Fiedler. Christentum und afrikanische Kultur: Konservative deutsche Missionare in Tanzania, 1900 bis 1940. 3. Aufl.: 1993. 220 S. Pb. vergriffen - ISBN 3-926105-13-5 (VKW)

Bd. 3: Hans Bär. Heilsgeschichtlicher Bibelunterricht. McIlwains Programm ‚Building on Firm Foundations' im Einsatz unter den Karen im Bezirk Omkoi (Nordthailand). 1998. 150 S. Pb. 20,00 € - ISBN 3-926105-90-9 (VKW)

Bd. 4: Lianne Roembke. Multikulturelle Teams. 2000. 332 S. Pb. 12,95 € - ISBN 3-88404-109-6 (Campus)]

Bd. 5: Stephan Holthaus, Klaus W. Müller (Hg.). Die Mission der Theologie: Festschrift für Hans Kasdorf zum 70. Geburtstag. 1998. 292 S. Pb. 30,00 € - ISBN 3-926105-96-8 (VKW)

Bd. 6: Jürgen Steinbach, Klaus W. Müller (Hg.). Theologie - Mission - Verkündigung: Festschrift zum 60. Geburtstag von Helmuth Egelkraut. 1998. 165 S. Pb. 25,00 € - ISBN 3-926105-97-6 (VKW)

Bd. 7: Philip M. Steyne. Schritt halten mit dem Gott der Völker: Weltmission im Alten und Neuen Testament. 1999. 300 S. Pb. 25,00 € - ISBN 3-932829-05-0 (VKW)

Bd. 8: Rainer Scheunemann. Mission und Evangelisation aus der Sicht indonesischer protestantischer Theologen. 1999. 624 S. Pb. 50,00 € - ISBN 3-932829-11-5 (VKW)

Bd. 9: Robert Badenberg. The Body, Soul and Spirit Concept of the Bemba in Zambia. Fundamental Characteristics of Being Human of an African Ethnic Group. 1999. 132 S. Pb. 15,00 € - ISBN 3-932829-14-X (VKW)

Bd. 10: Detlef Kapteina. Afrikanische Evangelikale Theologie: Plädoyer für das ganze Evangelium im Kontext Afrikas. 2001. 336 S. Pb. 24,95 € - ISBN 3-933372-44-5 (VTR)

Bd. 11: Robert Badenberg. Sickness and Healing: A Case Study on the Dialectic of Culture and Personality. 2003. 284 S. Pb. 22,80 € - ISBN 3-933372-70-4 (VTR)

Bd. 12: Beom-Seong Lee. Die politische Leistung der „evangelikalen" Kirchenführer in Korea: Der Beitrag der koreanischen Kirche zum nationalen Wiedervereinigungsgedanken vor dem Hintergrund der Erfahrung aus der japanischen Besatzungszeit von 1910-1945 (Die protestantische Kirchengeschichte in Korea von 1832 bis 1945). 2003. 252 S. Pb. 19,80 € - ISBN 3-933372-73-9 (VTR)

Bd. 13: Heinrich Klassen. Mission als Zeugnis: Zur missionarischen Existenz in der Sowjetunion nach dem zweiten Weltkrieg. 2003. 272 S. Pb. 19,80 € - ISBN 3-933372-84-4 (VTR) / ISBN 3-933828-95-3 (Logos)

Bd. 14: Heinrich Klassen / Johannes Reimer. Mission im Zeichen des Friedens: Beiträge zur Geschichte täuferisch-mennonitischer Mission. 2003. 275 S. Pb. 19,80 € - ISBN 3-933372-85-2 (VTR) / ISBN 3-933828-94-5 (Logos)

Bd. 15: Klaus W. Müller. Mission in fremden Kulturen - Beiträge zur Missionsethnologie. Festschrift für Lothar Käser zu seinem 65. Geburtstag. 2003. 423 S. Pb. 29,80 € - ISBN 3-933372-91-7 (VTR)

Bd. 16: Thomas Schirrmacher / Christof Sauer (Hg.). Mission verändert – Mission verändert sich / Mission Transformes – Mission is Transformed. Festschrift für Klaus Fiedler. 2005. 572 S. Pb. 39,80 € - ISBN 3-933372-77-1 (VTR) / ISBN 3-932829-87-5 (VKW)

Bd. 17: Heinrich Bammann. Inkulturation des Evangeliums unter den Batswana in Transvaal/Südafrika: Am Beispiel der Arbeit von Vätern und Söhnen der Hermannsburger Mission von 1857 – 1940. 2004. 348 S. Pb. 19,80 € - ISBN 3-937965-05-X (VTR)

Bd. 18: Lothar Käser. Körper, Seele und Geist bei den Insulanern von Chuuk (Mikronesien). 2004. ca. 250 S. Pb. 19,80 € - ISBN 3-937965-15-7 (VTR)

Bd. 19: Hans Ulrich Reifler. Handbuch der Missiologie: Missionarisches Handeln aus biblischer Perspektive. 2005. 630 S. Pb. 49,80 € - ISBN 3-933372-96-8 (VTR)

Bd. 20: Thomas Schirrmacher / Klaus W. Müller (Hg.). Das Gewissen in der Diskussion: Motivation, Funktion und Auswirkung. 2006. ca. 300 S. Pb. ca. 26,80 € - ISBN 3-938116-07-2 (VKW) / ISBN 3-937965-35-1 (VTR)

Bd. 21: Jürgen Stadler. Erste Schritte auf dem Weg zu einer einheimischen Kirche: Die Missionspraxis Christian Keyßers in Neuguinea 1899-1920. 2006. ca. 550 S. Pb. ca. 39,80 € - ISBN 3-937965-31-9 (VTR)

mission scripts

Bd. 1: Thomas Klammt. „Ist die Heidenmission zu empfehlen?": Die deutschen Baptisten und die Mission in der Ferne (1848-1913). 1994. 104 S. Pb. 13,00 € - ISBN 3-926105-17-8 (VKW)

Bd. 2: Peter James Spartalis. Karl Kumm - Last of the Livingstones: Pioneer Missionary Statesman. Nachwort von Eberhard Troeger. Englisch mit deutscher Zusammenfassung von Christof Sauer. 1994. 120 S. Pb. 10,00 € - ISBN 3-926105-18-6 (VKW)

Bd. 3: Thomas Schirrmacher (Hg.). „Die Zeit für die Bekehrung der Welt ist reif": Rufus Anderson und die Selbständigkeit der Kirche als Ziel der Mission. Mit Beiträgen von Rufus Anderson, Theodor Christlieb, Josef Josenhans, Hermann Gundert. 1993 (Nachdruck 1996). 136 S. Pb. 14,00 € - ISBN 3-926105-60-7 (VKW)

Bd. 4: Silke Sauer. Oralität und Literalität: Ihre Bedeutung für Kommunikation und Bibelübersetzung. 1995. 100 S. Pb. 12,00 € - ISBN 3-926105-37-2 (VKW)

Bd. 5: Christof Sauer. Mission und Martyrium: Studien zu Karl Hartenstein und zur Lausanner Bewegung. 1994. 148 S. Pb. vergriffen - ISBN 3-926105-42-9 (VKW)

Bd. 6: Elisabeth Wagner. Bei uns ist alles ganz anders: Handbuch für Ehefrauen in der Mission. 1995 (Nachdruck 1996). 214 S. Pb. (Deutsche Missionsgemeinschaft, Sinsheim)

Bd. 7: Klaus W. Müller, Annette Ley (Hg.). 1000 Quellen zur evangelikalen Missiologie: Bibliographie der Forschungsarbeiten an der Freien Hochschule für Mission bis 1993 mit Peter Beyerhaus-Brevier zum 65. Geburtstag. 1995. 208 S. Pb. 10,00 € - ISBN 3-926105-61-5 (VKW)

Bd. 8: Friso Melzer. Jesus Christus, der Erlöser der Welt: Erkenntnisse und Zeugnisse aus 60 Jahren missionarischer Dienste in Indien, Württemberg und anderswo. 1995. 140 S. Pb. 20,00 € - ISBN 3-926105-62-3 (VKW)

Bd. 9: Fritz H. Lamparter (Hg.). Karl Hartenstein - Leben in weltweitem Horizont: Beiträge zu seinem 100. Geburtstag. mit einem Vorwort von Landesbischof Eberhardt Renz. 1995. 176 S. Pb. 13,00 € - ISBN 3-926105-63-1 (VKW)

Bd. 10: Simone Jaumann-Wang. Changsha - mit Geduld und Gnade: Wie eine chinesische Provinzhauptstadt für das Evangelium geöffnet wurde. 1996. 183 S. Pb. 20,00 € - ISBN 3-926105-70-4 (VKW)

Bd. 11: Joost Reinke. Deutsche Pfingstmissionen. Geschichte - Theologie - Praxis. With an English summary. 1997. 90 S. Pb. 12,00 € - ISBN 3-926105-72-0 (VKW)

Bd. 12: Christa Conrad. Der Dienst der ledigen Frau in deutschen Glaubensmissionen: Geschichte und Beurteilung. 1998. 140 S. Pb. 16,00 € - ISBN 3-926105-92-5 (VKW)

Bd. 13: Rüdiger Nöh. Pietismus und Mission: Die Stellung der Weltmission in der Gemeinschaftsbewegung am Beispiel des Siegerländer Gemeinschaftsverbandes. 1998. 179 S. Pb. 16,00 € - ISBN 3-926105-94-1 (VKW)

Bd. 14: Hannes Wiher. Missionsdienst in Guinea: Das Evangelium für eine schamorientierte, von Animismus und Volksislam geprägte Gesellschaft. 1998. 125 S. Pb. 16,00 € - ISBN 3-926105-93-3 (VKW)

Bd. 15: Stefan Schmid. Mark Christian Hayford (1864-1935): Ein Pionier aus Westafrika. 1999 224 S. Pb. 20,00 € - ISBN 3-932829-08-5 (VKW)

Bd. 16: Markus Flückiger. Geschenk und Bestechung: Korruption im afrikanischen Kontext. 2000. 128 S. Pb. 15,00 € - ISBN 3-932829-17-4 (VKW)

Bd. 17: Mechthild Roth. Re-Integration: Missionare und ihre Rückkehr unter besonderer Berücksichtigung des deutschen Kontextes. 2003. 170 S. Pb. 16,80 € - ISBN 3-933372-69-0 (VTR)

Bd. 18: Thomas Schirrmacher. Weltmission - Das Herz des christlichen Glaubens: Beiträge aus ‚Evangelikale Missiologie'. 2001. 298 S. Pb. 18,00 € - ISBN 3-932829-28-X (VKW)

Bd. 19: Marcelo Abel. Indianer unter dem Einfluss christlicher Mission: Erfahrungen eines Einheimischen. 2002. 70 S. Pb. 9,80 € - ISBN 3-933372-65-8 (VTR)

Bd. 20: Edward Rommen. Namenschristentum: Theologisch-soziologische Erwägungen. 2003. 134 S. Pb. 14,80 € - ISBN 3-933372-74-4 (VTR)

Bd. 21: Martin Lomen. Sünde und Scham im biblischen und islamischen Kontext: Ein Beitrag zum christlich-islamischen Dialog. 2003. 190 S. Pb. 17,80 € - ISBN 3-933372-75-5 (VTR)

Bd. 22: Luis Bush. Wahre Partnerschaft: Aufruf zur finanziellen Unterstützung der Zweidrittelwelt-Missionen. 2003. 34 S. Pb. 5,80 € - ISBN 3-933372-93-3 (VTR)

Bd. 23: Annelie Schreiber. Das Evangelium im Kontext der Wirtschaftsform bei den Guarani: Überlegungen zur Kontextualisierung auf der Basis von literarischer Forschung und Feldforschung. 2004. 100 S. Pb. 12,80 € - ISBN 3-937965-08-4 (VTR)

Bd. 24: Carolin Steppat. Die Verkündigung des Evangeliums in animistisch orientierten Ethnien: am Beispiel indigener Ethnien in Brasilien und angrenzendem Tiefland. 2005. ca. 160 S. Pb. 16,80 € - ISBN ISBN 3-933372-95-X (VTR)

Bd. 25: Damaris Jahnke. Straßenkinder: Theologische Grundlagen und praktische Leitlinien in der neueren evangelikalen Missionsliteratur über sozial-missionarische Arbeit unter Straßenkindern in der Zwei-Drittel-Welt. 2006. ca. 190 S. Pb. ca. 19,80 € - ISBN 3-937965-19-X (VTR)

mission reports

Bd. 1: Klaus W. Müller (Hg.). Mission als Kampf mit den Mächten: Zum missiologischen Konzept des „Power Encounter": Referate der Jahrestagung des afem 1993. 2003[3]. 162 S. Pb. 16,80 € - ISBN 3-933372-92-5 (VTR) / ISBN 3-932829-86-7 (VKW)

Bd. 2: Klaus W. Müller, Christine Schirrmacher, Eberhard Troeger (Hg.). Der Islam als Herausforderung für die christliche Mission: Referate der Jahrestagung des afem 1994. 1996[1], 2000[2]. 110 S. Pb. 15,00 € - ISBN 3-932829-19-0 (VKW)

Bd. 3: nicht erschienen

Bd. 4: Klaus W. Müller (Hg.). Die Person des Missionars. Berufung – Sendung - Dienst. Referate der Jahrestagung 1996 des afem. 2003[2]. 117 S. Pb. 13,80 € - ISBN 3-933372-72-0 (VTR) / ISBN 3-932829-58-1 (VKW)

Bd. 5: Klaus Brinkmann (Hg.). Missionare und ihr Dienst im Gastland. Referate der Jahrestagung 1997 des afem. 1998. 175 S. Pb. 16,00 € - ISBN 3-926105-56-9 (VKW)

Bd. 6: Klaus W. Müller, Thomas Schirrmacher (Hg.). Werden alle gerettet? - Moderner Heilsuniversalismus als Infragestellung der christlichen Mission. Referate der Jahrestagung 1998 des afem. 1999. 152 S. Pb. 16,00 € - ISBN 3-932829-06-9 (VKW)

Bd. 7: Klaus W. Müller, Thomas Schirrmacher (Hg.). Ausbildung als missionarischer Auftrag. Referate der Jahrestagung 1999 des afem. 2000. 184 S. Pb. 18,00 € - ISBN 3-932829-09-3 (VKW)

Bd. 8: Klaus W. Müller, Thomas Schirrmacher (Hg.). Mission in der Spannung zwischen Hoffnung, Resignation und Endzeitenthusiasmus: Eschatologie als Missionsmotivation. Referate der Jahrestagung 2000 des afem. 2000. 220 S. Pb. 15,00 € - ISBN 3-932829-19-0 (VKW)

Bd. 9: Klaus W. Müller (Hg.). Mission im Kreuzfeuer. Referate der Jahrestagung 2001 des afem. 2001. 104 S. Pb. 12,80 € - ISBN 3-933372-39-9 (VTR)

Bd. 10: Klaus W. Müller (Hg.). Mission im Kontext der Globalisierung. Referate der Jahrestagung 2002 des afem. 2002. 148 S. Pb. 15,80 € - ISBN 3-933372-68-2 (VTR)

Bd. 11: Klaus W. Müller (Hg.). Gott zur Sprache bringen. Referate der Jahrestagung 2003 des afem. 2003. ca. 140 S. Pb. ca. 15,80 € - ISBN 3-933372-76-3 (VTR)

Bd. 12: Klaus W. Müller (Hg.). Missionare aus der Zweidrittel-Welt für Europa. Referate der Jahrestagung 2004 des afem. 2004. 141 S. Pb. 15,80 € - ISBN 3-937965-13-0 (VTR)

Bd. 13: Klaus W. Müller (Hg.). Westliche Missionswerke: Notwendigkeit, Strukturen und Chancen. Referate der Jahrestagung 2005 des afem. 2006. In Vorbereitung - ISBN 3-937965-13-0 (VTR)

mission specials

Bd. 1: Stefan Höschele. From the End of the World to the Ends of the Earth: The Development of Seventh-Day Adventist Missiology. 2004. 70 S. Pb. 9,80 € - ISBN 3-937965-14-9 (VTR)

Bd. 2: Hans Kasdorf. Design of My Journey: An Autobiography. 2005. 380 S. Pb. 25,80 € - ISBN 3-937965-07-6 (VTR)

Bd. 3: Heinrich Bammann. Grenzerfahrungen mit dem Bösen – Persönliche Erlebnisse und Deutungen mit Ausblick auf die beste Zusage des Lebens. 2005. 92 S. Pb. 11,80 € – ISBN 3-937965-28-9

Bd. 4: Peter Beyerhaus. Mission and Apologetics. 2006. ca. 290 S. Pb. ca. 25,80 € - ISBN 3-937965-44-0 (VTR)

Motivating Generation X

THE POTENTIAL OF GENERATION X
AS A CHALLENGE FOR CHRISTIANS AND FOR MISSIONS

by

JÜRG PFISTER

I am really praying that many people will read this futuristic, cutting-edge, strategic book. Let's make sure this book gets wide circulation.

George Verwer

Founder of Operation Mobilisation (OM)

Hope and help: such can I best describe the book "Motivating Generation X" by Jürg Pfister. I hope that "Motivating Generation X" will be read by responsible members of congregations and missions boards, that it will be heard and that its corresponding initiatives will be implemented.

Thomas Bucher
President of the Evangelical Alliance of Switzerland

Once I had begun to read Jürg Pfister's book, I could not put it down.
Dr. Roland Werner, Germany

Paperback 150 pp. $12,99 / £10,95 / €12,80
ISBN 3-937965-06-8

VTR Publications
vtr@compuserve.com
http://www.vtr-online.de

Lightning Source UK Ltd.
Milton Keynes UK
171820UK00001B/8/A